ROMAN IMPERIAL ARMOUR

THE PRODUCTION OF EARLY IMPERIAL MILITARY ARMOUR

D. Sim and J. Kaminski

OXBOW | books
Oxford & Philadelphia

First published in the United Kingdom in 2012. Reprinted in 2026 by
OXBOW BOOKS
81 St Clements, Oxford OX4 1AW

and in the United States by
OXBOW BOOKS
1950 Lawrence Road, Havertown, PA 19083

Paperback Edition: ISBN 978-1-84217-435-7
Digital Edition: ISBN 978-1-84217-702-0

A CIP record for this book is available from the British Library

Library of Congress Cataloging-in-Publication Data

Sim, David, 1947-
Roman imperial armour : the production of early imperial military armour / D. Sim and J. Kaminski.
p. cm.
Includes bibliographical references.
ISBN 978-1-84217-435-7
1. Armor, Ancient--Rome--Design and construction. 2. Armor making--Rome. 3. Rome--Army--Equipment. 4. Rome--Military antiquities. I. Kaminski, Jaime. II. Title.

U35.S54 2012
623.4'41--dc23

For a complete list of Oxbow titles, please contact:

UNITED KINGDOM
Oxbow Books
Telephone (0)1226 734350
Email: oxbow@oxbowbooks.com
www.oxbowbooks.com

UNITED STATES OF AMERICA
Oxbow Books
Telephone (610) 853-9131, Fax (610) 853-9146
Email: queries@casemateacademic.com
www.casemateacademic.com/oxbow

Oxbow Books is part of the Casemate Group

Front cover: A well preserved first century AD Imperial Gallic C (Weisenau-Guttmann) iron helmet with decorative red enamel studs. This helmet shows evidence of battle damage in the form of a blow to the front and a sword cut in the right ear section (private collection)

The Publisher's authorised representative in the EU for product safety is Authorised Rep Compliance Ltd.,
Ground Floor, 71 Lower Baggot Street, Dublin D02 P593, Ireland.
www.arccompliance.com

Contents

Foreword		vii
Acknowledgements		x
Abbreviations		xi
1	**The Evidence**	1
	Introduction	1
	Written and visual sources	1
	Metallographic and surface examination	2
	Experimental archaeology	3
	Conclusions	4
2	**Iron Production**	5
	Introduction	5
	Sources of iron in the Roman Empire	5
	Moving the ore	10
	Charcoal production	11
	Ore preparation	12
	Bloomery iron production	13
	Bloomsmithing (pimary smithing)	17
	Clean iron	18
	Conclusions	22
3	**Blacksmithing Techniques and Production Methods**	25
	Introduction	25
	Blacksmithing	25
	Welding	27
	Heat treatment	27
	Advantages of hot and cold working	31
	Work hardening	32
	Forming sheet metal hemispheres	32
	Producing holes in sheet metal	36
	Materials testing in antiquity	38
	Recycling metal	39
	Manufacture	40
	Economics	43
	Conclusions	46
4	**The Production of Sheet Metal**	49
	Methods of sheet iron production	49
	Conclusions	56

5 **Iron and Steel** 58
Introduction 58
Methods of making steel 59
Hardening and tempering 62
Conclusions 64

6 **Surface Treatment of Roman Armour** 65
Introduction 65
Rust prevention 65
The surface appearance of Roman armour 68
Polishing 69
Coatings 71
A comparison of different surface treatments 76
Preventing rusting during storage 77
Conclusions 77

7 **Helmets (*galea* or *cassis*)** 79
Introduction 79
Parts of the helmet 80
Methods of manufacture 82
Conclusions 92

8 **Scale Armour (*lorica squamata*)** 95
Body armour 95
Lorica squamata 95
Typology of *lorica squamata* 96
The nature of scale armour 97
Field repairs 100
Case study: The Carlisle shoulder piece 101
Metallography 101
Wire to join scales 102
Replication of scale armour 104
The future of scale armour 108
Conclusions 108

9 **Ring Mail (*lorica hamata*)** 111
Introduction 111
Wire production 112
Wire drawing 114
Type of metals used for wire 116
Experimental method for producing a draw plate 118
Wire drawing 121
Ring types 123
Non-ferrous rings 130
Riveted rings 132
Conclusions 132

10 Segmented Body Armour (*lorica segmentata*) 135
Introduction 135
Conclusions 137

11 Leg and Arm Armour 139
Arm armour 139
Greaves (*Ocrea*) 141
Method of manufacture 143
Conclusion 144

12 The Shield and Boss (*umbo*) 146
Introduction 146
Shield edging (guttering) 148
The construction typology of shield bosses 148
Double-skinned ferrous shield bosses 149
Laminated shield bosses (welded) 153
Other materials 156
Conclusions 157

13 Conclusions 159

Appendix 1: The Survival of Ancient Machines 163
Appendix 2: One-sided Carburization 165

Glossary 167
Latin terms 170

Bibliography 172

Plates **between pp. 116-117**

Foreword

By the beginning of the imperial age the equipment of the Roman army was already 'a composite of the best weapons of many tribes and nations, tested by several centuries of experience.' (McCartney 1912, 74). The Roman Empire depended on the power of its armies to defend and extend the imperial borders (Penrose 2005, 177). It was these armies that enabled the Roman state to dominate much of Europe, Northern Africa and the Middle East. The success was in a large part founded on well-trained, well-disciplined soldiers, who were equipped with the most advanced arms and armour available at that time.

It is this armour that this book will focus on – specifically, the manufacturing processes of metal armour and the metal components of armour by the Romans. To do this an examination will be made of the metals the armour was made from, of how the ores containing those metals were extracted from the earth and transformed into workable metal and of how that raw product was made into the armour of the Roman army. In so doing, new evidence of Roman armour production will be highlighted.

The study is predominantly restricted to the north-western part of the Roman Empire. The main consideration here has been the production of armour that has been made predominantly from sheet iron. However, where appropriate, reference has been made to sheet bronze armour. Armour (but not weapons) made from copper-alloys were used alongside that made from iron for most of the Roman period.

But this focus on metal armour should not detract from the fact that much armour may have been made from organic materials such as leather. By their very nature these materials are under-represented in the archaeological record.

Armour does not exist as an entity in its own right: it is there as a means of protection for those who wear it. It seems that an examination of the character of the Roman soldier would not be out of place here. He wore armour, it protected him – so what sort of a man wore armour? It is not in the scope of this volume to give a history of the Roman Empire or of the Roman army as a whole, but it is necessary for us to have some idea about the character of the men who fought wearing this armour.

The Roman soldier cannot be viewed in isolation, just as a man; we have to consider the world he inhabited. In so doing we will gain some insight into what he was fighting for. At the time considered in this book, the Roman Empire stretched from Northern Britain to the deserts of Syria. Estimates have put the population at 60 million (Lane Fox 2006, 5). This vast empire was connected by a system of well-built, well-maintained roads and by a complex of sea and river routes. This meant that troops could be deployed to trouble spots with ease, but it also meant that people, goods and ideas could also move easily around the Empire.

The policing and protecting of such a huge population required a large and well-organised force and the Roman army was such a force. It was made up of infantry, cavalry and the navy. Infantry and cavalry were comprised of legionaries and auxiliaries, and the navy was deployed in ships both at sea and on inland rivers (see Connolly 1988).

Although the number of personnel in the army and navy has been estimated to be as high as 500,000 under Hadrian (Lane Fox 2006, 6), the total number of men under arms (that is, the army, navy and marines) seems to be closer to a figure of around 350,000. This gives an indication of the number of personnel who would require armour.

The Roman army was a standing army (that is a permanent force) of professional soldiers who were supposed to be paid for out of the public purse. In reality the Imperial army was paid for out of the emperor's own money, which is part of the reason for their special bond (cf. Campbell 1984, 158). From the time of Gaius Marius onwards the rate of legionary pay was 225 *denarii* a year with deductions for clothing, as well as for food and arms (Watson 1969: 91). This increased to 300 *denari* under Domitian, and 500 *denari* under Septimus Severus.

There were many advantages to joining the Roman army: regular pay (which did not always happen and led to mutiny on occasions); a chance to accrue money from plunder, regular meals, clothing and shelter; a chance to escape from poverty – as the ordinary soldier was not accepted into the army because of his social rank, but upon his ability to meet a set of stringent requirements, both mental and physical. And if he survived his 25 years of service he would be given a plot of land to settle on.

Much of our information about the Roman soldier comes from Publius Flavius Vegetius Renatus a mid-fifth century writer. Of his two surviving works his *Epitoma rei militaris* (sometimes referred to as *De Re Militari*), is the most famous.[1] It focuses primarily on military organization and is the only ancient manual of Roman military organisation and institutions to have survived. However, caution needs to be applied in its use as he includes often contradictory material of different periods. These sources include Cato the Elder, Cornelius Celsus, Frontinus, Paternus and the imperial constitutions of Augustus, Trajan, and Hadrian (Vegetius 1: 8). However, within these limitations the *Epitoma* provides a useful guide to the world of the Roman soldier.

Not everyone was eligible to join the army. In the period 49–32 BC approximately 420,000 Italians were recruited into the army. However, by the time of Hadrian, the number of Italians formed only a small proportion of the legions; most legionaries were recruited from the provinces (Campbell 2000, 9).

Convicted felons were excluded as were, under normal circumstances, freedmen. Vegetius (1: 6) provides an indication of what was required from a soldier. He tells us that he should be at least 16 years old and 1.72m tall, but 1.77m was considered better. He should have:

> 'alert eyes, straight neck, broad chest, muscular shoulders, strong arms, long fingers, let him be small in the stomach, slender in the buttocks, and have calves and feet that are not swollen by surplus fat but firm with hard muscle – it is more useful that soldiers be strong than big.'

Why were these things important? Alert eyes – good vision would be essential on the battlefield. Broad chest – fit strong upper body to ensure a strong fighting man. Muscular shoulders – ability to fight with a sword, and carry the heavy weight when marching. Strong arms, for fighting. Long fingers – possibly ensuring a normal-sized hand, as opposed to a small hand with stubby fingers, possibly affecting fine finger control. Small in the stomach and slender in the buttocks – suggesting a basically fit man. Such men were thought to be found more frequently from the countryside rather than from the city.

'they are nurtured under the open sky, in a life of work, enduring the sun. With limbs toughened to endure every kind of toil and for whom wielding iron, digging a fosse and carrying a burden is what they are used to from the country. Skills that can easily be transferred to the art of soldiering.' (Vegetius 1: 3)

Vegetius was apparently not so concerned about feeding the soldiers as to training them to be self-sufficient. He suggested that the army had no need for men engaged in fishing or fowling nor for pastry cooks. Indeed, he said they should be rejected from the army. Presumably, he thought the Roman soldier should be a jack of all trades, and he would rather teach the soldiers to cook, than teach the cooks to be soldiers. However, stag and boar hunters and butchers were to be encouraged to join, along with blacksmiths and wainwrights. These craftsmen would have prior knowledge not only of the use of knives, but the forging of them as well.

To examine such qualities the recruit went before a panel of centurions. These men were the backbone of the Roman army. Leaders of men, their bravery was without question and their ability to judge a man's character and his potential as a soldier were essential to ensure that only those who were up to the task were selected for service.

Selection alone did not ensure entry into the army: it was followed by a four-month period of intensive training. Recruits were taught sword drill using a wooden sword that was twice the weight of the standard issue sword. It is also mentioned that they were encouraged to use the point, because it was more effective for the style of fighting, although the use of the edge was also taught (Vegetius 2: 23). Practice with the shield was also taught with wicker shields twice the weight of the standard issue, as was throwing a javelin. The use of the bow was taught to about a third of recruits – those who showed aptitude. They were also taught use of slings and lead-weighted darts, mounting a horse, marching, and running, jumping and swimming. They practised weapons drill every day of their time in the army. This not only involved weapons and battle drills, but many other skills required of the Roman soldier, such as the need to be able to prepare defensive positions and build camps. This training led Vegetius to state that:

'In every battle it is not numbers and untaught bravery so much as skill and training that generally produce victory.' (Vegetius1: 1)[2]

From this it is clear that not every recruit made it into the army. But those who passed out swore an oath of allegiance to their Eagle standard and to the Emperor. This oath was not just for the length of their service but for life. Even after an honourable discharge, they could, and often were, recalled to the army in times of need.

The Roman soldier practised weapons drill every day, as well as war manoeuvre drills; no-one was excused from drills. This constant and relentless drilling and its subsequent use in battle provoked the statement:

'Their drills were bloodless battles and their battles were bloody drills.'
(Josephus v, bk 1: 27)

A reform introduced by the Roman consul and general Gaius Marius made the legionaries carry all their own equipment and earned them the nick-name 'Marius Mules'. Every five or seven days cavalry and infantry were led out on *ambulatum*, in full armour and carrying full kit weighing 60lb and marched 20 miles at varying speeds. These were at military step (*militaris gradus*) 4.89km/h (3.04 mph); and full step (*plenus gradus*) 5.87km/h (3.65 mph) carrying all his equipment, weighing 45kg. During times of war he was expected to cover (march) 25 miles a day in full armour carrying all his equipment and food. It is likely that soldiers wore their body armour at all times when on duty, and this would accustom them to its weight (of course wearing armour was the easiest way of carrying it). After a time its weight would not even be noticed.

This intensive regime of training was expensive and the Roman state wanted to preserve its investment, so considerable measures were taken to ensure and maintain the health of legionary and auxiliary soldiers (Jackson 2000, 129).

Thus the man who had volunteered to be a soldier had to pass both physical and mental tests to determine his fitness to serve. He had to survive a harsh training regime before he was even admitted and demonstrate his dedication to the army and the Emperor. The Roman soldier was very fit, disciplined, highly trained in combat and kept at a constant state of alertness for war. Once admitted to the Roman army, such a man was protected by the most advanced armour of its day. This is the story of the production of that armour.

Notes

1 The other is a guide to veterinary medicine called the *Digesta Artis Mulomedicinae*.
2 Although note the contradiction in Vegetius (1:8).

Acknowledgements

In this endeavour many people and institutions have provided insights, support, and assistance. We should like to thank the following people for their help in the preparation of this book: Professor Richard Chaplin, Professor Anthony Atkins, and John Frew from the Engineering Department, University of Reading for their continuing encouragement and support; Dr Ralph Jackson and Dr Janet Lang, from the British Museum; Dr Alan Williams, from the Wallace collection; Dr Jerome M. Eisenberg of the Royal-Athena Galleries; Jenny Stevens, from the Museum of the Iron Age; Jenny Jones from the University of Durham. Furthermore, many others including David Cranham, Katherine Brown, Steve Champion, David Houghton, Guy Horwood, and Dr Henry Blyth; Clare Farley, for her proof-reading; and, of course, Mike Bishop for so many insightful comments during the production of this book.

Finally we should like to express our thanks to our friend Holger without whose encouragement, suggestions and insights this book would have been a lesser volume.

David Sim and Jaime Kaminski
Reading, UK

Abbreviations

BAf	Caesar: *Bellum Africum*
BAx	Caesar: *Bellum Alexandricum*
B.Civ	Appian: *Civil War*
BG	Caesar: *Bellum Gallicum*
Josephus	*Bellum Judicum*
Onasander	*Strategikos*
Pliny	*Natural History*
Polybius	*Histories*
Strabo	*Geography*
Vegetius	*Regnatus Epitomarei Militaris* (*De Re Militari*)
RIB	*Roman Inscriptions in Brtiain*

All other classical references are given in full in the text

1 The Evidence

Introduction

Iron and copper alloys underpinned the Roman armour industry. The extraction, processing and smithing of these metals[1] required a huge infrastructure. Long before a military smith could think about the production of a helmet or body armour, miners, charcoal burners, smelters, and bloomsmiths were required to convert ores into workable metal. This volume will consider the production of the metal components of Roman armour from a holistic perspective.

It is emerging that the level of technology and blacksmiths' understanding of the working and manipulation of iron was as advanced in the Roman period as it was in Europe, certainly up until the nineteenth century. Indeed most of the tools that are used by blacksmiths today have been found to have existed in the Roman period (e.g. Manning 1985a; 1985b).

A number of sources of evidence are available to study the level of technology and knowledge of Roman metalworkers and smiths. These include:

a) Written and visual sources.
b) Metallographic examination and interpretation of Roman artefacts.
c) Experimental archaeology.

Written and visual sources

Written sources have a number of advantages in understanding Roman smithing knowledge. They are the only means of hearing the voice of ancient society. In some instances ancient writers recorded the reasoning behind conducting certain activities. This differs from the study of the metallurgy of artefacts which involves the study of the end product, from which the reasoning behind production has to be inferred. While it has long been known that written sources could be manipulated by ancient writers, who may have had certain political or cultural biases, in contrast, there would be little motivation to manipulate factual quotations about iron and smithing technology.

Written sources have a number of limitations when it comes to understanding a Roman smith's level of metalworking knowledge. Writing in the ancient world was essentially the preserve of the elite. With a few exceptions these writers from the upper strata of society would have had little interest in processes as commonplace as blacksmithing and metal production. Furthermore, they may not have had access to the 'closed' society of the blacksmith. Much information was passed on by an oral tradition and experimentation by individual craftsmen. Sometimes this knowledge would not have been passed on and died with the craftsman.

However, Pliny the Elder[2] provides valuable information in his *Natural History*. Pliny was a member of the equestrian order and saw service in the army in Germany and held procuratorships in Gaul, Africa and Spain. His surviving work, *Natural History*, is an abundant source of information about iron, its sources in the Roman world and working techniques. Of course, not being a blacksmith, misinformation could creep into Pliny's work, for example, he believes that the quality of the water used to quench iron after forging is instrumental in determining the quality of the finished product. This is also mentioned in the *Suda*:[3]

> 'But the chief difference depends on the water in which at intervals the red hot metal is plunged; the water in some districts is more serviceable than in others, and has made places famous for the celebrity of their iron, for instance Bambola and Tarragona in Spain and Como in Italy, although there are no iron mines in those places.'
> (Pliny xxxiv: 142)

Other authors make some mention of iron, such as Philon who mentions ironworking methods, but these are comparatively rare. Roman and Greek writers also wrote a plethora of historical works which have proved fertile ground for incidental comments that relate to Roman armour. However, much of this literary work dates from the first century BC. Nevertheless, the commentaries provided can, with caution, be applied to the early Imperial period.

Epigraphic evidence also provides an additional source of information. For example, the monumental tombstone erected to Julius Vitali, the *fabriciesis* or *fabriciensis* (the smith or armourer) of the twentieth legion, V. V. (*Valeriana Vitrix*). Julius was of local Belgic origins, but died at Bath, aged 29, in the ninth year of his service. He was a member of the company of smiths, who provided his funeral (*ex colegio fabrice elatvs*) (Scarth 1864, 59; *RIB* 156). This kind of information builds a social picture of the Roman military that is lost in technical analysis of slag inclusions and tool marks.[4]

Another area where information regarding Roman metal workers can be found is in visual representations. Frescos such as the blacksmith and striker from the House of Vettii, Pompeii (see Figure 33) or the embossed image of the blacksmith from a late second–early third century ceramic vessel from Corbridge (see Figure 11), all provide indications of the tools used by smiths.

Literary and visual sources are, therefore, crucial for the historian but they only offer a limited window onto the past.

Metallographic and surface examination

The metallographic examination and interpretation of Roman artefacts is central to the understanding of Roman iron working methods. Metallography reveals the final stages of the processes that have contributed to the manufacture of an individual artefact. From this final stage it is possible to infer, with a considerable degree of accuracy, most of the processes that preceded it.[5] Metallography can reveal considerable information concerning the structure of the metal and the processes that have been employed in the manufacture of that particular artefact, such as heat treatments (Scott 1991).[6] It is, however, an invasive and partially destructive process that damages artefacts, and it is understandable that many museum curators are reluctant to allow metallographic examination of Roman material.

Although it is possible to deduce a certain amount of metallurgical information from fully mineralised iron artefacts, such information is only of partial use. Nevertheless, mineralised specimens can give a very good indication about the original shape and size of the artefact. Iron is subject to corrosion and will eventually degrade completely.

In addition to metallographic study surface examination can yield useful clues as to the final stages of the production process and post-production repairs. For example, although the outer surfaces of much Roman armour was polished, the inner surfaces often reveal tool marks from production.[7] The study of these tool marks can provide evidence regarding the final stages of production, for example if a helmet bowl was spun or raised, or the kind of hammers that were used to shape sheet metal. It is the combination of these data sources that helps to build up a body of evidence regarding the production of Roman armour.

Experimental archaeology

Experimental archaeology and the application of metallurgy to help the understanding of ancient technological processes had its beginnings in the late 1950s, with the work of researchers such as Henry Cleere, Peter Reynolds, John Anstee and John Coles. This broader experimental approach has been supplemented by the work of a plethora of re-enactment societies focusing on the Roman period.[8] The insights produced by these organisations complement the work of experimental archaeologists.

They realised the limitations of library-bound research. Although such research has an important part to play, it cannot on its own answer all the questions. Indeed, in many cases it can do no more than identify that there are questions to answer, but not be able to offer any explanation. The majority of production processes cannot be understood by reading a book, because most have degrees of subtlety that often are not even realised by their practitioners. They perform the task without thinking about what they are doing. This level of knowledge cannot be understood, unless the task is undertaken by those wishing to understand it.

The role of experimental archaeology is obvious when it is realised that most ancient artefacts cannot be tested satisfactorily because of their fragile nature and rarity. Experimental archaeologists can circumvent this issue by making a copy of the original and testing that. Criteria need to be established: the reconstruction must be made of the same metal as the original (the role of metallurgy is crucial here) and it must be made using only the technology available at that time. Then the reconstruction will be as close to the original as possible.

Experimental archaeology in the field of Roman armour has two functions: the reconstruction of the artefacts to determine the most likely methods of manufacture, and the testing of these same artefacts to determine their effectiveness in use. Testing allows quantification of impact resistance of armour, or general durability, etc.

Experiments to determine the most likely methods of manufacture also enable the researcher to make inferences about the production process, material loss, production time, fuel consumption and manpower requirements. These are crucial for understanding the nature of the Roman military production system. In experimental archaeology generally, the ability to put a time on production is perhaps one of the discipline's most valuable contributions.

Some armour was produced internally by the Roman military. In this case it is likely that speed, efficiency and efficient use of materials were a priority. This supply was supplemented by private manufacturers. Such manufacturers were in the business to make money and the faster a product could be produced the greater the potential for increased profit.

It is only through the process of reconstructing an artefact that it is possible to begin to understand the processes involved in its manufacture. For the research material referred to in this book armour was manufactured using only the technology that was known to have existed in the Roman period. Therefore, these items were produced using copies of Roman tools and forging equipment. No modern electrical devices or tools were employed. Previous studies of Roman armour have provided a deeper understanding of the materials used in its manufacture (Fulford *et al.* 2004). It has therefore been possible to produce sheet ferrous metal that is almost identical to that used in the manufacture of Roman armour.

Conclusions

Library-based research offers an important but limited perspective on the technology and techniques that produced Roman armour. There are few surviving ancient sources and these rarely provide information that is useful for the replication of manufacturing methods. Metallographic and surface examination of Roman armour provide crucial information regarding the techniques used in manufacture. This information can then be used to hypothesise a manufacturing sequence for a piece of armour. However, experimental reconstruction can corroborate if such hypotheses are valid. But reconstruction of armour using the tools and materials available to the Roman armourer yields more than just a confirmation of a manufacturing sequence. It can yield a product that is as close to the original as is possible, and this reproduction can then be tested as a proxy for the ancient artefact.

The study of technology is practical and needs practical input to answer questions. When studying the production of Roman armour it is the integration and assimilation of data from different sources that allows modern researchers to provide a guide to the manufacturing methods.

Notes

1 Iron, Copper and tin.

2 Pliny the Elder (AD 23–79), or Gaius Plinius Secundus was an author, naturalist and naval and military commander. His only surviving literary work is the *Naturalis Historia* (Natural History), an encyclopaedia written *c.* AD 77. Pliny devotes books xxxiii–xxxvii to mining and mineralogy. Iron forms an important component of books xxxix–xlvi.

3 *Suda s.v. Machaira.*

4 '*Julius Vitalis, armourer in the Twentieth Legion, Valiant and Victorious, with nine years service, twenty-nine years old, a citizen of the Belgae, formerly of the Elatus School of Craftsmen. He lies here.*' This highlights the Celtic origins of the armourer, his attendance at a Greek college and that there was a guild of armourers or smiths that had formed a society to cover the costs of burial (Carroll 2006, 186; Birley 1979, 85).

5 For example slag inclusions found in iron artefacts can be used to diagnose characteristics (Gordon 1997, 9).

6 For example, martensite an acicular structure, results from the rapid cooling (quenching) of steel without subsequent tempering. This produces a hard material but with a tendency to brittleness. Tempered martensite appears less distinct. The resulting metal is not as hard but much tougher. Cold worked metals that are not subsequently annealed have grains that are deformed and elongated. This increases the hardness of both iron and steel.

7 Especially on copper alloy artefacts that can be less prone to corrosion than those made of iron or steel.

8 By 2010 there are considerably over 80 such organisations worldwide.

2 Iron Production

Introduction

Iron is a widely distributed ore. With 5.06% of the earth's crust made of iron, it is the second most abundant metal in the crust (Alexander and Street 1979, 28). The ubiquity of iron was clearly understood by the Romans as Pliny notes:

> 'Deposits of iron are found almost everywhere … and there is very little difficulty in recognising them as they are indicated by the actual colour of the earth.' (xxxiv: 142)

Iron ore exists in different forms. The principal groups are those based on oxides (Fe_2O_3) and carbonates ($FeCO_3$). The oxide ores are hematite (ferric oxide, Fe_2O_3) and limonite (ferric oxide trihydrate, Fe_2O_3Â·$3H_2O$), and magnetite (ferrous-ferric oxide, Fe_3O_4). The carbonate form of iron ore is made up of siderite (ferrous carbonate, $FeCO_3$). There are also sulphide ores (pyrites FeS_2), but these were often rejected in the Roman period because of their undesirable sulphur content, which would produce a condition called 'hot shortness'.[1] Hot short iron will crack if heated and worked with a hammer. If it does crack then the exposed surface immediately oxidizes. This layer of oxide prevents the crack being easily repaired by welding. Large cracks can cause the iron or steel to fracture, while smaller cracks can cause the object to fail in use. Although hot short iron can be worked, it has to be worked at a lower temperature which requires more physical effort because the metal must be struck more often and harder to achieve the same result (Gordon 1996, 7).

However, it should be noted that natural weathering of sulphide ores such as marcasite can convert them to limonite. Weathered marcasite has been successfully smelted in experimental furnaces. Also, roasting would serve to expel much of the sulphur content of pyrites ores which would allow smeltings to produce usable iron (Pleiner 2000, 89–90). It is apparent that the properties of the ore will fundamentally affect the quality of the finished product (Salter and Ehrenrich 1984; Forbes 1950).

Sources of iron in the Roman Empire

Most iron products are easily portable and would be found far beyond the sites of mining and manufacture. The sheer geographic breadth of the Roman Empire would also have increased the scope of iron acquisition. But a number of sources for iron can be forwarded (see Figure 2).

- *Iron mined within the imperial borders*: The Roman Empire had a number of major iron producing regions within its borders, including Noricum, Spain, and Britain (Davies 1935; Pleiner 2000). The iron mined here would have been manufactured into goods for use within the Empire, with a small percentage being used for trade outside its borders.
- *Iron traded from regions outside the Empire*: The extensive trading links of the Roman Empire would have encompassed external iron producing regions. For example, there

Figure 1: Captured arms and armour shown on the base of Trajan's Column

is evidence for the trade in high quality steel with India (Schoff 1915; Bronson 1986; Cradock 1995, 245; Young 2001).[2] These would represent an additional input into the Empire.

- *Material acquired and lost during military conflict*: The aggressive acquisition of territory during the first century AD, prior to the stagnation of the second century, brought Rome into conflict with many nations and tribes on its borders. The conflicts and absorption of territories would have led to the acquisition of iron in the form of both the sources of production and captured weapons, tools, and other implements. Roman victory monuments such as Trajan's Column (Figure 1) show the variety of armour and weapons that would have been captured after conquest.

Some of this material would have been deposited in temples as offerings and some would have been taken as trophies by victorious soldiers, but the majority would have been recycled in some form. A valuable resource such as iron would have been important enough to prevent it falling into the hands of those unsympathetic to Rome. The movement of imperial troops around the Empire would have caused an efficient movement of iron products far from their source of origin.[3]

Aside from the increased demand for iron, as the Empire expanded there would also have been losses within the system. For example, just as the Empire could gain material through conquest so it could also lose material in catastrophic military defeat. For example, a serious defeat such as the Varus disaster in the Teutoburg Wald could have led to the irrecoverable loss of many tonnes of military equipment (much of it iron and copper-alloy). The loss of large numbers of military personnel and their equipment in battle was not unknown in the Roman period (French and Lightfoot 1989, 249).[4]

It is apparent that the Roman state went to considerable lengths in order to keep iron and other strategic goods out of enemy hands. The Regulae (Rules) of Q. Cervidius

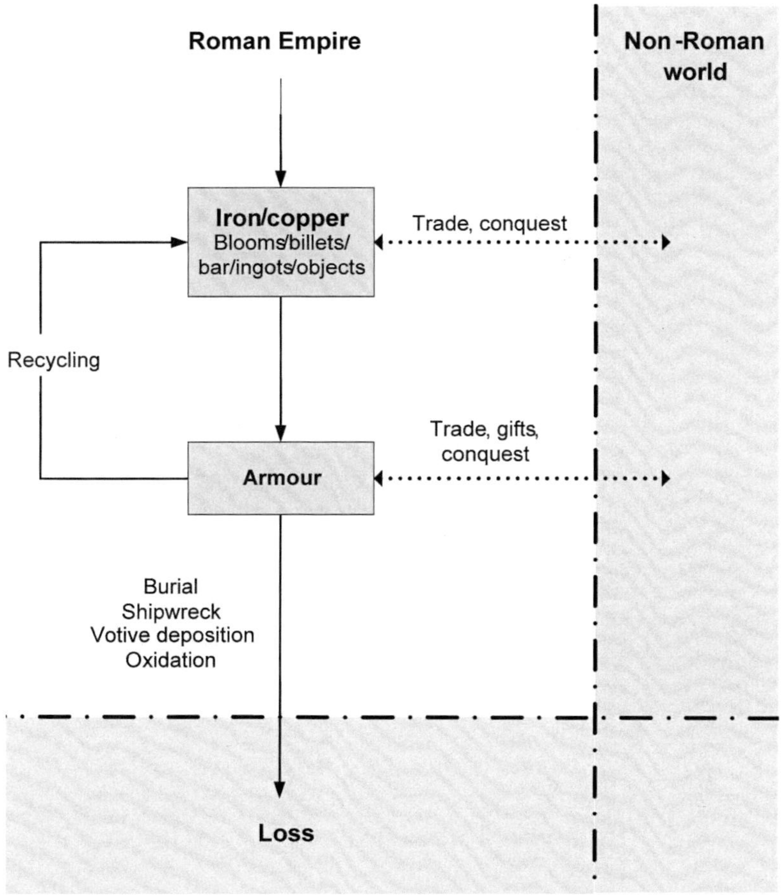

Figure 2: Metal inputs and outputs for armour production in the Roman Empire

Scaevola, a senior Jurist during the reign of Marcus Aurelius who eventually became praefectus vigilum around AD 175, highlights that:

> 'The sale of a whetstone to the enemy, just like the sale of iron and corn and salt, is not permissible without risk of capital punishment.' [5]

Some high-quality armour may have been presented to client kings or other nobles by Rome. In contrast, however, a silver-plated iron cavalry parade helmet from the so-called East Leicestershire hoard, recovered from near Market Harborough, comes from a late pre-Roman Iron Age context and is of very high quality.[6] It is a potential candidate for a pre-conquest diplomatic gift or traded goods. However, it is known that some client kings, especially those who had been brought up in Rome (*obsides*) and who had seen service with the Roman army, trained and equipped their own troops in Roman style. *Legio xxii Deiotariana* was raised from just such troops in Galatia (*Bellum Alexandrinum* 31–41, 65–77).

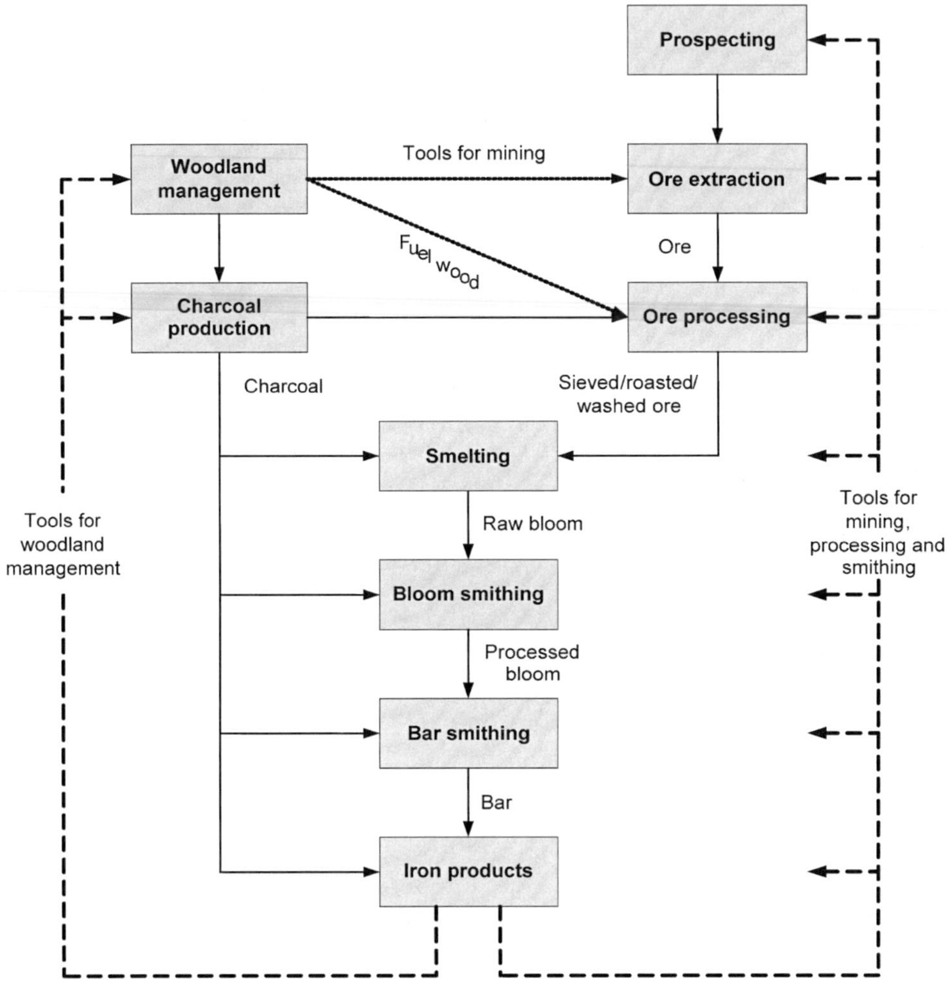

Figure 3: An overview of the bloomery iron production process (modified from Sim and Ridge 2002: 19)

The size of the Empire in the first and second centuries AD meant that it was a net consumer of iron and other metals. It is unlikely that much iron, copper or tin was traded to nations outside of the Empire.

All Roman iron armour began its existence as iron ore. Converting this iron ore into a billet of iron that was usable for armour production was a complicated process that required different skill sets ranging from charcoal production to smelting and smithing (Figure 3).

There were three principal methods of ore extraction available to Roman engineers. These were surface collection, open-cast quarrying, and underground mining (Healy 1978).

Surface collection

The collection of loose iron ore directly from the ground surface is the simplest of all methods of ore extraction. This will have been evident across the Roman world, from the gathering of weathered iron pyrites on the Downs of Southern England, to the surface use of exposed faults and pockets of ore in Spain. The use of surface deposits tends to be associated with small scale, often domestic, operations (e.g. Pliny xxxiv: 142). These sources would have had a negligible impact on military supply. However, such activities may have led to the discovery of larger ore pockets and seams which may have been later exploited using open cast or underground mining operations.

Open-cast quarrying

Open-cast quarrying was the most commonly used extraction method during the Roman period.[7] This varied considerably in scale from small extractions to extremely large quarries associated with industrial sites. Such industrial-scale quarry pits could be quite substantial. At the second century AD iron production site at Great Cansiron, in the Weald of Sussex, the open-cast quarries at Puckstye Farm and Tugmore Shaw cover a combined area of 2.5 hectares (Swift 1986, fig 1, 193). These quarries alone would have required the removal of over 100,000m^3 of material. At Footlands, the main quarry of Cinderbank Shaw would have required the removal of approximately 50,000m^3, while the quarry in Footland Wood, to the west, would have removed 40,000m^3 of material (Kaminski 1996, 353).

Underground mining

Underground mining was the most expensive of the ore extraction methods. It tended to be used for the extraction of the more valuable metals such as silver and gold. However, there is both literary and archaeological evidence for iron mining. Strabo's *Geography* includes references to 'mines' operated by the Chaldeans on the Black Sea coast of Asia Minor, near Pharnicia (12: 3.19); abandoned mines for iron and copper are mentioned on the Greek island of Chalkidiki (10: 1.9), and in the Iberian coast near Hemeroscopeion (3: 4.6).[8]

Strabo refers to Gaulish iron ore mines operated by the Bituriges Cubi and the Petrocorii (4: 2.2). In his *Bellum Gallicum* Caesar comments that the Bituriges of central Gaul were reputed for their underground iron ore-mining skills. During the siege of Avaricum (near Bourges) he noted that they were able to undermine the Roman siege works because of their knowledge of underground working that had been gained from operating their iron mines.[9]

> 'They have extensive iron mines in their country and are familiar with every kind of underground working' (*BG* 7: 22.2).

Archaeological evidence for Roman underground iron mines has been found. For example, in Noricum (modern Austria) the Roman mining operations are well attested (Strabo 5: 1.8). Roman galleries dating to the second part of the third century, reaching a depth of 22m below the surface have been discovered at Knicht, near Lölling, while others have been discovered near Wilde Keller, Zosnerkogel, near Hüttenberg (Schmid 1932, 177–80). These workings are referred to in the third century AD *Itinerarium Antonini*.[10]

	Surface collection	*Open cast*	*Underground mining*
Fixed infrastructure	No	Yes	Yes
Access to transport network	Unlikely	Yes	Yes
Accommodation for workers	Unlikely	Yes	Yes
Potential loss of personnel through accident	No	Unlikely	Possible
Potential yield	Low	High	Medium/high
Materials	Digging and collection equipment	Digging equipment	Digging/mining equipment, pit props, water pumps, ventilation equipment, lighting

Table 1: A comparison of different methods of ore acquisition

Other examples of underground iron mines have been discovered in Britain. For example, at Lydney, in the Forest of Dean, the entrance to a sloping shaft which followed an iron ore seam was sealed by a late third century hut (Wheeler and Wheeler 1932, 18; Schubert 1957, 42). There are other less-securely dated galleries that radiate from open-cast mines at Coleford and a cave-like aperture at Great Dowland (Bromehead 1947, 361). Underground mining of iron ore seems to have been focused in the major iron production centres of the Empire. It is apparent from a comparison of the three different ore extraction methods that each has differing requirements (Table 1). In the case of the extraction of non-precious metals such as iron and copper, open-cast extraction has the greatest potential return on investment. This is because of the higher fixed infrastructure costs of underground mining (pit props, ventilation, lighting), the increased danger to workers (collapse of mineshafts, noxious fumes), and the slower progress of mining (fewer miners can work a seam at any one time). Of course, there is evidence for underground mining highlighting that, in some instances, the geological environment made it necessary to follow underground seams.

Moving the ore

Iron-smelting sites were usually located close to the site of ore extraction. Iron ore is a heavy material of which at least 60% is waste. In most instances the movement of the ore would have been reduced as far as possible.

However, there is evidence of ore being moved greater distances by ship. In the Mediterranean, the Island of Elba produced high quality ores but deforestation caused by the fuel needs of the industry led to insufficient fuel for smelting. Ore had to be transported to the mainland for smelting where charcoal could be obtained from the Ligurian Mountains (Forbes 1958: 18). This kind of movement is revealed in the Adriatic where a shipwreck has been recovered containing iron ore (Jurisic 2000, 43).[11]

Little evidence exists for the method of transport of iron ore between the extraction sites and the smelting operations. However, both human and animal power was used for transporting materials. Pack animals are widely mentioned in the literary sources from the classical era (e.g. Euripides fr. 283 N2; Strabo 14: 2.24), but there appears to be a considerable reliance in the classical world on manual labour for the movement of wood and charcoal. This is seen both in the Greek literature (e.g. Homer's *Iliad* 23: 123; Aristophanes *Acharnians*: 272; Menander *Dyskolos*: 30–2) and in a number of Roman reliefs, such as Trajan's Column, and a Gaulish relief of the manual movement of a large tree-trunk (Meiggs 1982). Certainly, detailed examination of the Bardown iron production complex in the Weald (Cleere 1970, 13) revealed no evidence of wheel ruts in the excavated road surfaces. However, it has to be noted that the road systems on industrial sites were often resurfaced many times during their period of use (Cleere 1970, 9).

It appears likely that many methods were used to transport raw materials to the sites of production; however, they were probably dominated by the use of baskets[12] and pannier-type transport on manual or animal traffic.

Charcoal production

Before the discovery of the conversion of coal to coke by Abraham Derby at Coalbrookdale in 1709, charcoal was the only fuel available for iron-smelting operations although experimentation with other fuel sources almost certainly took place.[13] The fuel needs for smelting iron are highly specific. The impurities found in mineral coal, such as sulphur, can contaminate iron smelted with it, although this did not stop Roman metallurgists experimenting with coal, as attested by the finds of coal in a first century AD furnace and slag deposit at Icklesham, Sussex (Child 1983, 19). Furthermore, analysis of a fragment of cast iron discovered at a Roman iron production site in Wilderspool, Cheshire, revealed the presence of sulphur which, in conjunction with the presence of slag containing sulphur and coal on the site, has led Craddock and Lang (2005, 42–3) to suggest that some experimentation had been made to smelt iron with coal. However, the archaeological evidence from almost all Roman iron production sites is for charcoal being the main source of fuel (Kaminski 1996).

Dry wood by itself could not attain the temperatures required for smelting. To compensate for this, wood could be converted to charcoal. Charcoal is the carbon residue created by heating wood in the absence of sufficient air for complete combustion. Charcoal has two functions in iron smelting.

Its high calorific value provides an excellent source of heat for smelting. The absence of combined and uncombined water in charcoal compared to wood results in a hotter, more controllable heat than could be achieved with dry wood. Furthermore, charcoal is a source of almost pure carbon that can be converted first to carbon dioxide, then to carbon monoxide. This allows the chemical reduction of the ore to take place during smelting. The classical authors suggest that both charcoal kilns and pits were used. Theophrastus[14] in his *History of Plants* (v: 9.4) records the progress of a charcoal burn:

> 'They cut and require for the charcoal heap straight smooth billets: for they must be laid as close as possible for the smouldering process. When they have covered the kiln, they kindle the heap by degrees ... such is the wood required for the charcoal heap.'

This can be supplemented with Pliny's account in his *Natural History* (xvi: 23) of a clay structure used as a charcoal kiln:

> 'piles of freshly cut sticks are fitted closely together and made into an oven with clay, and the structure is set fire to, and the shell as it hardens is prodded with poles and discharges its moisture.'

However, evidence for pit structures is also recorded, by both Greek and Roman authors, including Theophrastus in his *History of Plants* (ix: 3.1–3) and Aelian[15] in his *On the Nature of Animals* (1.8)[16] (Olson 1991, 414).

This literary evidence compares well with the archaeological evidence from across Europe during the pre-Roman and Roman eras. Pleiner (2000, 121–5) distinguishes three types of charcoal production site: the pit, the charcoal pile, and a hybrid sunken charcoal pile. There seems to be little evidence for any chronological shift in the use of the different charcoal production methods. It is probable that local or regional traditions dictated the method employed.

Green wood is composed of an average of 50% water which can be reduced to 30% after exposure and seasoning. The removal of water during charring would result in some volumetric loss. In addition, the nature of wood does not allow for compact transport because of the large volume of air spaces that are created between the branches or timbers. Therefore, the transport of wood to the smelting site would result in the requirement of at least 40–50% more transport than if charcoal production were to occur in the woodlands. By contrast, the production of charcoal off-site and the transport of the product would result in a significantly lighter load and greater compaction, because of the smaller size of the charcoal pieces compared to branch wood, and the loss of volume because of charcoalification. However, because charcoal is so brittle its transport to iron production sites would result in much attrition. The carriage of charcoal was limited to some extent by the inherent fragility of the material and Crossley suggests that transport beyond 5–6km would considerably degrade the charcoal (Cleere and Crossley 1995, 133, 135).

Several stages are involved in the production of charcoal, not least the location of a suitable source of wood. Under ideal circumstances, a single person can cut a cord of wood in a day.[17] Once the wood has been cut, it has to be transported to the site of the charcoal clamp kiln. The clamp kiln is made by covering the wood-pile with sods of earth. This would normally be a minimal journey, because it would be in the interest of the operator to reduce the distance travelled. The clamp has to be constructed, which does not require a great deal of time. However, the extraction of the turfs or sods needed requires a significant input of labour. Once lit, the clamp has to be tended constantly to prevent accidental combustion of the charcoal. Although more than one clamp can be lit and observed at any one time, the charcoal maker cannot leave the area.

Ore preparation

After the physical extraction of iron-bearing materials, some preparatory measures would have been necessary before smelting. These could include washing, roasting, and grading the ore.

Washing

The need for washing was probably related to the nature of the geological matrix surrounding the ore-bearing strata. Washing would remove impurities which would increase the quality and, to some extent, the porosity, although the roasting of the ore would achieve this. The limited evidence for ore washing comes from the Near East, but there is no indication of the method of ore washing in Roman Europe, or whether it was perceived as necessary by the iron producers.

Roasting

Although some ores could have been smelted without preparatory measures, the yield would have been significantly reduced (Ehrenreich 1985: 20). Where a carbonate ore is smelted it must first be roasted to produce iron oxide which can then be reduced to iron:

$$FeCO_3 \rightarrow FeO + CO_2 \text{ (decomposition by heating)}$$
$$\downarrow$$
$$2FeO + \tfrac{1}{2}\,O_2 \rightarrow Fe_2O_3 \text{ (ready for reduction as above)}$$

This could be achieved through heating the ore in oxidising conditions. This would cause the expulsion of the vast majority of the water at approximately 105°C, although higher temperatures are required to remove it completely (Clough 1986, 16). The endothermic disassociation of the carbonates occurs between 200 and 750°C. The removal of the integral water helps to:

- increase the porosity of the ore allowing better reaction to the reducing conditions inside the furnace;
- make the ore nodules easier to break into manageable sizes for the most efficient flow of air through the furnace; and
- prevent the ore nodules exploding in the smelting furnace because of rapid expansion of the water into vapour (Gibson-Hill and Worssam 1976, 253–4).

The removal of the carbon dioxide from the iron carbonate ($FeCO_3$) requires heat though the temperatures required have not been fully established. Using experimental data, Cleere (1970) suggests that temperatures of 300–400°C were sufficient; however, Tylecote (1975, 26) suggests that temperatures in the range of 500–550°C are required (Gibson-Hill and Worssam 1976, 254).

There is no evidence to indicate if charcoal or dry wood were used in roasting operations. Since roasting only requires the removal of water, and intensive heating would result in excessive roasting that would produce unusable ore, dry wood would be adequate to reach the temperature required. Evidence for roasting hearths has been recorded in the Weald of southern Britain at Minepit Wood (Money 1974), Petley Wood (Lemmon 1952), Ridge Hill (Straker 1931, 234), Broadfields (Gibson-Hill and Worssam 1976, 255), and Bardown (Cleere 1970). Other examples of roasting hearths have been found on the Jurassic Ridge at Bedford Purlieus (Dakin 1968; Schrüfer-Kolb 2004).

Bloomery iron production

In the presence of reducing conditions, reduction of iron from its ores occurs at temperatures significantly below that of its melting point at 1535°C or of its oxides Fe_2O_3 at 1565°C, Fe_3O at 1594°C, and FeO at 1396°C (White 1968, 39). Naturally occurring iron ore is combined with waste material, or gangue, which consists predominantly of oxides of silicon, aluminium, and calcium. Sufficient heat has to be generated to liquefy the gangue during smelting. Charcoal is an ideal fuel for achieving the high temperatures necessary for smelting as it provides both a pure source of energy and a source of carbon monoxide for the reduction processes in the furnace.

The furnace charge would have consisted of charcoal and roasted ore. The reduction of the ore would have occurred in several forms, including the direct reduction by solid carbon derived from the charcoal. In addition to this, the combustion of the charcoal in the presence of the air blast induced from the *tuyères* would have resulted in the presence of carbon dioxide because of the combination of carbon (C) and oxygen (O2). This is converted in the presence of further carbon to carbon monoxide. This would have resulted in indirect reduction, allowing the removal of oxygen atoms in the following stages:

$$3Fe_2O_3 + CO \rightarrow Fe_3O_4 + CO_2$$
$$Fe_3O + CO \rightarrow 3FeO + CO_2$$
$$FeO + CO \rightarrow Fe + CO_2$$

The temperature must be sufficiently high to allow for the liquefaction and drainage of the slag and the combination of the iron particles by welding or sintering (Gibson-Hill and Worssam 1976, 257).

The smelting process separates the iron from the oxygen in iron oxide. The direct method of iron production involves heating the ore in an oxygen-starved atmosphere of carbon monoxide (CO) created through the combustion of charcoal. Carbon monoxide reacts with the oxygen in the iron to produce carbon dioxide to leave behind pure iron. This has a strong affinity with oxygen (O_2) and forms carbon dioxide (CO_2). Carbon monoxide reacts with the oxygen in the iron to produce carbon dioxide and leave behind pure iron.

In addition to the chemical process, the iron has to be physically separated from the other mineral impurities (slag). These can include silica (SiO_2) and alumina (Al_2O_3) which are the basic compounds found in sand and clay.

$$Fe_2O_3 + 3CO \rightarrow 2Fe + 3CO_2$$

This differs from the 'indirect' method of producing iron. Here, iron ore is heated with other materials to form a liquid, impurities float to the top and are removed. The liquid iron is then poured into a suitable mould, which goes on to be transformed into steel, cast iron, and other ferrous products.

Bloomery iron is the first product of the smelting process. Iron ore is put into a furnace with a flux, such as limestone. During the smelting process the flux absorbs everything that is not iron, forming a slag on top, with the iron underneath. In the currently held view of the Roman bloomery process fluxes were not used. And in order to produce iron a portion of the iron itself had to be sacrificed in order to make a slag compound. Seen below:

$$2FeO + SiO_2 \rightarrow Fe_2SiO_4$$

This process will produce a bloom that is comprised of iron and slag. Roman iron artefacts produced from bloomery iron should therefore contain some of the slag from the bloom.

However, metallurgical examination has revealed some examples of Roman iron artefacts that have a low slag content, and in some cases are almost slag-free.

Moreover, there is a belief that in the Roman period liquid iron was not intentionally produced, because it was assumed that the technology was not available to reach the necessary temperatures. A temperature of 1200°C is all that is required to bring about the production of iron by the direct method of iron making. Tylecote *et al.* (1971, 363) review experimental smelting and the figures obtained by early experimenters and it is clear that the production of liquid iron was achievable. Pleiner (1969) achieved a temperature of 1545°C, at which temperature cast iron can be produced.[18] Rehder (1986) argues that a simple charcoal furnace 30cm in diameter with a single *tuyère* easily powered by one man can reach a temperature of 1600°C. Tylecote *et al.* (1971) stated that a shaft furnace is capable of producing metal ranging from wrought iron up to cast iron, and that by altering the fuel-ore ratio, steel can be produced. A simple furnace, if handled correctly, is capable of producing a range of ferrous metals. According to Pausanius[19] (3: 12.10) it was 'Theodorus of Samos, who discovered the melting of iron and the moulding of images from it' in the sixth century BC. Interestingly, the reference to melting and moulding images suggests that iron was cast at this early date. The Romans were certainly aware of the properties of cast iron:

> 'it is remarkable that when a vein of ore is fused the iron becomes liquid like water and afterwards acquires a spongy and brittle texture.' (Pliny xxxiv: 146)

Fragments of cast iron have been discovered on Roman iron production sites (cf. Tylecote 1987, 325–6) although they are usually described as accidental production that has been discarded.

Furthermore, metallurgical examination conducted by the authors on various ferrous artefacts has established that steel was more commonly used by the Romans than previously thought. Roman smiths were able to produce high quality, low slag steel, used for tools, weapons, and domestic implements.

Tylecote suggested that most Roman blooms were small, in the region of 7kg at the largest (Tylecote 1987, 250). However, discoveries of furnaces at Laxton, Northamptonshire have shown that large furnaces producing large blooms were certainly in existence. The existence of large blooms certainly lends strength to the argument for the necessity of an iron industry that was able to produce iron in sufficient quantities to meet the needs of the Roman military and civil establishments. It is not known for certain what proportion of iron production went to the military for the use of weapons and armour but, given the size of the army, it is not unrealistic to suggest a figure of between 25% and 40% of iron produced. It must also be remembered that military establishments also consumed large quantities of iron in exactly the same way that a civilian establishment would, i.e. in the construction of buildings (nails, door fittings, grilles, etc).

Various materials were used in the construction of furnaces, but the linings of the furnace were made of clay. This was essential because the lining would interact with other materials inside the furnace during the smelting operation. Fulford and Allen (1992, 197) have shown that furnace linings were significantly consumed in the iron-making process. This was certainly true when rich ores were used. Examination of the third century furnaces at the Roman iron production site at Woolaston, on the edge of the

Forest of Dean iron field, revealed that the interior of the furnaces examined had been relined with clay that varied in thickness from 10mm to 30mm before refiring. During firing the clay changed into a glassy liquid which combined with the charge of iron ore and charcoal in the furnace. Analysis of the slags revealed the clay lining was essential for the formation of slag. Fulford and Allen add that, if clay had not been derived from the furnace walls, it would have been necessary to add it.

A typical cycle of smelting in a shaft furnace followed a general pattern although there were almost certainly different approaches on different sites. The furnace itself had to be preheated and this was usually achieved by burning wood. This removed any moisture from the furnace structure which would crack if rapidly heated to a high temperature, and partly baked the clay of the lining which made it more robust.

When the temperature was judged to be correct the furnace would have been charged with alternate layers of iron ore and charcoal. The charcoal burns and gives off carbon monoxide gas, which reacts with the oxygen in the iron oxide and forms carbon dioxide, leaving behind iron. As the temperature in the furnace rises, the materials in the ore melt. The impurities form a liquid at about 1135°C but iron does not become a liquid until 1530°C, so at a temperature of 1200°C the iron is not a liquid, but forms droplets, which concentrate near the *tuyère*. The liquid slag collects at the bottom of the hearth and is tapped off, in either a continuous or intermittent flow. This process is continued until the bloom which builds up below the *tuyère* is so large that the air will not circulate and the process stops. If the extraction of the bloom did not damage the furnace lining too badly, then another campaign of smelting could be conducted in the same furnace. Otherwise the furnace would need relining. It is difficult to quantify any of the times or weights involved because this kind of operation depended a great deal on the skill and experience of the operators. This is an area that relied heavily on experience and there are many subtleties that will escape the experimental smelter. The accumulated knowledge of the iron smelters is lost to contemporary society. Therefore, the results of experimental smelting need to be viewed with some caution.

The product of the bloomery furnace is a bloom of iron made up of pure iron and slag. Several factors contribute to the formation of the bloom including the furnace lining reacting during the smelt to form slags (Allan 1988).

The carbon content of the iron will be dependent on the ratio of iron ore to charcoal when the material was smelted. The impurities in the iron have to be removed and various suggestions have been forwarded as to how this was done. Experiments by the authors have shown that a very good yield can be achieved by breaking the bloom into small pieces, separating the iron and slag by hand, and welding the iron pieces back together again.

Experimental smithing of blooms has shown that heating and hammering can only lower the slag to around 5%. Beyond this level repeated hammering will not remove it (Figure 5). Metallurgical examination of Roman iron armour and other objects has revealed that some objects have little or no slag content (see Table 2). Therefore the method of producing such pure iron has to be considered.

Furnace types

A range of furnace types was available to Roman metal producers. Coghlan (1977) distinguishes between the simple bowl, the domed or pot furnace, and the shaft furnace.

Cleere (1972) classified furnaces on the presence or absence of slag tapping. His typology also divided furnaces into the groups: simple bowl, domed or pot furnace, and the shaft furnace.

The shaft furnace was widely used during the imperial period (cf. Gibson-Hill 1980). Shaft furnaces were an improvement on bowl furnaces. They were comparatively easy to construct and were relatively hard-wearing in use, as indicated by the numerous relining of shafts (Gibson-Hill 1980, 23). Shaft furnaces were often constructed into banks. They were in the form of hollow cylinders with an arched opening at the bottom. The arch was used for both the drainage of slag and for pumping air to heat the fire, possibly using bellows. It is possible that the bloom was extracted through the arch.

The size of bloom produced in the Roman period varied between 5kg and 10kg (Tylecote 1976, 56). However, evidence from the furnaces found at Laxton, in Northamptonshire indicates that blooms of considerably greater weight could be produced (Jackson and Tylecote 1988).

The Laxton furnace was 1.5m in diameter at its base and may have extended for 2m above ground level (see Figure 4). It has been estimated that 500kg of ore and 600kg of charcoal could be smelted in one operation to produce five blooms of 20kg each (Crew 1998). Blooms of this size contain only a small portion of slag and could be refined into bar iron with only 40% loss. Furthermore, the bloom formed freely in the lower charcoal bed, allowing easy removal through the furnace arch. The furnace did not need to cool down and, as there was no bloom sticking to the walls, the furnace lining was not damaged. The next smelt could start straight away, so supporting a continual process of smelting. It is likely that these types of furnace were in wide use in the Roman period and this means that production levels could have been very high.

Bloomsmithing (pimary smithing)

The product of the bloomery process is a mass of iron interspersed and held together by slag (the bloom). In this state the material is in a transitory state and has to be refined in order to produce workable iron (Rostoker 1990, 94). A process of heating and hammering is used to refine the bloom to a level where the slag inclusions are small enough to allow the iron to be worked. The refined bloom is referred to as a 'billet'. Some examples of blooms have been recovered as well as a number of billets such as those from Newstead (see Figure 29) and Strageath in Scotland (Frere and Wilkes 1989). At various periods in history workable iron has been supplied to the blacksmith in various forms ranging from billets to the so-called iron currency bars (Allan 1967; Brewer 1976).

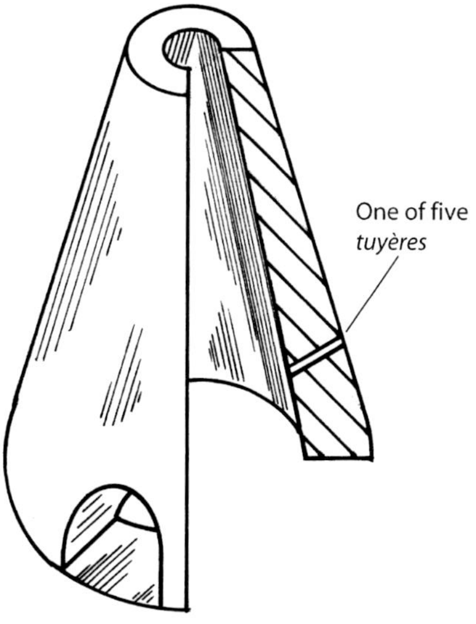

Figure 4: A schematic reconstruction of the Laxton furnace

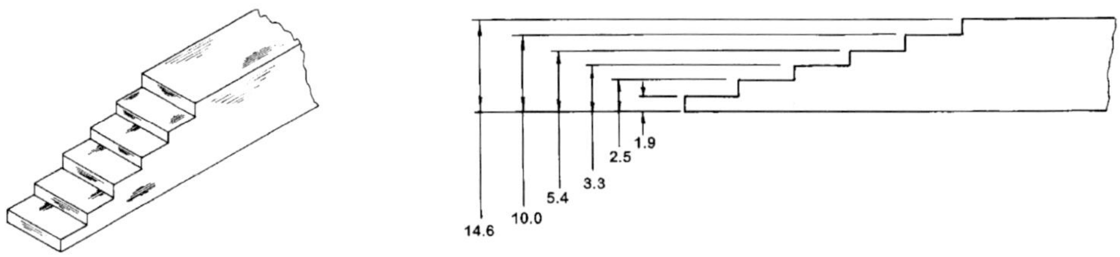

Figure 5: A 14.4mm square bar used for experiments on heating and hammering

Little remains in the archaeological record of the waste materials that were produced during the course of bloomsmithing. The principal product that remains is hammer scale. This is produced at high temperatures during the process of refining the bloom. It tends to have a large quantity of spheres together with flakes (Sim 1994). The difficulty arises that the same morphology of spheres and flakes is produced by fire welding of finished iron rather than that produced when forging a raw bloom.

It is the common assumption that repeated heating and hammering would expel the slag and weld the iron particles together. Initial experiments brought this assumption into doubt and so a campaign was mounted to test the various methods that could have been employed to expel slag from the body of the bloom.

A series of experiments was conducted to test the assertion that repeated heating and hammering could reduce the slag content of bloomery iron to the levels seen in some examples of Roman armour studied. In the first set of trials Victorian wrought iron was substituted for bloomery iron.[20] A 14.6mm square bar was forged down in a series of three steps (10.00mm, 5.4mm, 3.3mm, and 2.5mm, 1.9mm). In each separate heat the bar was heated to white heat, which is necessary for forging wrought iron (Figure 5).

Figure 6 shows a micrograph of the bar before forging and Figure 7 shows the same bar after it was forged from 14.6mm down to 1.9mm thick. The area fraction of slag remains the same in both samples. When the slag content falls below approximately 5% the slag is surrounded by iron and is trapped. It has no route by which it can be expelled from the iron. Hammering consolidates the outside surface layers of the iron forming a shell that seals the outside, trapping the slag within. Over 40 experiments were conducted using different methods of heating and hammering. Every sample revealed traces of slag in greater quantities than that seen in the examples of low slag-content Roman armour. The area fraction of slag remained the same from the start to the finish of each forging cycle. It is apparent that the low-slag content iron seen in a number of examples of Roman armour cannot be achieved by repeated heating and hammering.

Clean iron

Metallographic examination of armour and other iron artefacts reveals that some Roman iron is very pure (see Table 2) compared to wrought iron from the present era (Figure 8).

As this level of purity is evident in everything from armour (Figure 10) to nails (Figure 9) it indicates that the manufacturing process that produced this type of iron

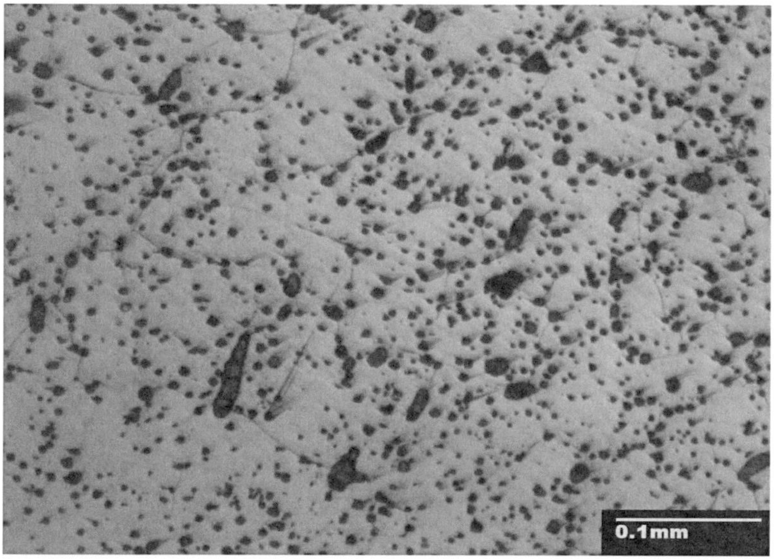

Figure 6: The slag inclusions seen in a sample of the 14.6mm square bar (magnification ×200)

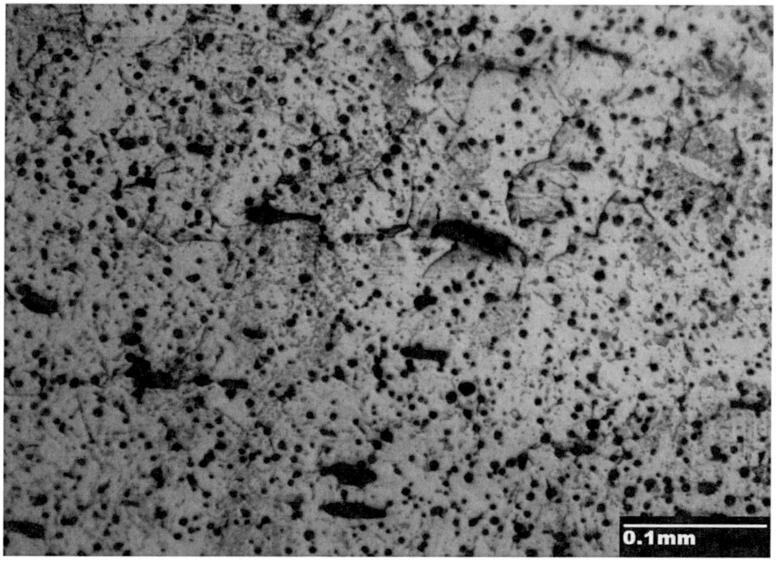

Figure 7: The slag inclusions seen in the same bar forged down to 1.9mm (magnification ×200)

was not restricted to military consumption and was used for producing many different types of artefact. The examples of armour are from various countries and the similarities between the iron indicates that, in those regions, the manufacturing process was similar, perhaps even identical.[21]

The experiments discussed above have highlighted the observation that repeated

Specimen	*Country*	*Location*	*Thickness (mm)*	*Mean hardness (Hv)*	*Non-metallic inclusions*	*Area fraction (Af)*
Ring mail	Denmark	Nydam B	2 × 1.3 oval	277	Quite clean, few slag stringers	1.2%
Ring mail	Germany	Stuttgart	0.80 diam. round	437	Quite clean, no slag stringers	2.2%
Ring mail	Germany	Stuttgart	0.95 diam. round	402	Quite clean, no slag stringers	2.8%
Ring mail	Germany	Stuttgart	0.85 diam. round	383	Quite clean, no slag stringers	2.0%
Ring mail	Germany	Thorsberg	0.90 diam. round	212	Quite clean	2.1%
Umbo	Germany	Xanten	0.64	201	Quite clean	2.5%
Manica	UK	Carlisle	0.87	258	Very few slag inclusions, no stringers	0.2%
Squamata	UK	Carlisle	0.37	266	A few slag inclusions, some slag stringers	3.3%
Squamata	UK	Carlisle	1.20	438	Few slag inclusions	1.3%
Ring mail	UK	Haltonchester	Badly corroded	211	Few slag inclusions, no stringers	0.5%
Umbo	UK	London	1.10	203	Very clean, few slag stringers	< 0.5%
Helmet	UK	Vindolanda	1.17	325	Few slag inclusions and stringers	2.9%
Lorica segmentata	UK	Vindolanda	0.50	215	Quite clean, few stringers	1.8%
Lorica segmentata	UK	Vindolanda	0.60	240	Few slag inclusions, no stringers	< 0.5%
Lorica	UK	Vindolanda	0.80	273	Few stringers	< 0.5%
Lorica	UK	Vindolanda	0.80	200	Very clean, few slag inclusions	< 0.5%
Lorica	UK	Vindolanda	0.60	208	Very clean, few slag inclusions	< 0.5%
Lorica	UK	Vindolanda	0.60	134	Quite clean, some stringers	2.0%

Table 2: Comparison of armour with a low area fraction (Af) of slag

heating and hammering will not remove the slag to levels seen in some iron artefacts, because once the slag content has been reduced to 5–10% more heating and hammering is not an effective means of removing further slag. Therefore it is unlikely that the slag present in a bloom can be removed by heating and hammering. This is because the slag is surrounded by iron and trapped with no escape route. It could be argued that

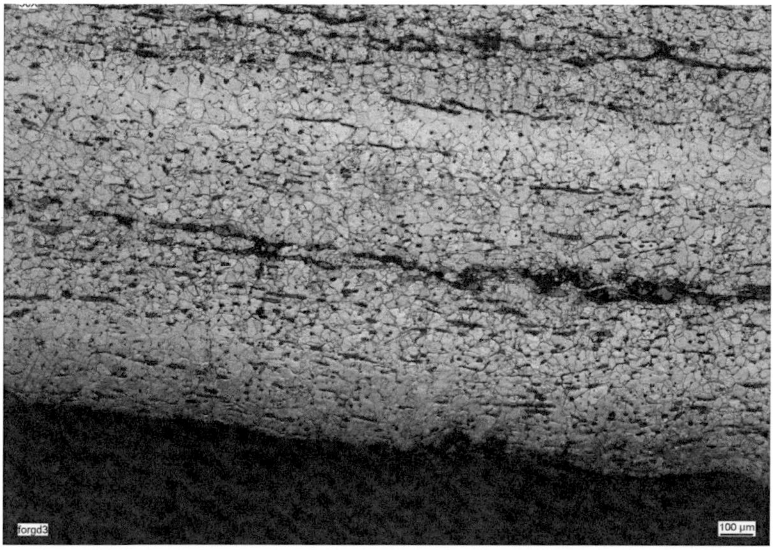

Figure 8: Micrograph of modern wrought iron showing slag inclusions

Figure 9: Micrograph of a nail from Pompeii Insula 9 showing very few slag inclusions (×100)

there is uncertainty, at present, as to the level of technology being used at this time.

It is apparent from the experiments that the slag in iron cannot be removed by heating and hammering and yet there are examples of Roman iron artefacts with very low slag content. The possibility has to be addressed that some iron was being produced with low slag content. It is conceivable that:

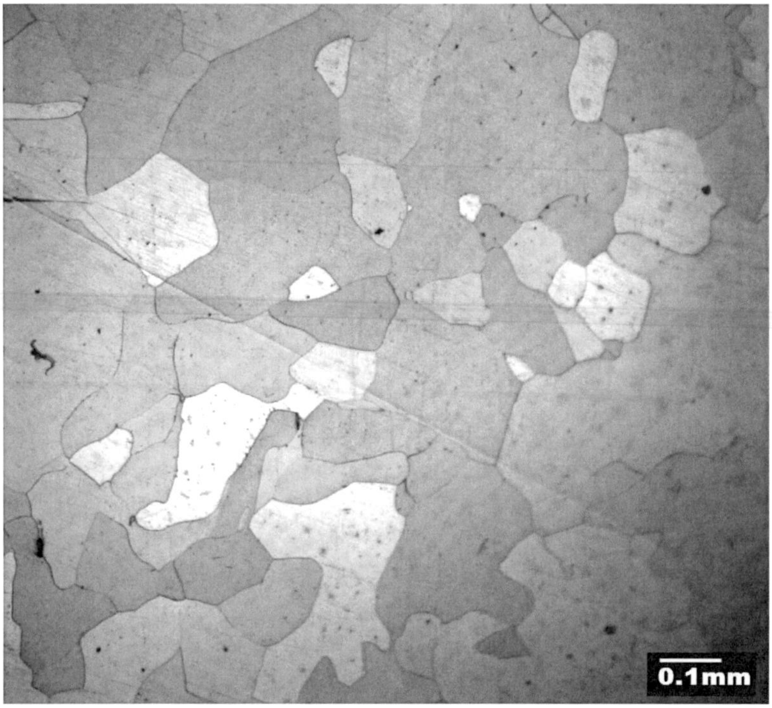

Figure 10: Micrograph of a greave from Carlisle showing very few slag inclusions

- The large smelting furnaces such as those at Laxton could produce a comparatively low slag bloom (Crew 1998), although little experimental evidence has been forwarded to support this hypothesis.
- Skilled smelters may have been able to reduce the slag content of their blooms through years of experience. Charles (1998) has determined that high quality bloomery iron can be comparatively clean.
- Some iron may have been made by a process that involved reducing the iron to a liquid (cf. Vetters 1996). This may have been a widespread process and one that was efficient enough to make it cheap enough for items such as nails to made from slag-free iron.

Conclusions

The production of iron suitable for artefact production was the result of many inter-related processes. The extraction of the ore through underground or open-cast mining was the most obvious manifestation of the iron industry. However, other operations such as charcoal production, with its attendant woodland management or clear cutting, were also essential for iron production. The smelting operation required that ore and fuel were brought together in the same place and, as such, it was usual for smelting to take place near to the site of ore extraction. This is because a large percentage of the material extracted during mining is waste product; it is not usually economically viable to move it. Charcoal would be brought to the smelting area. The end result of the bloomery process would be a bloom of slaggy iron that needed consolidating in order to produce a billet of iron that was usable by blacksmiths.

The accepted wisdom of the manufacturing processes used to remove the slag from the iron has been called into question. Numerous experiments have shown that, once the slag content has been reduced below 5%, repeated hammering will not remove it. The slag is completely surrounded by iron and has no means of escape. What happens is that the hammering simply elongates the slag and forms it into stringers. The quantity of clean iron that has been examined and its widespread use in many different types of iron artefact have shown that the production of very clean iron was easily achieved during the Roman period. The exact nature of the process is still a matter of debate.

Notes

1 Modern manufacturers avoid iron with over 0.03% sulphur (Gordon 1996, 7).

2 Of course there would have be losses in traded material, either through theft, military action or shipwreck. For example over a thousand ships are known to have been lost during the classical and Byzantine periods in the Mediterranean (Parker 1992, 1).

3 For example, an infantry soldier stationed in Dacia (contemporary Romania) might be re-equipped with armour that had been recycled from a combination of Roman and captured Dacian equipment, This soldier could then be deployed on Hadrian's Wall. When the armour reached the end of its effective life it could have been recycled into nails to furnish the fort.

4 The military established systems to try to prevent the loss of equipment in its ranks. Loss of armour or weapons could incur the death penalty, but more often flogging was the punishment (Southern 2006, 147).

5 The passage is found in the *Digest* published in AD 533. Although there is considerable debate as to the exact interpretation and legal standing of the passages in the *Digest* which was compiled for the Emperor Justinian (Rankov1999).

6 MLA (2004) *Portable Antiquities Scheme: Annual Report 2003/4*. MLA: London, 47–8.

7 See Schrüfer-Kolb (1999, 228) and Kaminski (1996). The dating of open-cast quarries is often problematic. Mine pits tend to be poor repositories for datable finds. Mine pits and quarries, by their very definition, result from the removal of material from a given location and, as a result, they do not tend to encourage the deposition of diagnostic material culture. Mining would tend to be an activity that brought workers to the extraction site on a daily basis, rather than requiring a permanent base around the site of extraction. The most frequent method of dating is that of proximity: the closeness of a mine pit or quarry to an iron production site is seen as an indication of the likelihood of its use by that site. Although this is fraught with difficulties, it has been the principal means of associating mine pits with working sites. In rare instances where modern survey and excavation techniques have been applied, it has been shown that some mine pits are linked to the site of production by slag-metalled roads. Examples of such sites include Bardown (Cleere and Crossley 1985, Fig. 10), and Great Cansiron (Rudling 1986, Fig. 1) in the Weald of Southern Britain.

8 These are assumed by modern historians to be underground workings rather than open-cast mines (Pleiner 2000, 95).

9 They also countermined the Roman siege tunnels, attempting to undermine the walls (*BG* 7: 22).

10 The *Antonini Itinerarium* or Antonine Itinerary is a register of the settlements and distances along the various roads of the Roman Empire. The original edition is thought to date to the beginning of the third century AD, while the extant version is dated to the reign of Diocletian. The author is unknown.

11 Certainly the products of the iron production sites were transported by ship as seen by the close association between iron production sites and the *Classis Britannica* in Britain (Cleere and Crossley 1995) and the presence of iron bars in shipwrecks in the Adriatic (Jurisic 2000).

12 Containers used to transport ore included leather bags, wooden buckets, and various forms of baskets. For example at Turners Green, Sussex, small deposits of ore were recovered over much of the site. This has been interpreted as resulting from the transport of ore to (or around) the site in panniers or other small containers.

13 Coal was extensively used in Roman Britain for a variety of processes (Cunnington 1933; Webster 1955; Dearne and Branigan 1995).

14 Theophrastus (371–*c.* 287 BC) was born under the name Tyrtamus in Eresos on the Island of Lesbos. His skills in oratory led to his nickname Euphrastos (the well-spoken) and then Theophrastus (divine spoken). He studied philosophy under Aristotle and succeeded him at the Lyceum. His interests ranged from biology and physics to ethics and metaphysics. He has two surviving works relating to the study of botany, *De Historia Plantarum* (The history of plants) and *De Causis Plantarum* (On the causes of plants). These works have led to Theophrastus being labelled the 'Father of botany.'

15 Claudius Aelianus (*c.* AD 175–235) was born in Praeneste to the east of Rome. His two principal works are the *Nature of Animals* and the *Various History*. The Nature of Animals (*De Natura Animalium*) is a collection of 17 books containing stories relating to natural history. As an author Aelian preferred to write in Greek.

16 A pit structure is indicated by Aelian, in his *Nature of Animals* 1: 8: '*While hunting, Nicias suddenly fell into a furnace for the production of charcoal*'.

17 A cord of wood is 128 cubic feet (3.62m^3). This corresponds to a wood-pile 4ft wide × 4ft high × 8ft long.

18 A review of the temperatures and yields achieved during experimental iron smelting can be found in Souchopova and Stransky (1989).

19 Pausanias was a second century AD Greek geographer. His *Description of Greece*, consists of ten books that describe aspects of ancient Greece.

20 Victorian wrought iron is a material that is comparable to some of the bloomery iron used in the Roman period.

21 While it is conceivable that armour could move great distances from the site of manufacture, objects such as nails are less likely to travel far.

3 Blacksmithing Techniques and Production Methods

Introduction

Iron was ubiquitous in Roman society. Metal-smithing would have been a feature of most Roman towns and cities (cf. Gralfs 1988; Boon 1974, 268). In both domestic and military contexts tools, fixtures and fittings, armour and weapons relied heavily on the material (cf. Rees 1979; Manning 1972; 1976; 1985a; 1985b). The huge volume of material produced is amply illustrated by the vast number of nails recovered from the legionary fortress at Inchtuthil, Perthshire (Angus *et al.* 1962) Similarly bronze and copper alloy was used in numerous applications especially those that required products that benefited from casting.[1] Indeed although there was considerable use of copper alloy in the manufacture of armour, Roman edged weapons from the time of the Principate were made from iron or steel (ferrous metal). Most military establishments would have had a smithy (cf. Schubert 1957: 59; Robertson *et al.* 1975, 16). In addition to blacksmiths (*ferrarrii*) the Roman military had craftsmen who specialised in bronze-working (*aerarii*). Military labourers were called *fabri* (Vegetius 2: 11), and would have been under the command of the *praefectus fabrum* (Sander 1962).

The tools of the blacksmith are the same today as they were in the Roman period although some subtle developments have occurred in heating technology since the Roman period.[2] The relief of the Roman blacksmith seen in Figure 11 was found on a late second/early third century vase from Corbridge, and highlights the similarities between contemporary blacksmiths and their Roman equivalents. The hammer (Sim 1998a), tongs (Sim 1992a) and anvil can all be found in a modern blacksmith's smithy. Iron tools because of the high labour cost of their provision are likely to have been well cared for (Shirley 2000, 171–172). The techniques of hot metal forging such as fire welding, flaring, drawing down, upsetting, etc (see glossary) are the same today as they were in the Roman period.[3] The production of Roman armour was reliant on certain basic blacksmithing techniques including welding, heat treatment, and work hardening.

Blacksmithing

Blacksmithing is reliant on the transformation of iron which takes place when it is exposed to high temperatures. When heated to temperatures in excess of 912°C iron undergoes a phase transformation. The hard ferrite which is the iron familiar to all, transforms into malleable and ductile austenite, which is the stable form up to 1400°C. It requires considerably less effort to transform into different shapes than ferrite. When cooled the austenite transforms back to the hard ferrite. Iron shaping and manipulation takes place best at temperatures in the range of 1000–1100°C. Hence Publilius Syrus, writing around 42 BC stated that '*you should hammer your iron when it is glowing hot*' (Maxim 262).[4]

Forging makes use of this phase transformation. The smith places the item to be forged

Figure 11: A Roman blacksmith, taken from a plaster cast of a late second early third century vessel from Corbridge (private collection)

in the fire and heats until red heat. Achieving this temperature is aided by the use of bellows. The smith can then work the forging on the anvil until it loses its heat through radiation and transforms back into the hard ferrite phase. Depending on the size of the forging and its temperature when removed from the fire a blacksmith can expect to have between 45 and 60 seconds of hot working time. The forging is then returned to the fire until it regains red heat, when working can continue. This sequence continues until the forging is complete (Buchwald 2005).

Although the shaping of parts by machining was carried out in the Roman period, it was a much slower process than today.[5] Complicated shaping was usually achieved in non-ferrous metals by casting and by forging in ferrous metals. A forging has advantages over a machined part.

- *Structural strength*: A forged component is stronger than a machined component, because the forging process causes the metal grain structure to flow in the direction of working, thus improving the strength.

- *Material loss*: Machining is more wasteful of material, because a machined component is produced by removing metal (swarf). Although it was possible to recycle non-ferrous metal swarf, ferrous swarf was not reused until much later, when it was incorporated into general scrap used in the indirect smelting process.[6]

Welding

Until the development of gas welding in the nineteenth century, iron and steel were welded by a process called fire welding. If a piece of iron is heated between 760°C and 1537°C it enters what is known as the plastic range (Bealer 1995, 124). At this temperature the material behaves as a semi-liquid. The blacksmith knows when the correct temperature has been reached by the appearance of white bursting sparks appearing in the fire. If two pieces of the same type of metal heated to this temperature are placed one above the other and struck with a hammer, they will fuse together to become a single solid mass.[7] In the Roman period this technique was used to produce large iron structures such as the so-called bathhouse beams (Wacher 1971; Wright 1972).[8]

As can be seen in the high-speed photographic sequence of a fire weld in Figure 12, and in detail in Figure 13, large quantities of slag are expelled during the operation. Depending on the size of the iron being welded, between 60% and 75% of the original volume of the metal is lost because of oxidization. These losses were such that Japanese sword makers covered their swords with slurry made of clay, to reduce the amount of loss during welding operations (Kapp *et al.* 1987, 71). It is not known if this was a practice used by Roman smiths. Many blacksmiths use a flux during welding. This helps to chemically dissolve the oxide formed on the surface of the iron, and to stop the formation of oxide during the heating prior to welding – although it is possible to produce fire welds that are virtually undetectable to the naked eye without the use of a flux.

Hammer scale is the formation of iron oxide on the surface of a piece of iron that has been heated to in excess of 700°C. When this heated metal is struck with a hammer, the force of the blow compresses the metal and also dislodges the oxide film that has been formed on the surface (Figure 13). This leaves a characteristic residue of iron oxide fragments on and around the anvil (Allan 1986; Sim 1998b, 97–145; Payne 2010).

In contrast to iron, copper and its alloys cannot be successfully joined by traditional welding, because a thin film of copper oxide covers each part of the heated metal preventing any close interlocking of the surfaces to be joined (Maryon 1949, 118–9).

Heat treatment

The properties of iron such as hardness, toughness, strength and ductility can be manipulated through heat treatment. The type of treatment will be governed by the carbon content of the metal; as such the properties of pure iron are not altered by heat treatment (Higgins 1976, 216). The ability to carry out these treatments is fundamental to the art of the blacksmith.

Artefacts crafted from iron are made for specific purposes and require particular properties to make them suitable for that purpose. For example, a metal cutting file can be left hard and need not be tempered, because it will not be subject to shock loads. In

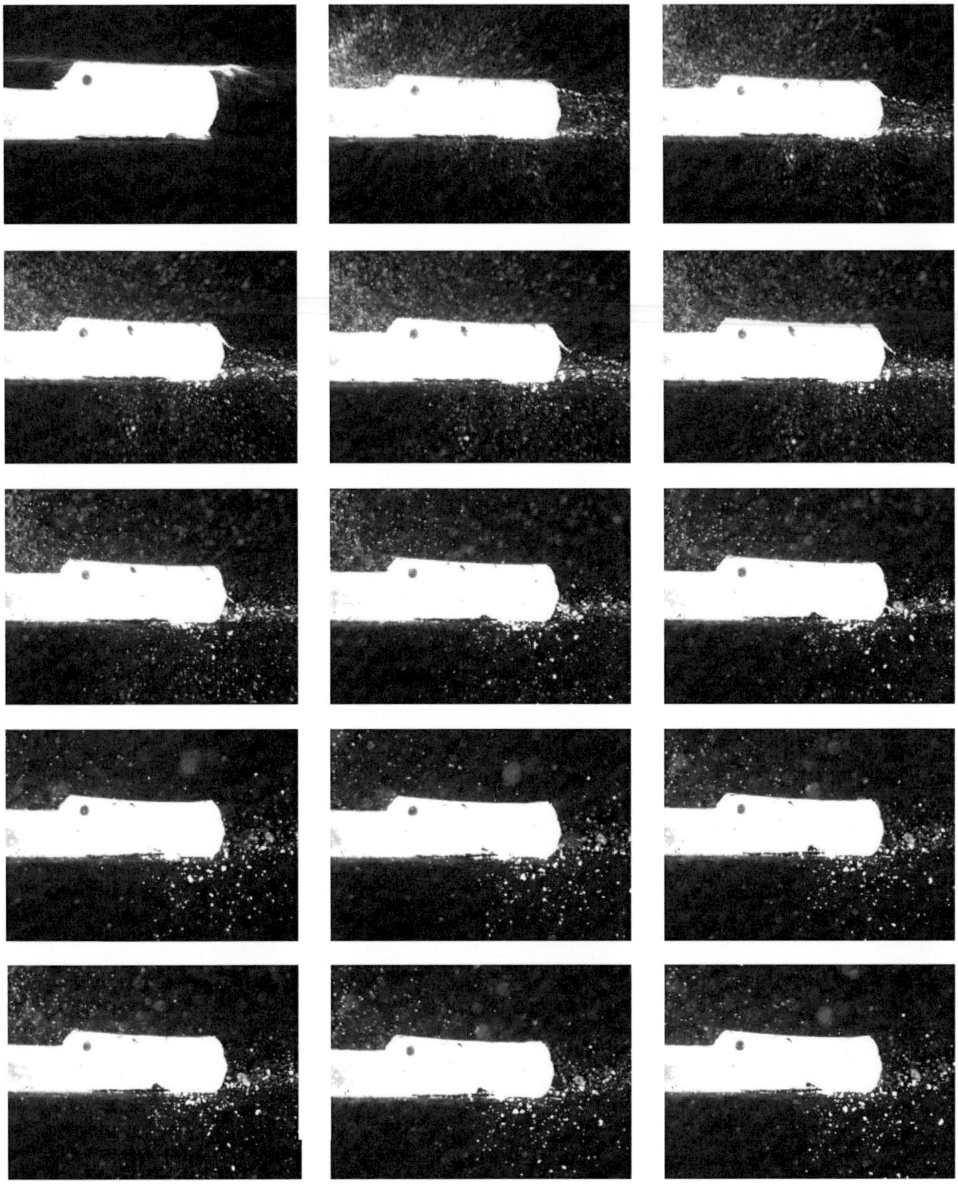

Figure 12: High speed photographic sequence of a fire weld showing the expulsion of hammer scale (side view). (Sequence should be viewed from left to right)

contrast, a mason's chisel will be subject to constant shock loads from hammering so it needs to be tough. Combining the properties of differently treated metals was sometimes done by Roman smiths to enhance the strength of armour. For example, some scale

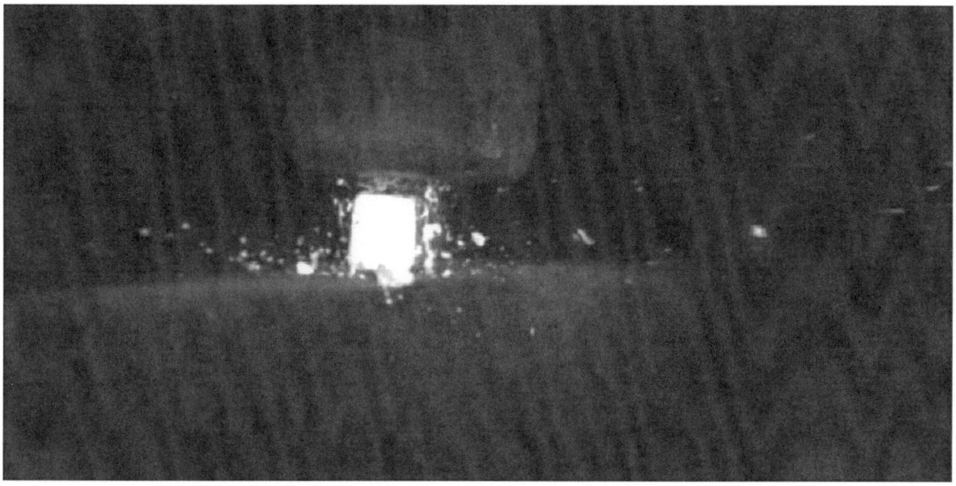

Figure 13: The expulsion of hammer scale (front view)

armour was made with a steel outer layer and an iron base, to provide a hard outer surface, strengthened by a tough backing.

In modern terms, heat treatment is the application of a specific temperature, followed by cooling at a specific rate to bring a metal to a particular microstructure. These changes cause the atoms within the structure to take up different positions and so change the properties of the metal (Alexander and Street 1979, 170). It was these changes in the property of the metal that the Roman blacksmiths were seeking. Both literary evidence and metallographic examination indicate that heat treatment was known to both Roman and pre-Roman societies.[9] There are four basic heat treatments that can be used to alter the properties of iron: hardening, tempering, annealing and normalising.

Hardening

Hardness can be defined as a metal's resistance to indentation or penetration. Metals are also hardened to reduce the rate at which they wear. Tools such as a shovel or a wood chisel are both constantly in contact with a material that is abrading the surface and causing the edge to blunt, because it wears away. Hardness increases a material's resistance to wear. However, constant wear of the outer surface is not a problem that is encountered in armour, although wear occurs when pieces of armour rub together. For example, articulated armour such as *lorica segmentata* or *manica*, scale armour (*lorica squamata*), or mail (*lorica hamata*), all have areas where there is metal-to-metal contact and consequently abrasion. Furthermore, cleaning can result in abrasion.

The hardening of plain carbon steel is carried out by heating to red heat, in the range between approximately 700°C to 900°C. When the correct temperature is obtained, the item is then quenched in oil or water. The choice of quenching medium is extremely important and will depending on the carbon content and thickness of the metal.

During quenching the heat energy in the item to be quenched is transferred to the medium in which it is immersed. If this rate is too fast the metal will crack, if too slow then it will not reach its full hardness. Items with high carbon content that require a slower rate of cooling will be quenched in oil (Plate 1a).

The cross-section of the product also plays an important role in the choice of quenching medium. Items with large cross-sections will often need more rapid quenching, because the centre of the piece can still remain at high temperature when the outside has cooled. Armour tends to have a smaller cross-section and cooling will be rapid. At a time when this type of knowledge was arrived at by trial and error the experience of a skilled craftsman was vital to ensure correct heat treatment.

Hardening leaves steel in a hard but brittle condition. For some iron tools, weapons and armour this brittleness has to be removed in order to make them serviceable. For example, a cold chisel which will be subject to shock forces would fracture at first use if it was in a fully hardened condition. The brittleness is removed by the process called tempering, but some of the hardness will be lost.

Until comparatively recently much craft knowledge was passed on from skilled craftsmen to apprentices by word-of-mouth, demonstration and on-the-job training. It is therefore difficult to be entirely certain of what knowledge the Roman blacksmith possessed. However, Pliny in his *Natural History* (xxxiv: 145–6) reveals that Roman smiths understood that different results would be achieved by quenching in water and quenching in oil.

> 'Quench small iron forgings with oil, for fear water might harden them and make them brittle.'

It is likely that the use of different quenching media was common knowledge to blacksmiths across the Roman world.

Tempering

Quenching induces internal stresses within the metal and tempering is carried out to relieve these stresses, reduce the brittleness[10] and toughen the steel. The process of tempering was known long before the Roman period for example Homer described the process in the *Odyssey*:

> 'when a smith plunges into cold water a mighty axe head or an adze to temper it – for this is what gives strength to the iron' (*Odyssey* 9: 391.ff)

Some items that are not subjected to shock forces, such as files, are left in the fully hardened condition. However, many other items need the brittleness removed in order to make them serviceable. Much of the panoply of Roman imperial armour falls within this category. The process is called tempering. It is carried out by heating the object to a lower temperature than for hardening, typically 230–320°C and then quenching it in oil or water. This removes the brittleness, but also reduces the original hardness; however, this loss of hardness does not significantly impede the effectiveness of the armour. These temperatures are indicated by a change in the colour of the oxide film on the surface of the metal (Table 3 and Plate 1c)

Temperature	*Temper colours*	*Applications*
290–330°C	Blues	Saws, stone chisels, cold chisels
270–290°C	Purples	Swords, knives, woodworking chisels
250–270°C	Browns	Axes, wood chisels, shears
220–250°C	Yellows	Razors, turning tools, scrapers, engraving tools

Table 3: Tempering colours and their applications (Healy 1978)

Annealing

The purpose of annealing is to reduce a metal to its softest possible condition (Sim 1998c). This improves the ease of working. Ferrous metals are annealed by heating them to a suitable temperature (depending on carbon content) and holding them at that temperature for a prolonged period. Non-ferrous metals are annealed by heating to the correct temperature and then quenching in cold water.

The production of some iron objects requires them to be worked at room temperature (cold working). In order to reduce the amount of force (effort) required to achieve this, the metal should be as soft as possible.

Normalizing

When a forging is going to be further heat-treated, normalizing is often carried out to relieve the stresses set up in forging. The process is carried out by heating to red heat (this will range from approximately 700°C to 900°C depending on carbon content and thickness) and cooling in air. This process produces maximum grain refinement, and consequently the steel is slightly harder and stronger than in the fully annealed condition. For example, a cold chisel has to be forged to shape; if it were hardened straight after forging, the stresses from forging would cause cracking. So it is forged, normalized, then hardened and tempered.

Advantages of hot and cold working

Iron can be worked cold and often is, particularly sheet iron. A modern example can be seen in the manufacture of car bodies, in particular hand-made cars – the bodywork is done cold. The advantage of cold work is that the sheet is easier to handle because it can be hand held, unlike hot worked material. The disadvantage is that it is slower to form the metal into a shape, because the malleability of cold iron is lower that hot iron. A further disadvantage is that as iron is worked cold, the metal itself gets harder due to work hardening (see below).

The malleability of iron increases, as the temperature it is worked at rises from room temperature. It is at its most malleable when heated to what is known as the forging range from approximately 700°C to 1200°C. When working sheet iron, as would be the case when making shield bosses, the volume of metal in a sheet is low and, this factor being combined with the large surface area, the heat is rapidly conducted to the surrounding air. This means the metal cools very quickly, leaving only a short time when it is at its most malleable – and therefore a short time when it can be worked.

It is also more difficult to manage when hot, as it has to be held in tongs; this reduces the manoeuvrability of the sheet and further impedes the working time. It is more difficult to manoeuvre sheet metal hot, than cold. The advantage of hot work is that production time is very quick, compared with cold work.[11]

After forging, the steel is left at room temperature to cool. On cooling the grains re-crystallise and retune to their original size and shape. If a shield boss is hot forged then left to normalise, then finished cold, it will have two effects.

1. It will reduce the hammer marks from hot working.
2. It will increase the hardness.

Work hardening

There are two methods of creating a hard surface on a piece of armour.

1. If it is made from carbon steel, it can be heat-treated to form a hard surface.
2. Work hardening (working metal cold). This is a deformation process. As the thickness of the metal decreases, the metal becomes harder and stronger, and a stage is reached when further deformation is impossible. At this stage, when the tensile strength and hardness are at a maximum and ductility at a minimum, the metal is said to be work hardened.

In this process the material is hammered or bent at room temperature, causing the individual grains to crack and break, thereby increasing the hardness of the material and decreasing its malleability and ductility. An example of this can be seen in the production of raised shield bosses. In this case sheet iron was formed into the rough shape of the boss. This may have been done hot, but the surface irregularities and bumps are removed by hammering the boss while cold (at room temperature). This produces a smooth finish but has the additional benefit that it work hardens the surface of the boss.

If shield bosses were to be made from heat-treated steel, and then damaged, they would need to be heated to red heat in order to repair them. Then they would need to be placed in a container of wood ash and allowed to cool overnight. This would make the material soft enough to be repaired. When the repair was completed, the boss would have to be heat treated to restore it to its former hardness. This would require the skills of a blacksmith. On the other hand, if armour were made from work hardened steel it could be easily repaired by semi-skilled workers and those repairs could be undertaken in the field.

Figure 14 shows a micrograph of a piece of non-work hardened low carbon steel; Figure 15 shows how the grains have been distorted after cold working. The hardness that results from work hardening is dependent on the metallurgical composition of the parent bar and the amount of cold work performed.[12]

Forming sheet metal hemispheres

Sheet metal hemispheres form the basis for both helmet bowls and shield bosses. There are two principal ways in which such hemispheres could be produced: raising and spinning.

Figure 14: Non work-hardened low carbon steel

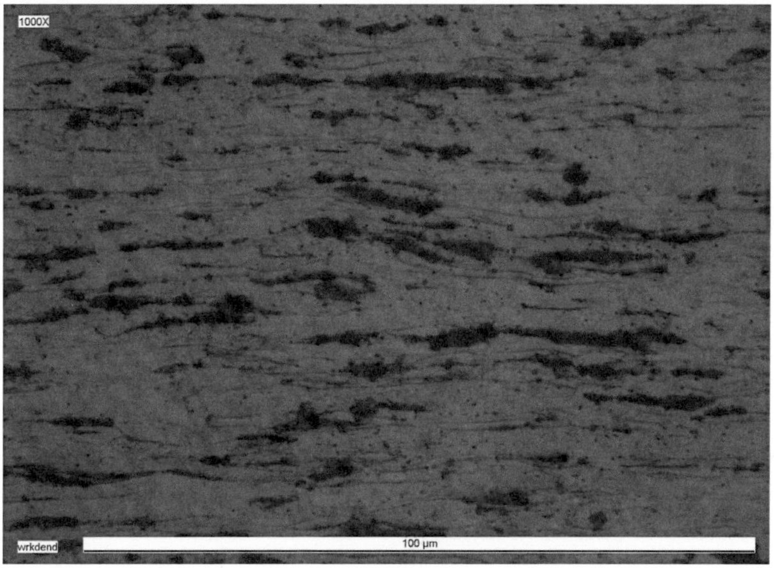

Figure 15: Work-hardened low carbon steel

Figure 16: Doming block used when raising

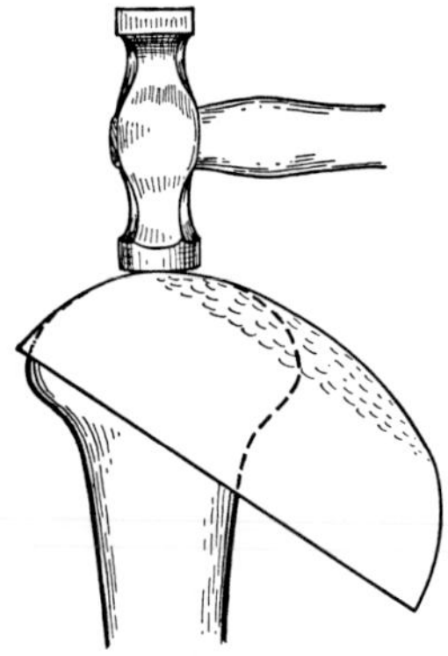

Figure 17: Planishing

Raising

Wooden doming blocks

The earliest helmets were produced by the technique of 'raising' (Hodges 1989: 74). This involves hammering a ferrous or copper alloy sheet into a wooden block with a hemispherical depression in it, called a doming block (Figure 16).

This operation is called sinking and needs to be done gradually; if the metal is struck with heavy blows it will distort. Furthermore, it has to be conducted in a systematic manner, working from the centre outwards. If this is not done evenly the metal can fold in on itself (creating a lap) which can then cause cracking. The hammering leaves a series of small but noticeable hemispherical depressions on the surface. These facets are removed by putting the blank over a ball stake, and hammering the surface using a hammer with a slightly curved striking face.[13] If a hammer with a flat surface is used, the edges of the hammer will dig in to the surface of the metal, leaving marks which will then have to be removed. This process is called planishing (Figure 17).

When the dome has been formed, the flange is shaped by flattening on the edge of a metal block or an anvil, and any holes are punched (see Sim and Ridge 2002, 96). This leaves the surface covered in small facets. These can be removed by mounting on a lathe and using a cutting tool or a file. This will usually leave concentric circles on the surface, which can then be removed using an abrasive. It is possible to train an operator to perform only this task. An alternative is that all marks are removed using abrasives. Although this is a very time consuming, it can be undertaken by unskilled labour. The production of helmet bowls using the sinking and raising method is both time consuming and requires a considerable amount of skill on the part of the operator. However, the technique requires much simpler equipment compared to spinning (see below).

Iron forming blocks

If a wooden doming block is used for the production of iron sheet products, it will wear out rapidly. This increases the cost of production because new tools need to be manufactured more often. And because the production of such tools is a skilled task they are expensive to make. Furthermore, a wooden block cannot be used to form hot iron. It would rapidly become unusable and would need frequent replacements. Wooden doming blocks are most effective when used on non-ferrous metal, which are softer than iron and can be cold formed easily. This gives the doming block a longer life.

It is possible that doming blocks were made of iron. An example is shown in Figure 18. This has been described as a socket for a door to pivot on; however, this shape of block could just as easily be used for forming shield bosses. It shows that the Roman blacksmith was capable of producing such blocks and it is not unreasonable to suggest that similar blocks could have been used for raising hemispheres for various applications.

Figure 18: An iron block with hemi-spherical depression from a second/third century context in Wroxeter (see Bushe-Fox 1914)

The manufacture of such a doming block is a simple task for a skilled blacksmith and the investment in time and materials is more than justified because, once made, such a block would need very little maintenance. Such blocks were and still are an essential piece of equipment in a blacksmith's workshop as many items produced by blacksmiths have a hemisphere as a component. These include domestic items such as ladles and spoons, as well as military equipment such as shield bosses and helmets – also other pieces of armour that make use of a dome. It is therefore likely that many blacksmiths would have had a metal doming block as part of their standard equipment.

Wooden block with steel insert

As an experiment a wooden block was made and a steel lining was placed inside it (Figure 19). This worked very well and is faster to produce than a solid iron block. However, the metal lining became very hot and the heat did not dissipate quickly because wood is a good heat insulator. This caused the block to shrink and split and, although it increased the life of the block, it required frequent immersion in water to stop the shrinkage. Nevertheless, if only a limited number of helmets or shield bosses were required, this would be a less expensive way to prolong the life of the doming block and enable the boss to be forged from hot metal.

It seems unlikely that such a system would have been used in a permanent workshop; however, it would be effective during campaigns when manufacture in the field was necessary. There is no firm evidence of this in the archaeological record; however, if such a device had been made, the wooden section would have decomposed and, if the metal lining remained intact, it would probably have been misidentified as a shield boss or not identified at all.

Spinning

Spinning is a production system where a thin sheet of metal is rotated and pressure is

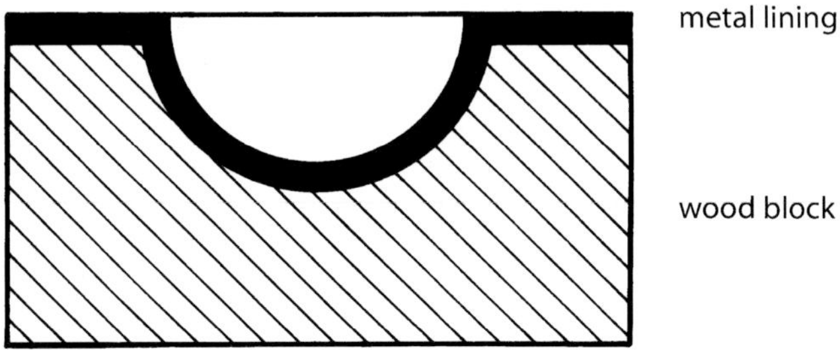

Figure 19: Wooden doming block with steel insert

applied to the sheet to force it against a wooden former (Hodges 1989, 74–5). The finished article will take the shape of the former. With this system it is possible to produce large quantities of identical objects. This differs from raising, which produces a series of objects, superficially similar, but unique.

Wrought iron with large quantities of slag inclusions is not suitable for spinning, because the slag inclusions act as stress raisers and cause cracking. However, it is apparent that much iron used for the production of Roman armour contains very low quantities of slag inclusions and this material can be spun into a bowl.

Up to the present no iron helmets have been recovered with spinning marks. However, the outer surfaces of most iron helmets have been subjected to polishing during manufacture and, subsequently, to corrosion. Both processes will remove the layer that contains the spinning marks. Plate 2 shows an example of spinning in a contemporary workshop. It is possible to spin iron sheet with simple lathes although it is much slower than the system used today. The starting point of production is a sheet of ferrous metal (probably steel) with low slag content. A disk of metal, the 'development', can then be spun on a lathe to form the characteristic helmet bowl. The methods of forming bowls in copper alloy or iron are in many ways the same but it is impossible to determine the exact sequence of operations because only the evidence for the final stage is visible.[14]

Both spinning and raising leave diagnostic surface marks (Plate 3a). Spinning results in characteristic concentric circles caused by the pressure of the spinning tool on the surface of the metal when it is rotating on the lathe. Raising leaves distinctive depressions caused by the hammer blows. In the case of Roman helmets and shield bosses these marks are almost universally removed from the outer surface; however, they are very rarely expunged from the inner surfaces which are not visible during normal use. It is on these inner surfaces that clues can be gleaned as to the production methods used to create the bowls. For example, Plate 3b shows the diagnostic spinning marks retained on the inside of the bowl of a mid-first century AD copper alloy Coolus helmet recovered from Chichester Harbour, UK.

Producing holes in sheet metal

It is evident from a visual examination of Roman armour that most holes were punched. This is usually manifested in the form of a burr on the inner surface that, in some cases, has been hammered flat and in others left as formed. This is hardly surprising because armour requires a considerable number of holes for articulations, attachments, attaching decorations, appliqués, etc. Some armour forms such as *lorica squamata* could require thousands of holes for attaching the individual scales to the backing and to each other. Punching is the most rapid mechanism for making holes in sheet.

Holes are usually made in thick iron by hot forging with a flat-faced punch followed by perforation with a pointed tool. This technique is, however, not suitable for the thin sheet of which armour is composed. Other methods for hole production have been proposed such as the use of a bow drill but the drilling times established from experimental evidence make it impractical (Rostoker 1986, 93–4).

Experimental research conducted by Rostoker (1986) suggests that small holes could be produced using a punch with a taper of about 60° at the tip. Copper alloy tools can easily be used effectively on copper alloy sheet and the punch point need not be sharp. The key to the method is the use of a flat, deformable backing surface upon which the sheet is laid. Rostoker (1986, 94) used a block of wood or a plate of lead. The punch is struck with a hammer while the sheet metal is laid flat on the deformable surface. The punch forms a dimple. The sheet metal is then reversed and the dimple is hammered flat. The sheet is then redimpled in the opposite direction and flattened. If this operation is carried out three or four times a small hole will form with little or no projection (burr) on the opposite side. Once the initial hole is formed its diameter can be expanded to the required size. This is achieved using a drift which is similar to the punch but with a longer taper at a smaller angle.

The sequence of operations is continued as before, the drift is used in the deformable backing and the sheet metal is reversed after each strike. The hole diameter increases the further the taper is driven in. This sequence of operations leaves a minimal burr on the opposite surface of the sheet. Should any develop, it can be suppressed by hammering them flat. This counterpunching procedure is simple and fast and allows holes to be positioned close to each other and close to the edge of the sheet.

However, tool marks found on the Thames Coolus helmet indicate that another method was also available to Roman armourers for producing larger diameter holes. The use of a plug cutting punch is evidenced by the impression of its tip on the surface of the copper alloy neck guard (Plate 3e). This is simply a punch with a hollow core that removes a plug of material from the sheet metal. This tool will produce holes more rapidly than counterpunching.

The inauspicious plug cutting tool mark on the Thames Coolus neck guard highlights the difficulties archaeologists face when attempting to recreate production processes. There is no literary evidence for the use of a plug-cutting punch, neither is such a tool represented pictorially but, more fundamentally, such a punch has not been recognised in the archaeological record. Yet the tool mark indicates that this tool was used. In the same way that spinning marks indicate that the some metal hemispheres were formed by spinning on a lathe, the plug cutting tool mark highlights the important of this kind of evidence for determining production methods. Sometimes indicators such as the consistency of thickness of sheet metal may be the only evidence for tools and machinery that has not survived in the archaeological record.

Materials testing in antiquity

Quality control and materials testing are an essential part of any successful manufacturing enterprise.[15] The earliest evidence of metallurgical quality control and materials testing comes from an inscribed Greek *stela* of the fourth century BC. This cites a decree concerning the manufacture of bronze fittings known as *empolia* and *poloi* required form the erection of columns of the Philoian Stoa. This inscription makes it abundantly clear that Greek metallurgists were aware of the relationship between the properties of copper alloys and their composition. It also highlights that a quality control system was in operation, otherwise the chemical specification provided would have been of little use (Varoufakis 1975).

An early military example of materials testing comes from Philon of Byzantium's *Mechanike Syntaxis.* In the 'artillery manual' (72: 11 f) section he describes the process in which Spanish *spatha* were tested for quality:[16]

> 'When they wish to test the excellence of these, they grasp the hilt in the right hand and the end of the blade in the left: then, laying it horizontally on their heads, they pull down at each end until they (i.e. the ends) touch their shoulders. Next, they let go sharply, removing both hands.
>
> When released, it straightens itself out again and so resumes its original shape, without retaining a suspicion of a bend. Though they repeat this frequently, the swords remain straight.'

In trying to understand why these swords were so resilient, Philon reveals that there was considerable understanding of the processes of heat treatment and work hardening:

> 'On investigation, they discovered that, first, the iron is exceedingly pure: second, that it is so worked after firing that no fold or other blemish remains in it, while the iron is of a kind that is neither too hard nor too soft, but somewhere in between...'

This reinforces the proposition that Iberian smiths were aware of the differing properties of iron from different ore sources.

> '... after that, they are subjected to a severe beating when cold, and this is what produces resilience. They are not beaten with heavy hammers or with powerful blows, for forceful and direct beating warps the shape and, by penetrating deeply, makes for too much hardness, so that swords so beaten, if one attempts to bend them, either do not give at all in the course of the test or, when forced, snap asunder, because all the material is tight, packed tight by beating.'

This clearly demonstrates knowledge of work hardening.

> 'Firings soften iron and bronze because the particles become less densely packed, so they say; while cooling and beatings harden them, for both processes cause the particles to become tightly packed, because the minute pieces of matter run together and the interstices of voids are removed.'

The use of the word particles indicates that Philon was aware that metal is made of what are now referred to as grains, and that heat treatment modifies the grain structure. This demonstrates an understanding that metals have a grain structure that can be modified by heat treatment.

> 'Therefore, we beat the plates, when cold, on both sides, and thus their surfaces naturally became hard; but the middle remained soft, because the beating, being gentle did not penetrate deeply. Therefore, they were composed of three layers, as it were, two hard and one in the middle softer. The natural result was resilience.'

This shows that it was clearly understood that the hammering process would change the physical properties of the outside surfaces, but that the centre remained unchanged. This indicates of a sophisticated level of understanding of the manipulation of the properties of metal.

Recycling metal

The recycling and reuse of metal was widely practiced during the Roman period. As highlighted in the evidence from hoards at Roman military sites such as Corbridge (Allason Jones and Bishop 1988) and Newstead (Curle 1911, 277). Reusing metal can take different forms; non-ferrous metal can be melted and recast to be formed into new objects. It can also be cut and reshaped to create new artefacts. The same can be applied to iron although iron scrap was probably not melted for re-use. Small pieces of scrap iron were fire welded to produce a new billet which was then processed into new artefacts.

Manufacturers often prefer to work with new metal rather than recycle scrap, because the quality of new material is usually known, while recycled material can be of variable quality.[17] The recycling of scrap metal can take a number of forms.

At its simplest, scrap metal can be reused by recutting it into a different shape. For example, a piece of *lorica segmentata* can be cut up to make scales of *lorica squamata*. Of course, it would be necessary to produce items that are the same size as, or smaller than, the original. Much ferrous metal recycling would have been in this form. Craftsmen would have kept damaged sections of armour and reused the parts that were still functional and remade the broken elements into other components when the need arose. This requires the least modification of the original components. The sheet metal has already been produced and this can then be adapted to another use.

However, much metal is recycled into items that are a different size and shape from the original. Most recycling requires the metal to be subjected to a series of processes to make it suitable for reuse.[18]

It is possible to fire-weld fragments and off-cuts of ferrous metal into a workable bar. Experiments have been conducted to determine the amount of fuel consumed, time required and metal lost when rewelding iron fragments back into just such workable size bars. These experiments shown in Table 4 give some indication of the requirements of recycling.[19]

From these two experiments, the average time required to produce one gram of recycled iron was 2 minutes 20 seconds. Therefore, 1.0kg of workable iron requires approximately 39 hours to produce, consumes nearly 34% of the original metal and requires 10kg of charcoal. Of course, 1.0kg of iron is insufficient to produce even a single Roman helmet

Experiment No.	*Starting wt frags (kg)*	*Finished wt (kg)*	*% wt loss after welding*	*No. heats*	*Running time of fire (minutes)*	*Charcoal fuel consumed*	*Production time (minutes)*	*Production time/g (minutes/*
Exp 260308	1.995	1.375	31.08	36	230	11	690	2.00
Exp 020408	1.520	0.960	36.84	28	122	9	366	2.40
Average	1.758	1.168	33.96	32	176	10	528	2.20

Table 4: Two experiments to determine production statistics for rewelding iron fragments into workable size bars

and, furthermore, the quality of iron recycled in this manner may not be as high as the original iron.

When scrap iron is welded together, rather than improving the quality of the metal, experimental evidence shows that more slag is actually integrated into the billet. This is because the metal is not in liquid form but a plastic state. At the interfaces between the individual pieces of metal there are layers of iron oxide and these are trapped inside the metal when it is forged, as can be seen in the photomicrographs in Figure 20.

This contrasts with cast iron which is produced by melting pig iron with scrap cast iron; the scrap cast iron has already had a large quantity of the impurities in it removed during its first smelting. Therefore, the quality of resmelted iron is often higher than the quality of pig iron.

Because of the number of variables, it is not possible to put an accurate figure on the amount of usable metal recoverable from scrap but, based on personal experience, a figure of 50% is reasonable.

Iron was not the only material that was recycled in the production of Roman armour. Copper alloys are easier to work than ferrous metals. For example, dents can be removed without seriously reducing the strength of the metal. Furthermore, recycling is simpler because these metals can be melted and recast.

Manufacture

One of the strengths of the Roman army was its discipline and employment of a system of fighting that involved every soldier knowing what his neighbour would do in a battle. Drill practice honed this system to perfection. It was said of the Roman army: *'Their drills were bloodless battles and their battles were bloody drills'* (Josephus v. bk 1:27).[20] Units were assigned special tasks, such as heavy infantry, light infantry, skirmishers or cavalry, but all acted together as a unit. This level of cohesion was enhanced by the use of standard (but not identical) equipment which was instrumental to their method of fighting.

In the early Republic, when the army was a militia, soldiers were responsible for procuring their own armour. It is likely that the manufacture of such a comparatively small amount of arms and armour could be achieved using the existing metalworkers in the

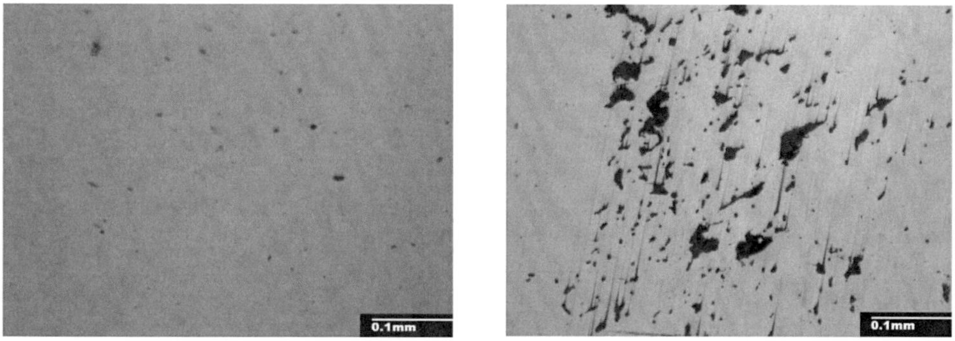

Figure 20: Roman nail as found (left), and after welding into billet (right)

local area. It would also mean that there would be differences in appearance of weapons and armour, as individual makers would have their own style. The reforms introduced by Gaius Gracchus made the state responsible for the supply of arms, armour and clothing to the legionaries. This was a major change of direction, and the procurement of arms by the state moves the whole of the manufacture and procurement of military equipment into a much larger sphere of activity.

When manufacturing on a large scale it is essential to reduce time and costs as far as possible and the most effective way to achieve this is to standardize the individual items being made. Weapons and armour of a standard size are essential when the soldiers within an army are fighting as a unit of men, not as individuals.

The Roman Imperial army was an army of professional soldiers. Augustus disbanded about half of the over 50 legions then in existence when he became sole ruler in 30 BC. The remaining 28 legions became the core of the early Imperial army of the Principate (27 BC–AD 284). This number fluctuated over time, but when supplemented by auxiliaries, cavalry and marines the Roman military fielded a huge number of men who would have been in constant need of new equipment, while existing equipment needed to be replaced because of losses or general wear and tear. Losses could be the result of:

- *Conflict*: equipment lost in conflict may not have been recoverable.
- *Broken or worn out*: general use either in combat or drilling will eventually cause some equipment to wear out and need replacing, because it no longer fulfils its function. Some parts of armour may have been lost in daily use such as *squamata* scales that became detached and lost.
- *Theft*: equipment had a value which could be realised through theft.
- *Ritual deposition*: there is increasing evidence that military equipment may have been used for votive offerings (cf. van Enkevort and Willems 1994).

Furthermore, it is impossible to be certain how many spare sets of armour were held by the Roman army. What is clear is that in order to produce armour in such large quantities it has to be mass-produced. The modern meaning of mass production is a system of making parts to a set of tolerances that make all parts interchangeable. For example, the crankshaft from a Model T Ford was designed to fit the engine of any other Model T Ford. However, the system employed by the Roman arms industry would have been of a different form; in modern terminology it would be called batch production. Jigs and templates would have been made to reduce production time and workers would have been given specific tasks to perform. When the task was completed the item would be passed on to another worker until complete. This would be the only way to meet the constant need for the larger numbers required.[21]

The manufacture of arrows is a good illustration of mass production. An arrow is made of three different parts: a wooden shaft, the feather fletchings and the metal head. Many different craftsmen were employed, each with a separate set of skills. The wood was cut, split and sawn into the appropriate length. The feathers were collected. The blacksmith (arrow smith) forged the points. The shafts, feathers and points were given to the fletcher who assembled them onto arrows. Harnessing the skills of several craftspeople makes mass production possible. The same principle would have applied to the making of armour. For example, in the case of *lorica segmentata*, the brass hinges were made from sheet metal made from a billet that had been reduced in cross-section to make sheet. They were cut and bent and the holes were made but they were possibly polished in a separate workshop. It is likely that individual personnel had specific tasks to enable large numbers to be produced.

The philosophy of manufacture

A high standard of production can be seen in the manufacture of highly-decorated arms and armour, as well as the high prestige items of arms and armour manufactured personally for the officer classes (e.g. see Plate 6c).

Such items have been made by highly skilled craftsmen who were employed to produce small quantities of prestige items. The priority was to produce a beautifully made and finished object. These criteria, however, do not apply to the manufacture of arms and armour for the use of ordinary infantry soldiers. It is clear from the examinations of many examples that the standard of workmanship was set at a level that could be considered to be fit for purpose. For example:

- *Working marks*: helmets have the marks left by manufacture removed from the areas that are visible, but the undersides are left as worked.
- *Alignment*: components were often misaligned, such as plume holders on helmets or hinges on *lorica segmentata.*
- *Corrections*: errors in production like the mispunched hole seen in Figure 24 were rarely corrected.

There are several explanations for this, one of which is that the manufacturer was anxious to produce the items in the minimum time possible. The items would fulfil their purpose irrespective of the amount of time that could have been devoted to finishing them. Close examination reveals all these flaws, but when viewed from a distance they are too insignificant to be noticeable.

Economics

In Roman society one of the principal consumers of manufactured goods was the army (Cornel and Matthews 1992, 56). It has been estimated that as early as the second century AD 75–80% of Rome's state budget was devoted to military expenditure (Cornell 1995, 130). The production of arms and armour by private manufacturers for the Roman army was subject to the same laws of supply and demand as any other production process. The product had to be made in such a way that the manufacturers could make a profit. Manufacturing cost can be divided into three broad categories:

1. Direct materials cost.
2. Direct labour cost.
3. Indirect manufacturing overhead cost.

The direct costs included: material, fuel and labour.[22] Labour is usually an important contributory cost in a manufacturing process and a major factor in that cost is the time it takes to make an item. All labour has a cost; if it is slave-labour the cost is in kind because the slave has to be fed, housed, clothed and purchased in the first place. If the labour is from free men then they have to be paid a wage.[23] This makes it inevitable that manufacturers will try to find ways to reduce production times. Wilson (2002) has argued convincingly that some Romans were not at all averse to making large investments in equipment in order to increase production.

Manufacturing times

Reconstruction allows a greater understanding of the following:

- *The production process*: in any manufacturing process there are always several ways to arrive at the finished item. Some methods will be unnecessarily slow and expensive in terms of labour and material consumption and these will usually be rejected. Two equally skilled craftsmen can often produce identical artefacts in the same time but using slightly different methods. This research adheres to the following criteria: the item should be made in the shortest possible time with the minimum use of fuel and minimum wastage of material. This is a set of criteria that would be familiar to manufacturers.
- *Material loss*: by careful weighing at the beginning and end of the manufacturing process it is possible to determine the amount of material lost during manufacture, which then makes it possible to determine how much metal will be needed to produce a finished artefact of a particular weight. In the Roman period the most widely used method of producing arms and armour was by forge work, either hot or cold, and sometimes a combination of both. The forging had to be further processed by metal removal to produce the finished item. Experiments have shown that during the forging process 11–20% of material is lost because of oxidization. This is considerably higher when fire-welding takes place, where material loss can be up to 60%. A further 30–50% of material can be lost during the cleaning and polishing process.Table 5 shows the amount of material that is lost during the forging the finishing processes on Roman armaments.

Item	*% loss in forging*	*% loss in finishing*	*Total % loss*
Gladius	9.9	24.28	34.27
Pilum	19.79	18.12	37.91
Spear	26.34	11.73	38.07
Bolt head (flat)	13.15	No finishing required	13.15
Incendiary arrow	27.47	1.0	28.47
Bolt head (pyramid)	20.00	No finishing required	20.00
Arrow (flat)	13.00	1.0	14.00

Table 5: Material losses in weapon manufacture (after Sim 1992b: 114 with additions)

Item	*Forging blank from the billet*	*Forge billet into a weapon*	*Metal removal for finishing*	*Total*
Gladius	63	125	1860	2048*
Pilum	278	127	221	626
Spear head	54	46	79	179
Bolt head (flat)	31	5	0	36
Incendiary arrow	149	23	7	179
Bolt head (pyramid)	35	18	0	53
Arrow (flat)	30	5	2	37

Table 6: Production times in minutes of selected Roman weaponry (after Sim 1992b: 114 with additions)

*The *gladius* was finished using only hand-held tools. The blade was elongated diamond in cross-section, therefore there were four surfaces to be treated. The cross-section of *gladius* blades varies. With the current state of knowledge, the use of mechanically aided abrasives (such as grinding wheels) has not been proved in the Roman period, but given that the finishing time of 31 hours for a single sword is unlikely, even if such work was conducted by unskilled labour – we are led to the conclusion that a mechanical device must have been used in order to satisfy production.

- *Production time*: production time was a consideration for Roman smiths. Roman armour was generally fit for purpose and often appears to have been constructed rapidly.[24] Using experimental techniques to determine production times is therefore a key component of the study of Roman arms and armour production (Table 6). In order to determine how long any artefact takes to make it is essential to reproduce a considerable number of the object being studied. There is a learning curve associated with producing objects but practice will improve the manufacturing time. Eventually, as experience is gained, the manufacturer will reach a plateau and the production for a particular object time will remain approximately at that level. Figure 21 shows how the production time for *lorica squamata* scales reduces significantly until a plateau is reached after the production of seven scales. At this stage the production time stabilises at approximately 70 seconds per scale. Production time can also be reduced through the use of templates and jigs (see Figure 22).
- *Fuel consumption:* charcoal was the most commonly used fuel in forge work although the use of other fuels such as peat, or even coal cannot be ruled out. Although fuel costs may have been low compared to the other raw materials in iron smithing they cannot be discounted. The availability of costs of fuels may have influenced manufacturers to consume the minimum amount of fuel.

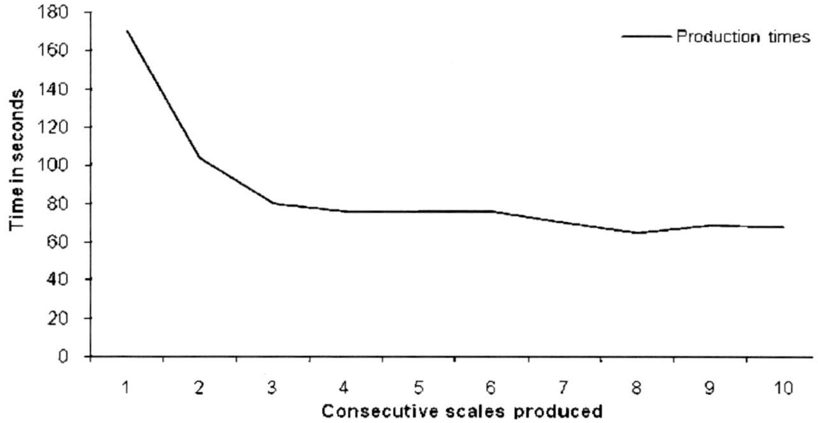

*Figure 21: How practice producing an item reduces the production time (*lorica squamata *scales)*

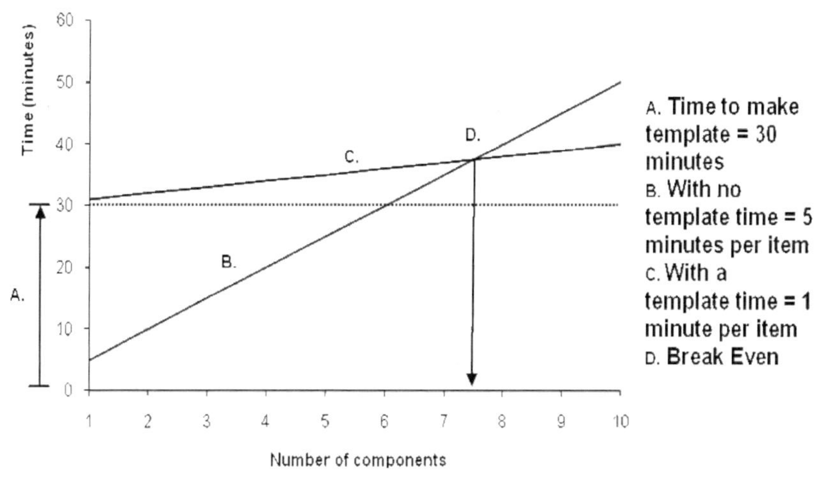

Figure 22: A comparison of relative production times using templates and unaided production

- *Manpower requirements*: there are two factors to consider with manpower: first, the number of man-hours required to produce an object and, secondly, the differential cost of the type of labour employed. Take the example of a blacksmith – a skilled manufacturer – who, working alone, produces an artefact in one hour. If this same blacksmith works with a striker as his assistant – an unskilled labourer – he can produce the same artefact in half an hour. This has taken two men the same equivalent of one man-hour. In private armour factories this will have a cost benefit because the skilled blacksmith is paid at a much higher rate than the striker, who is paid as unskilled labour.[25] Therefore, the cost of the artefact is lower.[26] In military establishments there is an opportunity for cost saving because the need for skilled

> blacksmiths is reduced. These craftsmen can be devoted to tasks more appropriate to their level of skill.

A striker will use sledge hammers of different weights depending on the work being conducted. When the hammer weight ranges between 5kg and 8kg then the work output is approximately double that of a smith working alone, although the total man-hours remain the same because two people are working.[27] However, experiments have shown that when a striker is using a 15kg sledge hammer, the work output is considerably changed. For example, if a blacksmith can work a billet into a bar in approximately 10 hours, then if he were to use a striker with a 15kg hammer, the same output could be achieved in approximately 3 hours. This is simply because each downward blow of the heavier sledge hammer will achieve greater compression or manipulation of the metal compared to a lighter hammer. Although a striker with a lighter hammer may achieve a few extra blows this does not compensate for the greater work achieved with the heavier hammer.[28]

Conclusions

The extensive use of iron in Roman society meant that there was a large body of both civilian and military smiths in that society who could manipulate, shape and repair iron objects. The limited literary sources and the metallurgical evidence reveal that all of the basic methods of heat treatment of iron were known and used by Roman blacksmiths. It is unclear how widespread particular processes were, because there are still very few examples of Roman ferrous metals that have been examined metallurgically.

Notes

1 For example machinery (Schioler 1980).
2 These are the use of electrically driven rotary fans to deliver air to the fuel and the use of coke as a fuel. Pliny describes the use of steel and flint for the lighting of fires (xvi: 208).
3 Further definitions can be found in Gale (1971) and Congdon (1971).
4 Publilius Syrus, was a first century BC Latin writer of maxims. Of Syrian origin he was brought to Italy as a slave, but was freed by his master and educated. All that survives of his works is a collection, a series of moral maxims. Each consists of a single verse, and the verses are arranged in alphabetical order according to their initial letters.
5 It was limited by its reliance on water or animal power.
6 An experiment was undertaken by the authors to compare the losses of machining over forging. A piece of 25mm diameter bar was machined down to a diameter of 12.5mm. For a length of 25mm the amount of material lost was 50%. The same size and shape was produced by forging, but the percentage loss of metal was only 4%.
7 Certainly slagged material that had been recovered from beside a Roman rampart at the fort at Loughor, Wales, has been interpreted as waste from a blacksmith's forge which had been used for welding (Greenough 1987).
8 It is more complex to weld different metals such as wrought iron to steel together, In this case each component has to be heated separately before being brought together for welding, because they have to be at different temperatures (Frankland 1795).
9 Cf. examples of hardening and tempering on a knife blade and carburisation from another object from Late Bronze Age Cyprus (Thorland 1971), hardening Roman iron tools from Saalburg (Maddin *et al.* 1991, 15), the quenching and tempering of Roman swords (Lang 1988, 216).
10 Brittleness is usually associated with hardness, for example glass is a hard, brittle material. However, not all brittle materials are hard; for example chalk is a soft, brittle material.

11 Experiments by the authors have shown that a shield boss can be made in a third of the time – hot, compared to cold.

12 An experiment was conducted to demonstrate this. A piece of 0.20% carbon steel that had a hardness of 69 VPN was forged and cooled in air. This caused the hardness to rise to 153 VPN. After further cold working the finished hardness was 268 VPN.

13 One of the earliest representations of the use of a ball stake can be seen in a bronze geometric statuette of a Greek helmet-maker from the late eighth or early seventh century BC. The craftsman is sitting on the ground and holding the helmet over the ball stake, in preparation for striking it with a mallet (Richter 1944, 1–5, figs 1–4).

14 It is quite possible that a helmet or shield boss could be drop-forged then finished with a hand-held hammer over a steel ball. In this case only the marks of the hand-held hammer and the steel ball will be visible. Given this limitation with the evidence, it is necessary to examine the possible methods that could have been employed in the production of helmets. Some potential production methods are based on accepted methods of sheet metal working, and others are based on the need to produce large quantities, and therefore make use of machines. Indeed it is quite possible that different methods were employed at different locations depending on the preference of the manufacture.

15 An example can be found on the edges of anvils; a blacksmith manufacturing chisels will often test them on the edge of his anvil to determine if they have been properly hardened and tempered. This can be shown by the number of small notches seen on the edge of many anvils.

16 Philon of Byzantium (*c.* 280–*c.* 220 BC), was also known as Philon Mechanicus. Philon was a Greek writer on mechanics, who published the *Mechanike Syntaxis* (a compendium of mechanics). This was divided into eight sections: *Isagoge*, an introduction to mathematics; *Mochlica*, general mechanics; *Limenopoeica*, harbour building; *Belopoeica*, artillery manual; *Pneumatica*, devices operated by air or water pressure; *Automatiopoeica*, mechanical toys; *Poliorcetica*, siege warfare, and *Peri Epistolon*, secret letters. The military sections *Belopoeica* and *Poliorcetica* survive in Greek, as do fragments of *Isagoge* and *Automatiopoeica*.

17 Scrap material usually has to be passed through a number of different stages to render it fit to be reworked and this can often take a considerable number of hours. Scrap metal often has damage not visible to the naked eye that often will only appear when a considerable amount of work has already been done. Such damage will result in the scrapping of the piece and the time taken is lost.

18 For example, a broken file cannot simply be re-forged into a knife. If this was attempted, the metal would probably crack during the second forging process, because of the stresses set up when it was initially forged into a file. It has to be annealed. When it has cooled the teeth will have to be removed (if it is forged with the teeth still on, they will act as laps and the metal will break during forging). In the above example, between 11% and 20% of the metal will be lost, depending on the time required for annealing. These figures will apply for any metal needing annealing.

19 In experiments 260308 and 020408 off-cuts of mild steel and EN42J were welded into a billet using a skilled blacksmith and two strikers. In experiment 020408 an attempt was made to produce a cleaner bar by washing down the anvil and hammers before each weld.

20 Josephus (*c.* AD 37–100) was governor of Galilee during the Jewish revolt. He was captured by the Romans in AD 67, whence he went over to the Roman side. As such he was in the Roman camp at the time of the fall of Jerusalem and the destruction of the Temple. His two most important works are the *The Jewish War* (*c.* AD 75) and *Antiquities of the Jews* (*c.* AD 94).

21 Evidence from the Roman period suggests that military mass production was employed in areas as diverse as ship building (Goldsworthy 2003, 42) and weapons manufacture (Sim 1992b; 1995a; 1995b).

22 There are also indirect costs (overheads) which could include repairs on equipment, building rental, lighting, etc.

23 It is problematic to give a precise figure for costs and wages as there is very little documentary evidence; one of the few covering this is the *Edict of Diocletian* (Frank 1940).

24 Often parts such as hinges on *lorica segmentata* or plume holders on helmets were poorly fitted and aligned. This could be a function of rapid production or the use of unskilled labour to assemble the pre-produced components. Either way this will result in the simple reduction in time required to produce an artefact or the reduction in skilled manufacturers time and its replacement with semi-skilled and unskilled labour.

25 Private manufacturers were well aware of the concept of profit making (Bradley 1994, 14).

26 To put this in context; if a blacksmith were paid ten units of currency per hour, and required 1 hour to

produce a greave, the labour cost for the item would be ten units of currency. If the same blacksmith were to use a striker to help produce the greave and this reduced the production time to half an hour, then the labour cost would be only 30 minutes of the blacksmith's time and 30 minutes of the striker's time. If the labour cost of the striker was two units of currency per hour then the cost to produce the artefact would be one unit of currency for the striker's time and five units of currency for the blacksmith, giving a total of six units of currency to produce the artefact. In this context the use of unskilled labour to supplement the blacksmith's time provides a net saving of four units of currency.

27 However, this is usually cheaper because one of the workers is less skilled than the other and so may have a reduced wage rate.

28 Experiments conducted by the authors.

4 The Production of Sheet Metal

Methods of sheet iron production

There is an increasing body of evidence to show that, in many cases, there is little variation in the thickness of the sheet metal used for Roman armour (see Table 7 and Fulford *et al.* 2004, 200, fig. 3). Such uniformity of thickness has been noted by other researchers such as Clemetson with *lorica squamata* (1993, 9). It cannot be ruled out that sheet iron destined for military applications was produced to much tighter tolerances compared with civilian uses.[1]

This does, however, raise the question of how such thin sheet could be produced to such a high degree of accuracy. If the sheet were hammered flat then there would be much greater variation in thickness. Furthermore, it would be expected that tool marks would remain on the inner surface. Objects such as helmets retain production tool marks on the inside of the bowl because it was simply too time consuming to remove them

Origin	*Description*	*Mean (mm)*	*Range (mm)*	*Max. thickness (mm)*	*Min. thickness (mm)*
Vindolanda 4656	Armour Fragment	0.87	0.76	1.27	0.51
Vindolanda 5061a	Armour (*lorica segmentata*)	0.67	0.30	0.82	0.52
Vindolanda 5061b	Armour (possible *manica*)	0.83	0.83	1.20	0.50
Vindolanda 4141	Possible *lorica segmentata*	1.06	0.63	1.45	0.82
Vindolanda 5799	Armour fragment	0.55	0.61	0.96	0.35
Vindolanda 4544a	Armour fragment	1.21	1.04	1.85	0.81
Vindolanda 4544b	Armour fragment	1.52	1.16	1.80	0.64
Vindolanda 4544c	Armour fragment	1.06	0.38	1.27	0.89
Vindolanda 2199	*Manica*	1.13	1.18	1.71	0.53
Vindolanda 3662	Armour fragment	1.47	1.14	2.03	0.89
Vindolanda 4672	Armour fragment	1.18	0.90	1.78	0.88
Melrose FRA 167	Shield boss	0.86	0.80	1.36	0.56
Melrose FRA 177	*Manica*	0.92	0.60	1.16	0.56
Cramond 1	*Lorica segmentata*	1.00	0.80	1.50	0.70
Cramond≠2	*Lorica segmentata*	0.79	0.60	1.05	0.45
Cramond 3	*Lorica segmentata*	1.00	0.75	1.40	0.65
Cramond 4	*Lorica segmentata*	0.89	0.88	1.50	0.62
Cramond 5	*Lorica segmentata*	0.81	1.15	1.66	0.51
Cramond 6	*Lorica segmentata*	1.00	0.75	1.40	0.40
Balkans	*Lorica squamata* (complete)	1.27	0.27	1.12	1.15
Balkans	*Lorica squamata* (scale fragment)	1.27	1.01	1.52	0.51
Average		1.02	0.79	1.42	0.64

Table 7: The comparative thickness of samples of Roman iron armour

Figure 23: A Roman iron billet from Newstead Scotland (© Trustees of the National Museum of Scotland)

when they would not be seen in normal use. Yet the examples of sheet-based armour examined show no examples of production tool marks on the inner surfaces.[2] This either indicates that Roman smiths went against normal practice and expended a considerable degree of time and effort removing tool marks on the inner surface of body armour (but not helmets), or there were no tool marks in the first place. If there were no tool marks then it has to be considered how sheet could have been produced to high tolerances without leaving such marks.

Producing thin sheet metal of a relatively constant thickness (*c.* 1.0mm) without tool marks is only achievable in a consistent and sustained manner with the use of mechanical means. A number of methods can be used,[3] such as drop hammers and trip hammers, six-man hammers, or even rollers. Certainly in the context of mass production of sheet, time-consuming techniques such as hand production will not support a constant supply of sheet needed for military purposes. Mass production relies on the supply of materials that are of consistent dimensions. The need for standardization is paramount in mass production and a degree of standardization is a factor of Roman military organisation (Baker 2004, 1).[4]

Each method will be recreated and experiments conducted. The results of these experiments will be compared to existing Roman armour to determine which method could have been used to create the finished artefact. With all methods of sheet production, however, the starting point is a billet of iron such as the example from Newstead shown in Figure 23.

This could then have been coonverted into sheet iron using:

1. A one man hand-held hammer.
2. A blacksmith and striker using a flatter.
3. A multi-man hammer (vertical drop).
4. Power hammers.
5. A hammer based on pile drivers.
6. Rollers.[5]

One man hand-held hammer

With this method the billet is forged down to sheet by a blacksmith working alone.

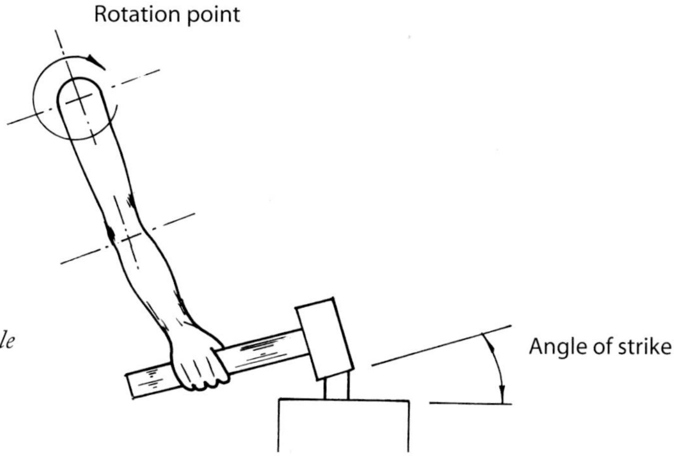

Figure 24: The hand-held hammer arrives at an angle to the work surface

Figure 25: Close up of a hammer head arriving at an angle to the surface of the work. The cross-section of the face of the hammer is considerably smaller than that of the sheet it is striking, and it leaves hammer marks on the surface. No matter how carefully the blacksmith places his blows, some hammer marks will always remain visible. These hammer marks are sufficiently deep as to be almost impossible to remove using only a hammer, and are too deep to be easily removed by polishing.

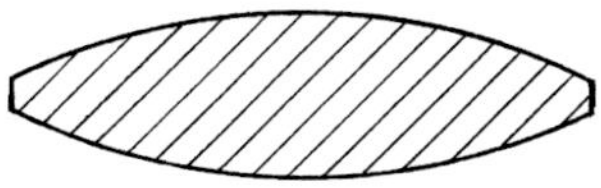

Figure 26: Exaggerated schematic view of the tapering effect of hand-hammered sheet

This is considered unlikely because, even in antiquity, most blacksmiths would have been assisted by at least one striker (cf. Plate 8a). However, a series of experiments was conducted to determine whether this method could be used to produce sheet with the consistent thickness seen in the Roman originals. In every case the profile of the sheet was that of a lens as shown in Figure 26. Hammer marks were also evident. This is because, when held in the hand, the hammer head strikes the metal at an angle to the horizontal because the hammer swings through an arc (see Figures 24 and 25).

Blacksmith and striker using a flatter

The majority of a blacksmith's tools require the hot iron to be held with one hand and the tool to be positioned using the other. The tool is either manually operated by the blacksmith or force is applied to the tool by a striker using a sledge hammer (Plate 8a).

Artefacts are forged from either sheet or bar, and these are produced by blacksmiths and strikers working a billet into the required form. An experiment was carried out by a blacksmith working with two strikers. Each of the strikers wielded a sledgehammer that weighed 10kg. A piece of 25mm square wrought iron bar was forged down to form sheet. The sheet was forged to 2mm thick. On examination it was found that the centre of the sheet was 2mm thick but it tapered to 0.9mm towards the outside, the experimenters were unable to produce a sheet with a cross-section with parallel sides using this method.

Multi-man hammer (vertical drop)

Two and three-handled sledge hammers were in common use in the ship building industry until well into the twentieth century and the idea of a multi-handled hammer cannot have been unknown to blacksmiths in antiquity (Figure 27). It was hypothesized that such a hammer would descend vertically and would arrive parallel to the surface of the anvil. When the hammer head strikes the surface of the anvil the flexing of the wooden handle causes the head to rebound. The recoil is, however, not in a vertical plane, and when it strikes the next time the head then hits the work at an angle. Although the tapering effect was reduced using this system, it was not possible to produce a sheet of the same dimensional accuracy as the Roman originals.

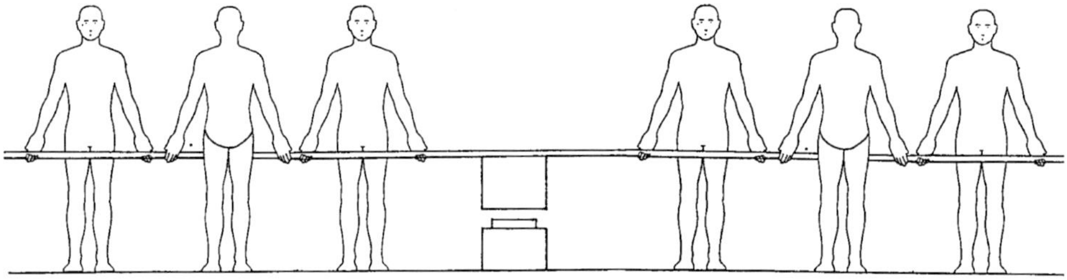

Figure 27: Six-man hammer (schematic view)

Power hammers

The billet is forged down to sheet by a blacksmith working with a power-assisted drop hammer. In order to produce sheet, the striking face of the hammer has to arrive parallel to the surface of the anvil. Using scaffold poles a model of the set-up shown in Figure 28 was constructed and a weight of 30kg was used. This proved to be a fairly dangerous machine, but sheet was produced. However, it had the same lens-shaped profile as the previous experiments. With some modifications this could be turned into a much safer machine, and it is possible that this may have been done in the Roman period. However, it was shown that this set-up would not produce sheet to the same dimensional accuracy as seen in the Roman armour examined.

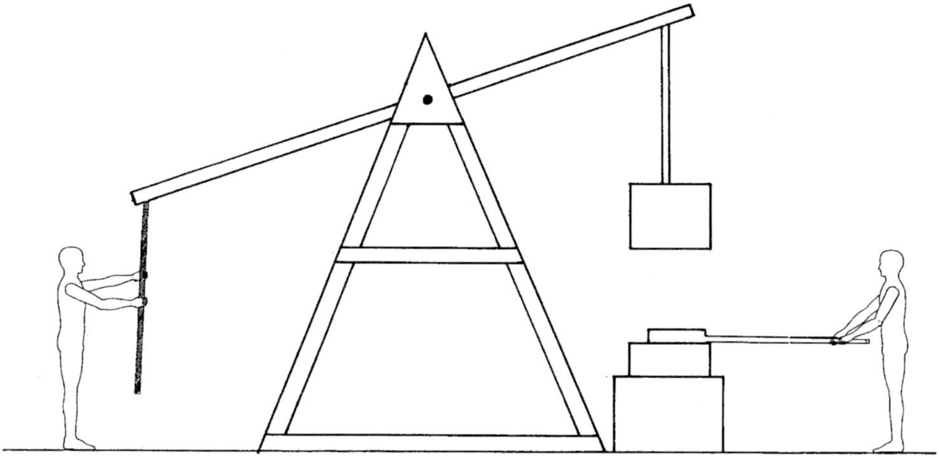

Figure 28: Power drop hammer (schematic view)

A drop hammer based on a pile driver

Pile drivers are attested in the Roman period[6] and it is likely that such a device could have been used for the processing of iron into sheet. It was found that by dropping a weight that was constrained in a simple cage and raising it with a single pulley, a large amount of work could be done by two men – and quite good quality sheet could be produced (Figure 29). However, this method still did not produce sheet with perfectly parallel faces.

Working with any of the above methods the billet can be forged down to a thickness of approximately 4.0mm. Any of the above methods used on material of this thickness produces the tapering effect shown in Figure 26.

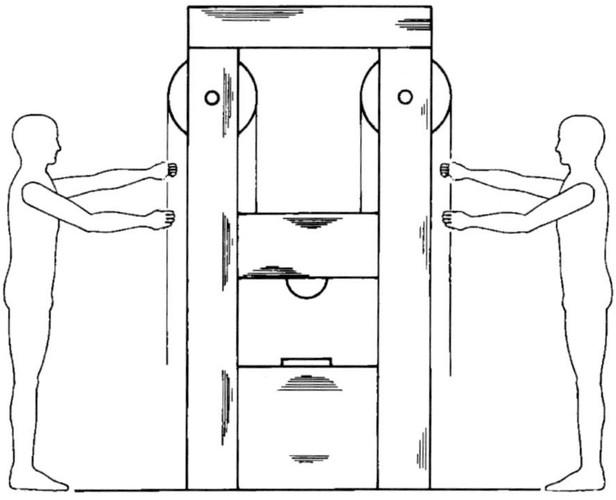

Figure 29: An experimental drop hammer for forming hemispheres (schematic view)

A machine based on the principle of a dropped weight could have been used to form shield bosses and helmet bowls. Experiments have been conducted which produced effective devices.

Rollers

The above experiments have shown that any of these techniques can be used to bring the iron close to the thickness required for sheet but will not produce sheet of the dimensional accuracy that has been found. It is apparent that the sub-millimetre sheet found in some examples of Roman armour was unlikely to have been produced consistently in any quantity by these methods. It may be that mechanical devices were used to speed up the amount of time taken to reduce the billet to the required size. For example, the billet could be reduced to a dimension of approximately 4.0mm, which could then be passed between a system of rollers to reduce it to its finished thickness.

With the modern system, huge rollers reduce ingots that weigh several tonnes down to sheet. Each roller is individually machine powered. When hand rollers are used, the two rollers are geared together. It has been assumed that these simple systems were used in antiquity and could have been used to produce sheet iron. However, there is no literary or archaeological evidence for rollers.

This system could be based on the same principle as the quern (Figure 30). The offset handle shown in Figure 30 is a form of crank. Cranks were known in the fourth century AD, as seen in writings of the Emperor Julian's physician Oreibasios mentioned the use of the crank (Sprague de Camp 1963).[7]

The top stone has a handle and is rotated about a central axis while the bottom stone is fixed. Using this mechanism as a basis for a system of rollers, each roller is fitted with a handle and they are mounted above each other so the axis of each stone is parallel with the other. This enables each stone to be rotated independently by hand – material passing between them being rolled into sheets.

Rollers of 75mm diameter will perform sheet production very well. It is also possible that rollers were made from iron. An experiment was conducted to demonstrate the ease with which a pair of rollers could be made, and to use the rollers to produce sheet iron. A roller made from iron or steel can easily be produced using very simple technology. All the tools required were known to have existed in the Roman period. Rollers could be produced by forging, followed by turning on a pole lathe (see Sim 1997b) and finally lapping (see Figure 32).[8]

The experimental set of rollers was found to operate with ease with two men driving the rollers and one feeding the metal. The initial reduction is done when the metal is at red heat; when the material is within a millimetre of the finished size it is allowed to cool. The surface oxide film is easily removed and the final reductions required to bring the material to its final thickness is done cold. This has the advantage of producing a clean, smooth surface and also work hardens the metal.

This is unskilled work, which greatly reduces the amount of skilled labour needed, and does not require great physical strength. The surface finish is very good and considerably reduces the amount of time needed to finish it off (there are fewer depressions which are not as deep as forging, so it takes less time to remove them.)

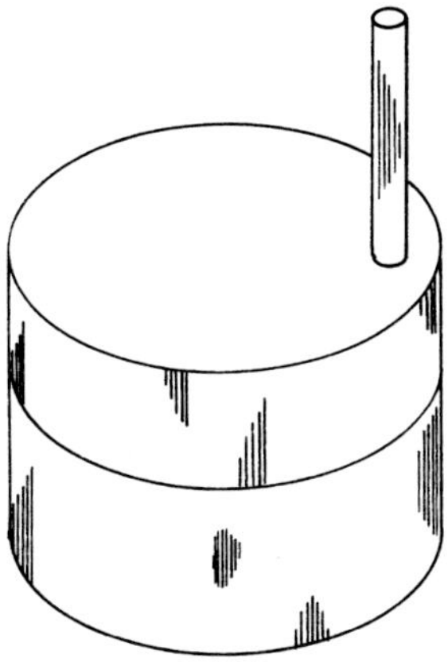

Figure 30: Schematic view of a Roman quern

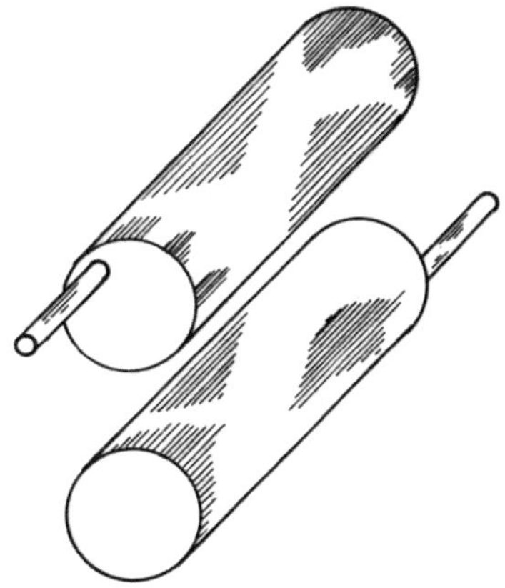

Figure 31: Schematic view of experimental rollers

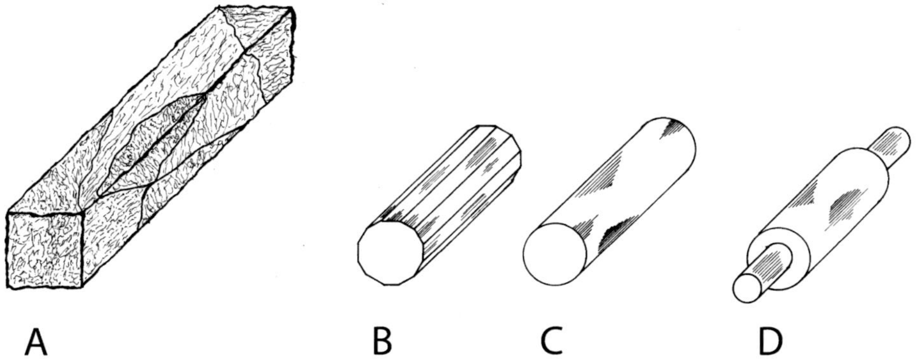

Figure 32: Schematic view of a potential roller system

It has been demonstrated that the other methods of sheet production do not produce sheet of the same dimensional accuracy as the system of rollers proposed. The rollers also produce sheet without tool marks, as seen on the originals. It is a very simple system, and to make it only requires machinery that was known to exist in the Roman period.

Roman rollers are unlikely to survive in the archaeological record or be recognized by archaeologists. The rollers would be recycled if they were made of bronze (which is and always has been expensive). If they were made of iron they would have been recycled, because it is unlikely that a blacksmith would leave so much iron tied up in an unused form for long. If they were made from stone they could be misidentified as architectural features. The wooden superstructure associated with a rolling machine would be unlikely to survive in the archaeological record (Figure 33).

Figure 33: Wooden machinery from Luxor, Egypt, in 2007

Conclusions

Much Roman armour was made from sheet metal. This could be produced using straightforward (sheet) metalworking techniques. The Roman army was a huge organisation that was in a state of war in many different parts of the Empire for most of its existence. The sheer volume of armour that was needed to keep such an army equipped for war was vast, and the requirement for armour was unending. There was a need for systems of production that could meet those requirements and, in many cases, those systems were based on making armour using mass production methods. Such a production system needs a constant reliable and steady supply of both materials and manpower. If either of these is not available then production is likely to be curtailed.

Manpower alone would not meet the needs and it seems that systems of machines could have supplemented the effort from the labour force. Furthermore, hand production was not an effective way to produce sheet of a consistent thickness without tool marks. The use of machinery would have been a possible mechanism to produce some of the sheet seen in the archaeological record, however, poor visibility of machines (from spinning lathes to pile drivers) is due to most machines being made from wood at this time. When this is considered in conjunction with the lack of literary evidence, this has created a skewed perspective of Roman technology.

Notes

1 For example, the lock plate from Wroxeter had an average thickness of 1.58mm but a tolerance range of +1.74 to–0.95mm.
2 This is further reinforced by the use of thin sheets that were required for the construction of some types of shield boss (see Chapter 13).
3 Much Roman armour was made from ferrous or copper alloy sheet metal. The production of sheet metal is similar irrespective of the material used.
4 Standardisation can be traced to even bar iron as seen in iron bars from Pannonia (Durman 2002).
5 It has become established wisdom that the Romans did not use rolling machinery for producing sheet metal, because there is no archaeological or literary evidence for rollers. However, most machinery is poorly represented in the archaeological record. This is especially pertinent when archaeologists are not looking for specific machine components, because according to established wisdom the machine was not used by the Romans. By ruling out a technology exclusively on these grounds (literature and archaeology) it would be necessary to exclude spinning lathes from a study of Roman helmet making technology.
6 Vitruvius' ten books on architecture (bk 3: 4, 2) alludes to pile drivers in his description of construction on marshy ground in the 1st century BC: '*If we could not find the right ground, and the place was only boggy ground, the alder or oak piles, a little bit burnt, should be driven by the machines very close to each other, then the spaces between could be filled with coal so that a very strong stonework could be built.*'
7 Julian or Flavius Claudius Julianus (*c.* AD 331–63), was emperor AD 361–3.
8 A set of experimental rollers was made using only the tools and techniques available to the Roman blacksmith. The billet was forged into two separate cylinders using swages. A tenon was forged on the end of each bar using swages. One tenon had a square section forged on the end. Each roller was mounted between centres and turned on a bow lathe, until it was smooth and concentric. Any eccentricity would result in reduced efficiency and loss of accuracy in the roller system. The bearings were hot forged and made from steel. The hole for the tenon was punched with a punch that was the same diameter as the finished tenon. When the bearing cooled the hole shrank to a diameter that was smaller than the tenon. This allowed the tenon to be lapped to fit the bearing with only a small amount of material being removed from the tenon and the hole in the bearing, resulting in a sliding fit (this is a fit that allows the two parts to go together and rotate with no sideways movement). The use of lapping to make sliding fits between male and female cylinders has been demonstrated by Sim (1997a). The frame and base used to support this pair of rollers was made from oak. This hardwood stood up very well to the extended heavy work to which it was subjected. In use the rollers did not become very hot as the metal was only in contact with them for less than a second during each pass. It was immediately apparent that the framework of such a machine would be unlikely to survive in the archaeological record. The wooden framework would almost certainly decompose, and the rollers, depending on the material of construction, would either be recycled or would not be recognised if they were excavated.

5 Iron and Steel

Introduction

As a material iron is strong, tough, and relatively easily worked; its limitations are its relative weight, and propensity to rust. However, the advantages of iron significantly outweigh its limitations, hence the metal has been widely used. At the atomic level iron is composed of 26 protons combined with 26 neutrons making it one of the most electro-statically stable elements in the universe. This stability also makes it one of the most abundant elements in the universe.

Iron's comparative softness yields cutting properties that are similar to those of bronze, but because it is soft, its ability to cut other materials is limited to those that are softer than iron. In addition, it will not hold a cutting edge for long and will require frequent sharpening. The addition of carbon to iron produces the alloy steel. With a hardness of 235 VPN for 0.4% carbon steel compared to 100 VPN for pure iron, steel was the hardest metal alloy known in antiquity. This meant it could be used for cutting other metallic and non-metallic materials. Its hardness also made it ideal for both weapons and tools.

The difference between iron and steel was clearly understood by the Romans, as demonstrated by the poet Propertius (Bk 1. poem 16: line 30) who notes: 'Harder be she than iron and steel'. Furthermore, the use of steel for the edges of pattern-welded swords shows clearly that it was understood that this material had different properties from the materials used for the rest of the sword. Similarly, other cutting tools such as chisels, saws, gravers, gauges and die-sinking tools were made of steel. Alternatively, some tools such as hammers were 'steeled', by having steel plate welded to the working surface (Ward 1911, 195).

In addition, Pliny demonstrates that the Romans were aware that iron from different ore sources could have different properties:

> 'Some lands only yield a soft iron closely allied to lead, others a brittle and coppery kind that is specially to be avoided for the requirements of wheels and for nails for which purpose the former quality is suitable; another variety of iron finds favour in short lengths only and in nails for soldiers' boots; another variety experiences rust more quickly.' (xxxiv: 143)

He considered that the best iron comes from the Seric (thought by Pliny to have been brought overland from China through a network of intermediaries). This, however, seems to have been *Wootz* steel from India (Healy 1978, 215); the second best iron was from Parthia, in what is now north-eastern Iran. Pliny also thought the iron from Noricum (now in modern Austria) to be of good quality. Analysis of iron from this region of Austria showed the ore to have high manganese content (Tylecote 1987, 169). Manganese increases the strength and hardness of steels and also forms carbides. It lowers the critical cooling rate, thus increasing the potential of the steel to harden and gives rise to steels that can be air hardened (Bailey 1967, 68). Pliny considered that in other places, the quality of the iron produced was dependent on the method of working.

Methods of making steel

Iron is an element while steel is an alloy of iron and carbon. The carbon atoms are smaller than the iron atoms and fit into the spaces between the atoms of the parent iron. Once the carbon content exceeds 1.9% then the material is classified as ultra-high carbon steel and beyond 2.0% it becomes cast iron. The carbon can be introduced into the iron by various methods, either when the iron ore is being smelted or by introducing it when the iron is in a solid state. Some of the methods of producing steel include:

1. Smelting, to produce a steel bloom.
2. Carburisation, carbon introduced when iron is in a solid state.
3. Crucible, melting iron into a liquid.
4. Hardening from carbon absorption during the forging process.

Smelting (to produce a steel bloom)

The process of smelting iron by the bloomery process can be used to produce steel by changing the ratio of charcoal to iron ore. The carbon present in bloomery steel is dependent on the ratio of charcoal to iron ore and, if the charcoal component is high enough during smelting, the bloom that is produced is steel. It is unclear if the full significance of changing the ratio of fuel to ore was fully understood by the manufacturers because it is only since the nineteenth century that the role of carbon has been understood in the metallurgy of steel (France-Lanord 1980). In such a bloom the carbon content may vary in different places within the same bloom.[1] It is likely that steel blooms contain less slag than pure iron blooms and will require less work to remove slag. The carbon in four hammer heads from Iron Age contexts at Bredon Hill, Herefordshire, was interpreted as coming from the bloomery process rather than secondary carburization (Fell 1993). In the Japanese Tatara process,[2] the carbon from the charcoal combines with the iron to produce a homogeneous mass of steel (Kapp *et al.* 1987). The carbon content of the bloom is variable with pure iron at one end and cast iron at the other. These are big blooms that have to be broken into small pieces to make them workable. Those pieces of similar carbon content are separated into discrete piles and then welded back into a single billet. This is then used to make swords. The bloomery process can be used to produce a bloom that is all steel (although the carbon content will vary within the bloom) and simply forged into a workable bar. This will be steel but with slag inclusions that are a source of weakness because they act as stress raisers.

Solid state (carburization)

Cementation, case hardening or forge hardening are all names for the same process that converts iron into steel when the iron is in a solid state (Wagner 1990). When iron is heated to a temperature of 900–950°C it will absorb carbon. The rate of absorption is approximately 1.0mm per hour for the first three to four hours and this rate gradually falls off (Figure 34).

The iron is immersed in a carbon-rich material. Some of the carbon-rich materials used included charcoal, leather, hoof and horn. Indeed, these were still in use for carburizing well into the middle of the twentieth century. The army would have had a plentiful supply

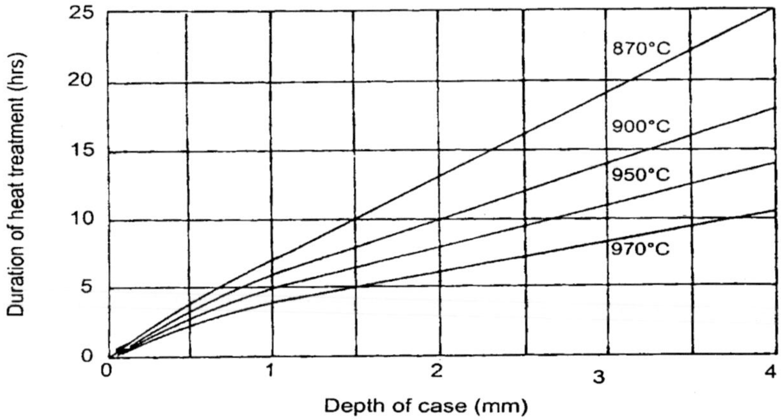

Figure 34: The depth of case as a function of time and temperature

of hoof and horn as a by-product from tanning. Indeed there are instances of leather works next to metal-working areas, such as at Hofheim near Weisbaden, in Germany. It is also likely that, by experimenting with various mixtures, some manufacturers would have been able to produce steel of better quality than others. Ultimately Roman military manufacturers would be attempting to produce iron and steel products of better quality than their opponents. This would account for the wide differences in quality and slag inclusions found in Roman iron.

The conversion of iron into steel can be carried out by immersing the iron in a carbon-rich material, then placing it in a suitable container that has been sealed to prevent the access of any oxygen. The sealed container is then heated for a prescribed time, depending on the depth of carbon penetration required.

It is unknown what thickness of material was carburized in the Roman period, but it is possible to make an educated guess. The thicker the metal the longer carburization takes and the more fuel that is required, which adds to the cost. Steel is not generally used for large metal components such as bathhouse beams or ships' anchors and so it is possible to infer that the material thickness could be quite small. A 3mm thick piece of iron can be converted into solid steel in approximately three hours. The fuel consumption for this is not onerous; however, if 12mm thick iron is converted the process will take approximately three days, which has considerable implications for fuel consumption. Although there is no evidence of this process being used in the Roman period on such a large scale, it is apparent that steel was used much more widely than once thought. Consideration must be given to the techniques that were available to make steel.

Cementation as a method of producing steel was known in antiquity and it is quite possible that blacksmiths could make their own steel. Any blacksmith's forge is quite capable of obtaining the temperatures required and charcoal was probably the main source of fuel. In this way a Roman blacksmith could make sufficient amounts of steel for personal requirements. This method of steel making would not have been able to keep pace when large amounts of steel were required in times of war.

Making crucible steel

A method that will produce homogeneous (slag-free) steel is by using a crucible to melt it in. Crucible steel was known to have been manufactured in India in the Roman period and continued to be manufactured after the collapse of the Western Roman Empire. The process involves taking good quality bloomery iron which is then broken into small pieces and placed inside a crucible, with organic material, together with a small amount of slag. The crucibles are sealed and fired for many hours at temperatures in excess of 1400°C. As the iron absorbs carbon from the organic material it lowers the melting point of the iron and it becomes a liquid. The impurities will rise up through the liquid and form a layer that floats on top of it. Some of the components of the slag will act as a flux to help this process. When the process is complete the crucibles are left to cool, which can take several hours. They are then broken open and the ingots of crucible steel extracted. This is a high carbon steel with few slag inclusions.

Rome had extensive trading networks. During the first and second centuries AD Roman trade with India was at its height (Schoff 1915; Bronson 1986; Craddock 1995, 245, 278; Young 2001). Both Pliny's *Natural History* (xlv: 145) and the *Periplus of the Erythraean Sea* (Huntingford 1980) record that good quality iron and steel were made in the East and traded with the classical world, and that some of the steel supplied to the Roman world was crucible steel. Furthermore, there is an unequivocal reference to making crucible steel by the third century AD Alexandrian alchemist, Zosimos of Panopolis. Therefore, the principle of crucible steel production was clearly understood at this time.

Craddock (1995, 245, 278) also argues convincingly that the crucible process that produced *Wootz* was not exclusively for the production of *Wootz* and that it was used to make good quality carbon steels that did not have the very high carbon content of *Wootz*.

The impracticalities of carbon absorption during the forging process

It is not possible to harden iron by carbon absorption during the forging process. Experiments by the authors have shown that in most forging operations the iron remains in the fire for not longer than two minutes. The rate of carbon absorption by iron during cementation is approximately 1.0mm per hour. Using these figures it can be shown that if any carburization takes place, it will only penetrate to a depth of 0.03mm.

Absorption would be in the outside surface of the iron and this surface is oxidized in the fire and then in the air on its way from the fire to the anvil. The outside surface layers are then dislodged as hammer scale, when the iron is struck with a hammer. Given that the forge fire is usually an oxidizing atmosphere, it is more likely that surface layers will decarburize during forging. Thickness of hammer scale is dependent on several factors such as the temperature of the metal, the force of hammer blows, etc, but a typical range examined after forging a piece of steel at bright red heat recorded thickness in the range 0.02–0.90mm. Any carburized material will be removed when this surface layer is removed, and it will be so every time the metal is placed in the fire.

Absorption during annealing

It has been claimed that carbon can be absorbed into iron during the annealing process. It is necessary to differentiate here between the annealing that takes place in modern metal processing plants, that bring about the desired structure that conforms to the metallurgical requirements of modern production processes, and the practicalities and limitations of the working practices of a blacksmith. Modern annealing requires the metal to be heated to a prescribed level, held at this temperature for a certain time, and then slowly cooled. A blacksmith anneals carbon steel after it has been forged to soften it and to relieve the stresses set up during forging, before it is further heat treated. If heat treatment is carried out without annealing, it will lead to cracking. This is, and was, a basic technique that all smiths are, and were, taught.

In a blacksmith's forge annealing is conducted by heating the artefact to red heat and removing it from the fire; then it is buried in an insulating material such as wood ash or sand to cool very slowly. It is not left in the fire for prolonged periods because the fire is needed for forging and cannot be cluttered up with pieces of metal. Prolonged heating is expensive on fuel. It is also unnecessary, because all that the blacksmith needs to do is bury it in sand to slow cool it, in order to produce a metal that can be further heat treated without cracking. It may not be considered to be properly heated by modern metallurgical standards, but that would not have been a consideration in the Roman period. It was only necessary that the metal would be in a suitable condition for further treatment and it would not crack during further processing.

Hardening and tempering

- *Hardening*: steel can be made hard by heating to 30°–50°C above the upper critical range for its carbon content, holding at this temperature for a time depending on thickness, and then rapidly cooling it in water or oil. This leaves the steel very hard but brittle. If the steel item is to be subjected to shock impact, then the brittleness has to be removed by tempering (items such as files that are not subject to shock are left hard and not tempered).
- *Tempering*: this is achieved by heating the item to a suitable temperature for its specific use. Items such as scribers are heated at a lower temperature than hammers. The range of temperature is from 210°–330°C. As can be seen in Figure 35 there is a marked lowering of hardness as the temperature rises.

In their normalized condition, steels of different carbon content have different hardness values. The higher the carbon content, the higher the hardness. When heat treated, the hardness value will depend on carbon content: the higher the carbon content the higher the hardness value. Low carbon steel cannot be made as hard as high carbon steel. Pure iron has a hardness value of 100 VPN[3] whereas non-heat treated 0.4% carbon steel has a hardness of 235 VPN, and the same steel when hardened has a hardness of 600 VPN.

Heat treatment is not the only way to increase hardness; it can be increased by cold working (hammering) but this will not produce the same degree of hardness as heat treatment. The amount of energy to bring about work hardening increases with a rise

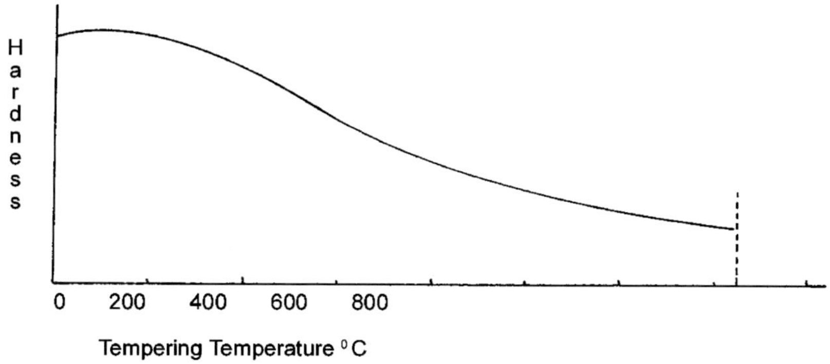

Figure 35: Variations of hardness with tempering temperature for 0.8% carbon steel

in carbon content, but it can still be done by hand hammering and will not require a significant amount of extra work.

Unhardened steel and armour

Armour is best produced from a material that combines both toughness and hardness. Hardness alone is not enough. Glass is a very hard material but is also highly brittle and would be of no use as armour.

Toughness is a material's ability to resist sudden shock loads. Hardness is a material's ability to resist deformation and penetration. Hardness is usually required from a surface that is subject to constant wear. Sudden shock load is the force both weapons and armour are most likely to be subject to during combat, and armour that is tough is more likely to offer a better level of protection than one that is hard.

In some situations armour or weapons require toughness to perform properly rather than hardness. Armour has to remain effective for the duration of combat. If it stops a blow but is destroyed in doing so then it will be of no more use in that combat and puts the wearer at risk. Tough armour might distort but not fracture, and even if damaged will still give protection. Hard armour is more likely to fracture after one blow.

Comparing modern wrought iron with modern black mild steel it can be seen that the steel is superior in both yield strength and ultimate tensile stress (see glossary). Modern black mild steel has very few slag inclusions. In other respects it is almost pure iron, and it can be seen from the figures in Table 8 that this material, because it is slag-free, is superior to wrought iron that has a higher slag content.

Armour made from hardened steel

When hardened steel armour needs repair the operations will require the expertise of a skilled blacksmith. Because steel is hard, it needs to be made soft enough to work. This is done by normalizing – heating to red heat and leaving it to cool in still air; it is often left on the side of the forge fire so cooling is not rapid. Alternatively, it can be annealed to bring it to its softest possible condition. As described above, this is done by heating

	Yield Strength (YS) N/mm	*Ultimate Tensile Stress (UTS) N/mm³*
Modern wrought iron	228	273
Pure wrought iron (i.e. v. low inclusion count)	192	329
Black steel (EN 10025)	335	489

Table 8: Mechanical properties of iron and low carbon steel (J. Hošek et al. 2011). Note that these figures will vary with the composition of the metal

to red heat and burying the item in wood ash or dry sand. The ash or sand are heat insulators and allow the metal to cool slowly making it soft. This process takes several hours so typically it is done at the end of a day's work so the metal can cool overnight. Often the metal is still warm to the touch next morning.

The damage can then be corrected using hammers, files, etc. The edge is made sharp but cannot be fully sharpened at this stage. The metal is then heated to red heat and quenched in water or oil to harden it. This is followed by heating to a tempering temperature suitable for its purpose and again quenching. These heats will have burnt some metal off the cutting edge, reducing its sharpness (this is why it cannot be fully sharpened before heat treatment) and the cutting edge will have to be sharpened with an abrasive stone (a file is not hard enough to cut the hardened steel edge). This is a slow business and requires some skill. The surface of the metal will be covered with a black scale and, if a shining appearance is required, this too will have to be removed with scrapers, files and, finally, an abrasive of some sort. From this it can be seen that in some instances unhardened steel has advantages over hardened steel.

Conclusions

It is clear that the difference between iron and steel was clearly understood in the Roman period. Roman metallurgists also understood the difference between the properties of different ores. It is evident that there was a well-established trade in both iron and high quality steels from India at this time. However, it seems unlikely that a valuable commodity transported from the Indian sub-continent would end up being used for the production of domestic nails. It therefore seems likely that steel was being deliberately produced within the Empire.

Notes

1 It is possible for Roman individual iron artefacts to contain microstructures that range from ferrite (pure iron) to high carbon steel such as the pile shoes from the Roman bridge at Minturnae, Italy (Campbell and Fahy 1984, 29).

2 The tatara method is named after the traditional Japanese furnace used for smelting iron and steel. The tatara is a clay vessel into which ironsand (*satetsu*) is added in layers with charcoal and smelted. When the process is complete the tatara is broken and the steel bloom (*kera*) is removed. The end product is extremely pure steel, or *tamahagane*.

3 Developed by Smith and Sandland (1922) at Vickers Ltd the Vickers hardness test is a method to measure the hardness of materials. The technique observes the ability of a material to resist plastic deformation from a standard source. It can be applied to all metals and has one of the largest scale range among the hardness tests. The Vickers Pyramid Number (HV) or Diamond Pyramid Hardness (DPH) is the unit of hardness given by the test.

6 Surface Treatment of Roman Armour

Introduction

Roman iron armour was often treated to prevent rusting and to enhance its physical appearance. Iron armour in particular can deteriorate very quickly if it is not given constant attention, especially in the damp climate of Europe. According to Vegetius, overseeing the maintenance of the good order of equipment was the responsibility of the decurions and centurions. Polished armour was perceived to be both morale boosting to the wearers and intimidating to the enemy. As Vegetius (2: 14) states: 'who can believe in the warlike nature of a soldier whose equipment is neglected and marred by rust?'

Rust prevention

Rust is the reddish-brown oxide of iron formed by the action of moisture and oxygen on the surface of iron. It consists mainly of hydrated iron(III) oxide ($Fe_2O_3.H_2O$) and iron(III) hydroxide ($FeO(OH)$, $Fe(OH)_3$. It was a phenomenon that Romans were well aware of although its cause was not fully understood.

> 'The same benevolence of nature has limited the power of iron itself by inflicting on it the penalty of rust, and the same foresight by making nothing in the world more mortal than that which is most hostile to mortality.' (Pliny xxxiv: 141)[1]

Untreated iron armour will rust during normal use. This is detrimental to the long-term functionality of the armour. As it rusts the surface layer of the armour is converted to iron oxide, which has no structural integrity. This rust layer is usually only a few microns thick unless it is left unchecked when it will gradually consume the metal; this of course is unlikely in armour that is being used on a daily basis. Cleaning the rust off using an abrasive removes the iron oxide layer, but also some of the ferrous metal from the body of the armour.

There are a number of mechanisms through which moisture can interact with the iron to form rust. For example Figure 36 shows a broken oxide layer on the surface of a piece of iron. In this case atmospheric moisture forms the electrolyte. One mechanism is as follows. Atmospheric moisture contains carbonic acid, because of the presence of carbon dioxide from the atmosphere going into solution with the water:

$$H_2O + CO_2 \rightarrow H_2CO_3$$

Furthermore, it also contains sulphuric acid, caused by the dissolution of sulphur dioxide in this moisture:

$$SO_2 + H_2O \rightarrow H_2SO_3$$

Ferrous ions leave the iron and migrate into the electrolyte leaving the electrons behind. These electrons flow from the iron to the oxide coating. The electrons then take part in the following reaction:

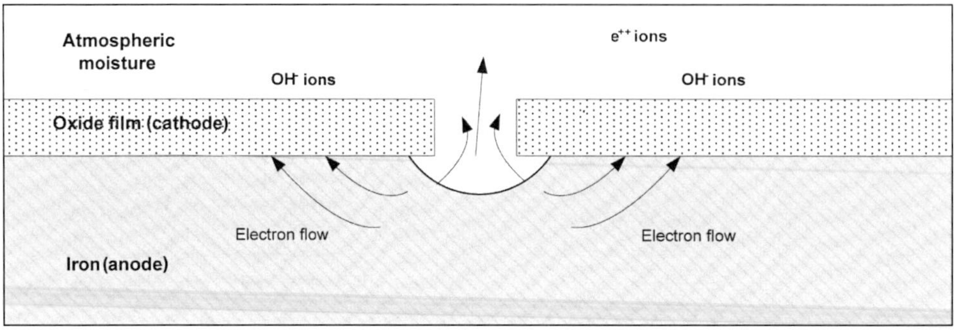

Figure 36: The basic principles of electrolytic corrosion

$$H_2O + \tfrac{1}{2}O_2 \rightarrow 2 \text{ electrons} \rightarrow 2OH^-$$
(from atmosphere) (hydroxyl ions)

The ferrous ions and the hydroxyl ions then react in a region away from the electrolytic action, to form ferrous hydroxide ($Fe(OH)_2$) as shown:

$$Fe^{++} + 2OH^- \rightarrow Fe(OH)_2$$
(ferrous ion) (hydroxyl ions) (ferrous hydroxyl)

The ferrous hydroxide is quickly oxidised by atmospheric oxygen to form ferric hydroxide, ($Fe(OH)_3$) which is precipitated as a reddish brown substance. This is the main constituent of rust.

Considerable effort has been expended on the prevention of rusting in antiquity, as it has today.[2] Rusting of iron and carbon steel can be minimized through the use of protective coatings, such as paints, varnishes, lacquers, oils. The Romans were familiar with these methods as Pliny records that smiths varnish iron and the heads of nails with bitumen (xxxv: 182). Longer lasting and more archaeologically visible protections could be achieved through the use of metallic coatings applied as liquids (tin, silver or gold) or as leaf (gold and silver).

Other surface treatments such as blueing or blacking will slow down the formation of rust. All of these methods are based on the creation of a barrier layer between the atmospheric moisture and oxygen, and the surface of the metal. Such surface treatments are applied to prevent surface deterioration, because of atmospheric corrosion, but they could also have the beneficial effect of enhancing the surface appearance of the armour.

No surface treatment

It is possible that some armour was deliberately left without surface protection. Brightly polished armour will look splendid both on the parade ground and on the battlefield. Constant cleaning is a good way to keep soldiers occupied when they are not on campaign. Of course, cleaning different forms of armour presents its own challenges. Some items such as helmets or greaves are relatively straightforward to clean. However, some types of body armour present their own challenges. Some are based on plate (sheet metal), such as *lorica musculata* (cuirass), *lorica segmentata* (segmented armour) and *lorica squamata* (scale). Of these forms *lorica musculata* is the easiest to clean because it is essentially a single sheet of metal. *Lorica segmentata* and *squamata* are more difficult to clean because many of the plates overlap. However, during everyday use, the overlapping components rub together which leads to self-cleaning. Nevertheless, much of the exposed surface of the articulated plate in *lorica segmentata* or scales in *squamata* will need cleaning. With *segmentata* this is relatively straightforward because of the size of the articulations. However, *lorica squamata* presents an entirely different problem to clean effectively. The individual scales are difficult to clean because of their imbricated structure; furthermore the use of joining wire on some scale armour further complicates the cleaning operation. In contrast, mail (*lorica hamata*) if worn regularly is to some extent self-cleaning because of the constant movement and abrasion of the individual rings (Garlick 1980, 8).

It has been shown that some Roman armour was made from a low slag-free iron (Fulford *et al.* 2004). This material is almost identical to modern pure iron. Plate 3d shows pure iron after only seven days exposure to the atmosphere. The rust that has formed on the surface in this short time would need to be cleaned off.

It is likely that soldiers wearing untreated iron armour would have applied some form of treatment such as the dregs of olive oil or other vegetable or animal based oil. Experimental evidence has shown that the application of olive oil to wrought iron as a barrier method is highly effective. If allowed to dry thoroughly, the oil can form a varnish-like coating that is very difficult to remove. Oils and waxes would have also been required to maintain the leather fittings found in the soldier's accoutrements as well as to lubricate hinges. It is apparent that the smell in use would have been somewhat interesting (cf. Debrebant 2009).

Blueing and blacking

Another method to slow down the onset of rust formation is to exploit the oxide layer that forms on the surface of the iron when it is heated. Between 220°C and 320°C the surface colour changes with changes in temperature, these colours are known as *temper colours*. The colours range from light straw at the lower end, to deep blue to black at the upper temperature.

Before the invention of thermometers and thermocouples to measure high temperatures, the blacksmith had to rely on the changes in colour that iron undergoes as its temperature rises as an indicator of that temperature. Indeed this change of colour is still the blacksmith's main guide to temperature and would have been so for Roman blacksmiths. These colours can be seen in Plate 1c. Other metals give off different coloured flames as temperature rises. The tinsmith uses the colour given off by copper when heated to indicate that the soldering iron has reached the required temperature. The colour of the flame is blue-green as can be seen in Plate 1b.

With the processes of blueing and blacking, the metal is heated until the required colour is evident on the surface, at which point the item is quenched in oil. The oxide layer is porous and the oil is absorbed into it. This form of coating will provide a protective layer and will last for many years before it needs recoating, provided it is given proper maintenance by keeping it as dry as possible. Of course, under field conditions, it would have been difficult to keep armour dry for any prolonged period of time, especially in the European theatre.

The principle behind this process is that an oxide layer is deliberately created in order to prevent the formation of further oxide. This is possible because the oxide formed by heating is Fe_3O_4 while the oxide layer formed by exposure to the atmosphere (rust) is hydrated oxide in the form FeO(OH). A rust retarding surface that is also very hard can be produced by forging the item and quenching it in cold water. The surface appearance will be a dull black, but this is easily enhanced by the application of oils or fats. The Fe_3O_4 oxide layer formed on the surface has a rough black appearance and is very hard. This effectively creates an additional layer a few microns thick of very hard material on the surface with a tough back.

In addition to providing a degree of rust proofing, these colours can also be used to enhance the surface appearance of iron. The colour range is from light straw through blue to black, hence the traditional name of blueing or blacking for this process.

When a smooth surface is required, the oxide film formed in forging has to be removed completely. This requires a considerable commitment of time. To clean a surface of $25cm^2$ to a polished finish using files and scrapers takes approximately 1 hour and 16 minutes. The smooth clean surface can then be heated until the required colour is obtained and then quenched in oil.

Plate 5a shows scale armour that has been blued, and Plate 5b shows scale that has been heated to a higher temperature forming a black oxide layer.

The surface appearance of Roman armour

The primary function of armour is to protect the wearer. There are, however, other secondary factors that influence its design. The importance of the appearance of armour was well understood by the Roman military. Onasander[3] (bk 28) tells us:

> 'The general should make it a point to draw up his line of battle resplendent in armour – an easy matter, requiring the command to sharpen swords and to clean helmets and breast-plates. For the advancing companies appear more dangerous by the gleam of weapons, and the terrible sight brings fear and confusion to the hearts of the enemy.'

He goes on to say (bk 29) that:

> 'the polished spear points and flashing swords, shining in the thick array and reflecting the light of the sun, send ahead a terrible lighting-flash of war.'

It is evident that the psychological impact of polished armour, and even weapons, was well understood by the Roman army. This impact could be two-fold: intimidating to the enemy and morale-boosting to the soldiers wearing the armour.

The current evidence seems to indicate that Roman armour was polished rather than blacked or blued. There is considerable literary evidence for polished armour. For example during the Civil War an attempted ambush by two of Antony's legions was exposed by the: 'suspicious agitation of the rushes, and the gleam here and there of shield and helmet.' *(B. Civ.* 3: 67)

Furthermore, where colour representations of armour do exist in fresco and mosaics, armour is represented as white or silver (for iron armour), or yellow/gold (for copper alloys or iron armour with a surface coating such as gold).

Unfortunately, the third strand of evidence, archaeological finds, is far less helpful. It is not usually possible to identify these treatments in the archaeological record. Many archaeological contexts do not allow for the preservation of surface finishes as ephemeral as blacking or bluing. It cannot therefore be ruled out that blacked or blued finishes were not used during the first or second centuries. Certainly such finishes confer considerable advantages:

- *Cost*: black armour is cheaper to manufacture because no time has to be spent removing the oxide layer from the surface before polishing.
- *Rust resistance*: blacking helps improve the rust resistance of the armour.
- *Camouflage*: the muted black colour of black armour will have conferred some degree of camouflage compared to highly polished armour.
- *Appearance*: the black colour can be used as a contrast to other metals for decorative effect. Gold, polished brass, tinned or silvered detailing would provide a striking contrast with a black background.

The possibility also has to be addressed that some armour was blacked or blued on the inside but polished on the exterior.

Polishing

When a piece of iron is forged, the reaction of the iron with the oxygen in the fire causes a layer of oxide to form on the surface of the metal. During forging much of this layer is dislodged by hammer blows, but while the metal is still hot it reforms almost immediately (Figure 37).

Usually the last forging operations are performed at a low temperature and only light blows are used; these will not dislodge the surface oxide. This will form a black layer on the surface and, if this hot metal is quenched in oil, a rough black surface is created that will adhere strongly to the parent metal. To produce a smooth black finish the original hammer scale has to be removed and the metal polished. This is then reheated to a suitable temperature and quenched in oil. The rough black finish is obviously easier to produce,

Figure 37: Surface of iron after forging

requiring less labour and time, but the smooth black surface confers certain advantages compared to a rough surface. These include:

- Increased efficiency to deflect blows.[4]
- Easier to keep clean.
- More pleasing appearance.

The principle of polishing

Any product of forging will have marks on its surface from the tools used in its production (Figure 38). This is also true of items that have been machined on a lathe or spun.

Blacksmiths endeavour to leave the forging with as smooth a finish as possible. This will reduce the amount of metal that has to be removed to bring the surface of the item to a smooth, clean appearance. In the Roman period this was done using a variety of tools, most of which are still in use today.

In order to bring a forged or machined item to a polished finish it is necessary to remove all surface coatings created during forging (such as oxides) and all marks from working. The method is to use files, scrapers, polishing stones and abrasive compounds, each in consecutively finer sequence.

A good example is a helmet that has been cold worked to shape, so hammer marks have been left on the surface. No matter how careful the craftsman is who made them, these hammer marks are too deep to be removed by polishing alone. The indentations viewed in the schematic section shown in Figure 39 can be seen to be a series of troughs and peaks. These can be flattened by removing the peaks (Figure 40).

In the first operation, a file with coarse teeth is used to remove all the peak tops. This will leave the helmet with a series of grooves left by the file. These are removed using a file with fine teeth and filing at an angle of 90° to the original file marks. These marks are removed by using a scraper made of hard steel. The finishing is done by using a series of abrasive grits, starting with coarse and finishing with fine, each episode of polishing removing progressively fewer microns of material. It is also possible that honing stones were used. The final polishing was probably done using a variety of media.

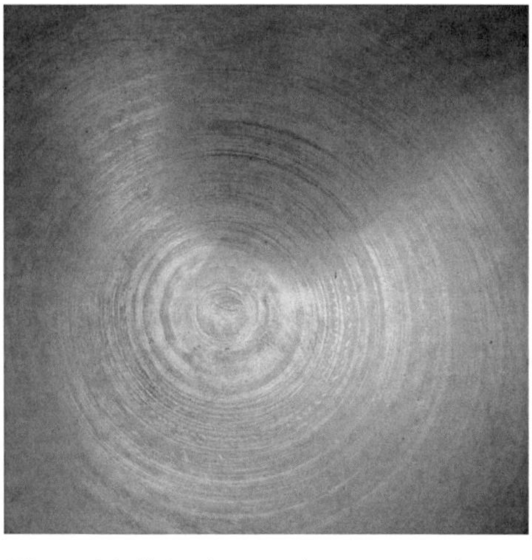

Figure 38: Spinning marks on a reproduction helmet

Modern polishing is done using wheels that rotate at high speed; this makes polishing a fairly quick process. The same level of polish can be achieved by using a leather strap. The ends of the strap are held and the strap positioned across the work and then reciprocated. If the leather was dipped in abrasive paste this would considerably enhance the polishing process. Experiments have shown that

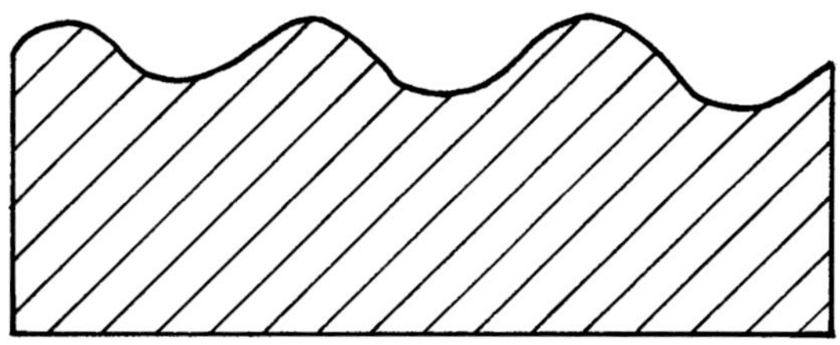

Figure 39: Enlarged schematic section of a forged surface showing troughs and peaks from working

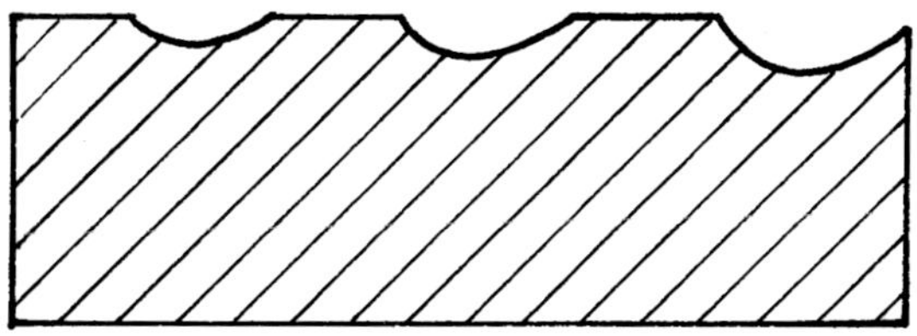

Figure 40: Enlarged schematic section of a forged surface showing troughs and peaks after first filing

sand, hammer scale, powdered glass and ground pottery are all abrasives that can be used successfully as a lapping medium (Sim 1997a) and subsequent experiments have shown all these materials are effective for the removal of hammer scale. In these experiments, the abrasives were mixed with animal fats to form a paste. All of these can be ground in a mortar and pestle to produce ever finer grades of abrasives. All the abrasives tested were found to have similar qualities of metal removal, although sand was the easiest to use because it required no preparation prior to use.

Removing scale using mechanical means

A series of experiments was conducted to determine if the oxide film left by forging could be removed by the use of simple machines. A wheel can be made quickly with little effort. Mounted on a wooden shaft and rotated with a bow lathe it will satisfactorily remove scale. It can also be used to sharpen and shape items. It was of course found that a crank speeds up production but a quern system of drive turned through 90° will do as well. Depending on the abrasive used, the removal time can be halved. Furthermore, it does not need skilled workers.

Abrasives have to be used with caution. Surface finishes such as blueing, blacking, tinning and gliding can be removed with harsh abrasives. It is necessary to remove surface soiling without removing excessive amounts of the underlying protective coating. This can be achieved using a finer grade of polishing compound. These are surprisingly easy to make. A fine polish can be made by grinding charcoal into a fine powder (the same consistency as talcum powder) and mixing this together with waste cooking oil to form a paste. This is applied using a strip of leather. It was found that this only removes the thinnest of layers – in the region of a few microns thick.

Coatings

Metallic coatings were widely used during the Roman period. The object of a coating is to separate the surface of the metal from the oxygen present in the atmosphere, thereby preventing its corrosion. The secondary effect of many of these coatings is to enhance the appearance of the surface of the metal. As Onasander (bk 1: 20) notes:

> 'armour inlaid with gold and silver surpasses that of bronze and iron – the former have the advantage in ornamentation but the latter prove superior in efficiency.'

Coatings could be applied as a liquid or paste to the surface of the metal such as with mercury-gilding (Tylecote 1987, 240) or tinning. Alternatively, metal leaf could be applied to the surface.

Tinning

Tin is a soft, weak metal, slightly less dense (7.5g/cm^3) than iron (7.9g/cm^3) with a melting point of 232°C. Tin is unsuitable for armour, being too weak to afford protection, but when applied as a protective coat on iron, the strength of iron and the corrosion resistance of tin are a perfect complement to each other. Tin is, however, a very expensive metal, because its ores have a low metal content, often less than 1% (furthermore, tin ores are often embedded in granite). This being so, it makes it likely that tin was added to lead to make an alloy that was cheaper and also better for tinning.

Prior to the invention of electro-plating in the nineteenth century, tinning was carried out either by immersion, or wiping. With immersion, the item is dipped in a container of liquid tin-lead alloy (Figure 41). With wiping, the surface of the item is heated, tin is run onto its surface from a stick of the alloy and then wiped with a cloth, spreading the tinning material over the surface (Figure 42).

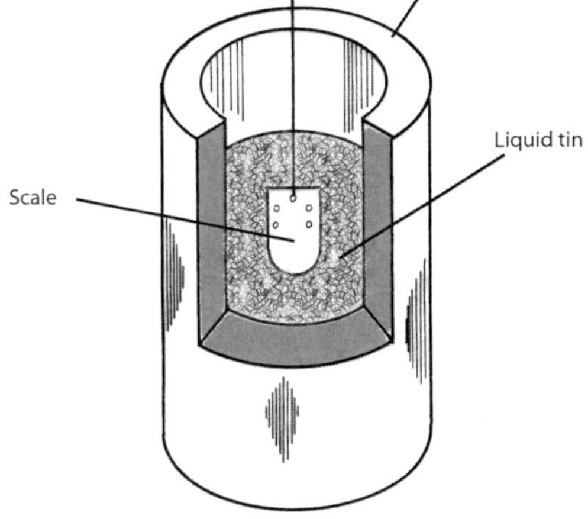

Figure 41: Dipping scale of lorica squamata *in a crucible of liquid tin*

If an alloy of 62% tin and 38% lead is made, this is the eutectic of the lead-tin alloy range. This alloy has a melting point of 183°C and is very fluid at this temperature, making it ideal for tinning by immersion (see Figure 43).

Using an alloy is therefore advantageous because:

- less tin is required, and
- less fuel is required to keep the alloy liquid compared to pure tin.

Dipping and wiping lead to different results. Dipping causes both sides of the object to be tinned, which consumes more of the expensive tin alloy compared to wiping. In most cases there was no need to tin the underside of armour because this was usually left in an unfinished state and would not be seen.

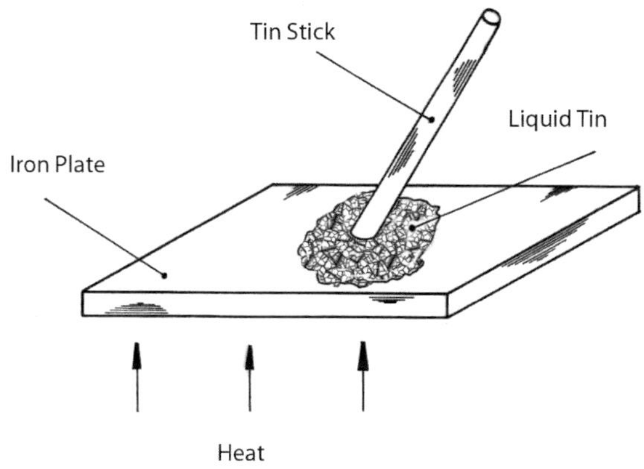

Figure 42: Traditional tinning method. If an alloy of 62% tin and 38% lead is made, this is the eutectic of the lead-tin alloy range. This alloy has a melting point of 183°C and is very fluid at this temperature, making it ideal for tinning by immersion (see Figure 43).

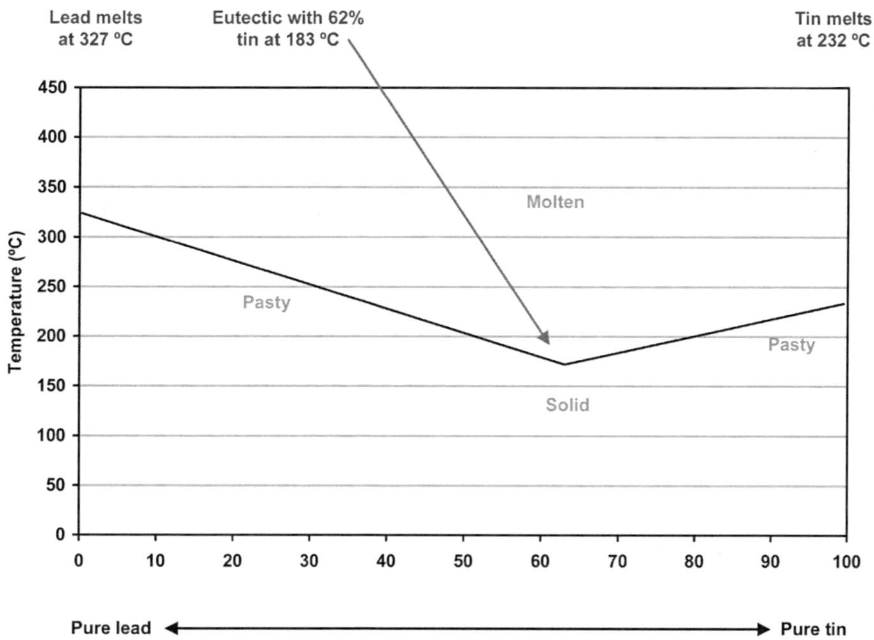

Figure 43: Thermal equilibrium diagram of the lead-tin alloy range (showing melting points)

So although dipping is potentially a rapid means of tinning it may have had limited application to armour. Certainly, with larger items such as helmets, the dipping of individual components may be more problematic. A large container of tin alloy would be required and would also require considerable fuel to keep it liquid. Larger items may have been wiped with tin.

There are many examples of Roman artefacts and armour that have been tinned (cf. Clay 1984). Most tinsmiths will have their own 'recipe' for the alloy they use for tinning and it is unlikely that there was ever a universal recipe. These recipes will vary from individual to individual because one particular kind of alloy will suit the working practice of one particular worker, and may not suit others. Therefore, it is likely that individual manufacturers produced tinning alloys to their own specifications, and kept these recipes a closely guarded secret. Pliny (xxxiv: 150) considered tinning to be principally for rust prevention:

> 'It (iron) can be protected from rust by means of tin (Pliny calls it white lead) gypsum and vegetable pitch.'

However, tinning would have conferred the dual advantage of both rust prevention and decoration. The tin on the surface of the metal retains all the properties of tin; it is corrosion resistant, but it is also soft. Soft metal can easily be damaged in service. If the coating of a 'tinned' article is scratched or abraded then it will not protect the exposed iron surface, in fact the steel will then corrode in preference to the remaining 'tinned' surface. This is because tin is less reactive, i.e. lower in the electro-chemical series, than is iron, and the iron becomes the anode (iron is anodic to tin). The benefits and technique of tinning was widely established from an early date with fine examples of tinned helmets being produced such as the fifth to early fourth century BC Chalcidian tinned bronze helmet shown in Plate 7a. A first century AD Imperial Gallic Type tinned bronze helmet is also shown in Plate 7b. In this example detailed examination shows that abrasion caused by cleaning has removed some of the surface tinning exposing the bronze core.

Some examples of armour have a covering of silver sheet, such as the Kalkriese face mask (Franzius 1995: 72). Such armour would have been expensive to produce. However, the application of high-quality tinning to armour could give the impression of a much more expensive silvered product at a fraction of the cost. Both silver sheet and tinning would have conferred rust proofing to the armour in addition to a spectacular appearance.

Gilding

Mercury-gilding (also known as fire-gilding) was widely practised during the second and third centuries AD (Oddy 1991; Tylecote 1987, 240). In this process, powdered gold and mercury are mixed to form a solution. This amalgam is spread over the surface of the metal. The item is then heated indirectly causing the mercury to evaporate. The deposit of gold left behind is initially dull but, with burnishing, reveals a shine. This is an effective method of decoration as can be seen from the late third to early fourth century Roman helmet crest rib shown in Figure 44 and the shield boss in Figure 45. Furthermore, the inert gold will provide good protection for the underlying metal. However, the use of gold makes this method expensive. It was probably reserved for high-status armour, such as parade armour, and for those with sufficient means to afford this type of finish.

But as Onasander (bk 1: 20) states the application of precious metal coatings and inlays to armour may increase the visual appeal of the object but not its effectiveness.

Leaf finishes

Leaf finishes were often retained for highly prestigious items. Precious metals such as silver and gold were most commonly applied as leaf. Such metals would be beaten into extremely thin sheet and this leaf applied to the surface of the armour during leafing or gilding. Alternatively more mundane metals such as copper alloys could be applied in leaf form to simulate more expensive gold.

An example of a bespoke officer's pseudo-Attic helmet has been recovered from Xanten, Germany. It is of iron construction with silver leaf. The bowl is decorated with embossed hair and a relief of a laurel crown. This particular helmet was specially shaped to accommodate a deformity in the skull possibly resulting from a battle injury (Fuegère 1994, 106–7).

An example of what appears to be a centurion's helmet dating to the second quarter of the first century AD with *crista transversa* recovered from Sisak, on the Kupa river, is of iron with three layers of decoration including silver gilding, leaf silver and later repairs (Radman-Livaja 2004, 71–2).

Heavy foil finishes

In contrast to leaf finishes the heavy foil surfaces have a structural integrity of their own. Usually these are of copper alloy. Examples of *squamae* surfaced with heavy foil have been recovered from the armourer's workshop from Carlisle dated to the first half of the second century AD (McCarthy *et al.* 2001).

A number of examples have been recovered of very thin copper alloy *squamae.* A set of ten undecorated copper alloy *squamae* and *squamae* fragments comes from the Romano-British villa site at Rockbourne, Hampshire (see Figure 46).[5] This is complemented by a further set of two copper alloy *squamae* with an embossed helmeted head on that have been recovered from the Balkans (Figure 47).

These *squamae* are little more than the thickness of heavy foil and would have no defensive capacity whatsoever. Furthermore, they are so fragile that they could not be worn under any practical circumstance. Two options could be hypothesized for these thin *squamae*. It may be that they were for purely decorative use, possibly adorning statues

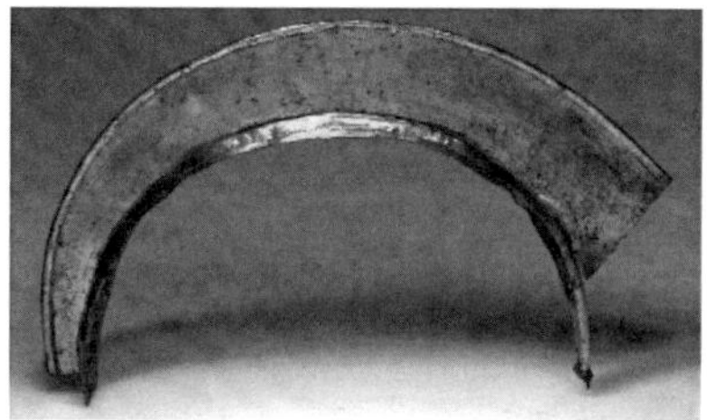

Figure 44: Crest of the late third/ early fourth century AD now in a private collection

Figure 45: A late 3rd/4th century Roman shield boss. Bronze fire gilded

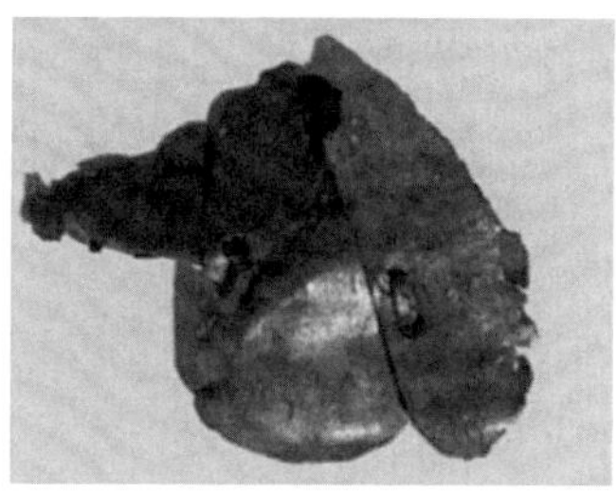

Figure 46: Thin copper alloy squamae *from the Romano-British villa site at Rockbourne, Hampshire, (© Hampshire County Council)*

Figure 47: Squamae *from the Balkans (Private collection)*

Surface treatment	*Description*	*Labour cost*	*Material cost*
Untreated	Left as forged	Low	Low
Blacking	Quenching in oil	Medium	Medium
Blueing	Quenching in oil	Medium	Medium
Polished	Surface abrasion	High	Low
Polished (oiled)	Surface abrasion and coated in oil	High	Low
Polished blacking	Polished then quenched in oil	High	Low
Polished blueing	Polished then quenched in oil	High	Low
Tinned	Polished then dipped in liquid tin	High	High
Silver/gold leaf	Polished then gilding with leaf	High	High
Gilding	Polished then gilded with gold/ silver and mercury amalgam	High	High
Composite metal	Two layers of different metal joined together	High	High

Table 9: The comparative costs of different surface treatments

or for limited ceremonial wear, although no such uses have been recorded in the literary or archaeological records. Alternatively they could be the outer surface of a composite bi-metal scale which has seen the iron core corroded away. Although no evidence of rust remains on the inner surface the looseness of the remaining wire joining links seems to indicate that thicker *squamae* could have been accommodated.

Composite metal construction

There is increasing evidence for some armour that is composed of an iron core with an outer surface of another metal such as copper alloy. Because this involves the attachment of two separate metal layers the technique moves beyond the realms of simple surface treatment to structural composition, however it is relevant to the surface finish. Usually the smith has exploited the properties of the metals to great effect. The strength and rigidity of the iron core is complemented by the flexibility of the copper alloy surface which can be finely worked and retain the comparative corrosion resistance that eludes iron.

This composite metal construction technique is most widely used in helmets, especially finely ornamented cavalry helmets, as in the Weiler form in Plate 6c or the Guisborough helmet (Cavalry Sports type 1). Measurement of the thickness of the Guisborough helmet indicates that the outer copper alloy sheet is less than 1.0mm and this emphasises the reason for the composite construction. The thin copper alloy sheet has been extensively worked using repousé, punching and engraving. The use of repousé especially would not be possible on thicker metal or iron. However, the copper alloy structure would simply have been too fragile to wear unless there was an inner core to support it. Solder marks on the inner surface indicate that it was attached to some form of metal inner core although this is now lost.

A comparison of different surface treatments

As can be seen from Table 9, the cost of labour for surface treatment is high for 70% of the treatments considered, although high labour costs and high material costs account

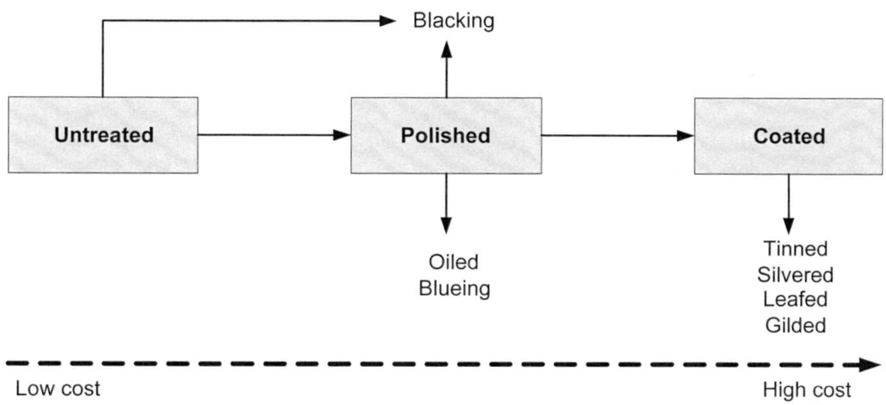

Figure 48: Schematic view of the relationship between surface treatment and cost

for only the top 30%. All treatments incur some cost, but if the top three high-cost items (tinning, leafing and gilding) are considered, these do not improve the effectiveness of the armour; they improve the appearance. In fact, with the exception of leaving a forging black from the forge, most of these treatments make little significant difference to the defensive index of the armour. Their role is decorative, and protective against oxidation, and it must be assumed that those who paid for these treatments considered it a worthwhile expense. It may be that the finer finishes were the speciality of private suppliers to the army rather than mass-produced army products (Figure 48).

Preventing rusting during storage

The prevention of rust is also of importance when iron items have to be stored after manufacture. When supplying an army, many items may need to be stockpiled prior to use. It is likely that items such as nails could have been used as forged, as they would have had an oxide film on them, and this would give protection from rust. Other items would have been forged but would require cleaning and polishing before storage, such as swords and spear heads. Experimental research has shown that gypsum, wood ash, dry earth and animal fat all prevent rusting. Pliny indicates that gypsum and vegetable pitch were used (xxxiv: 150). Clearly they would not have been suitable for protecting equipment in everyday use, and therefore it can be assumed that they provided protection during storage.

Conclusions

There are two main reasons to surface-treat armour: to prevent rusting and to enhance its appearance. The psychological effect of the appearance of armour was clearly understood by the Roman military establishment, as is attested by Roman writers such as Onasander (bk 28), describing the '*lightening flash of war*'. Armour was treated in many different ways, ranging in cost from methods such as blueing or blacking to the most expensive of gilding or gold leafing.

Armour left untreated will quickly rust and this will have to be removed. All surface treatment, even gold leaf, will need to be polished from time to time. Tinning will dull over time and even blue or black finishes will lose their lustre. It is not known what the Roman armourer or soldier used for cleaning armour, but many materials such as sand, ground ceramic, ground charcoal or wood ash mixed with a carrier such as animal fat or discarded cooking oil were cheap and readily available.

It is also probable that any soldier would have examples of several different types of surface treatment on various pieces of his armour. It is also likely that more expensive types of finish were not the sole prerogative of the officer class, but also the ordinary soldier, who wanted to demonstrate his personal wealth, and would spend his own money enhancing his own armour, thus improving his personal appearance and making the soldier more identifiable on the battlefield. This way soldiers wishing to rise through the ranks could be observed by comrades and officers and so enhance their chances of promotion (cf. Lendon 2005).

Notes

1 See also Pliny (xxxiv, 146).

2 If wrought iron is used in the condition in which it emerged for the forge (i.e. scale covered) this would help the iron to resist attack in environments which were mild enough not to cause descaling. Even in rather corrosive conditions the scale slows down the initial rusting of iron (Chilton and Evans 1955, 120). However, it is unclear if this was applied to Roman armour.

3 Onasander was a first century AD Greek philosopher. His *Strategikos* was a comprehensive treatise on military topics, including the use of infantry. The work was dedicated to Quintus Veranius Nepos, consul in AD 49, and legate of Britain.

4 The rough surface gives edged weapons a greater chance to 'bite' into the metal of the armour, compared to a smooth surface, which is more likely to allow the blade or edge to slide off.

5 First–fourth century AD.

7. Helmets (*galea* or *cassis*)

Introduction

Helmets are designed to give protection to the wearer's head, which makes the helmet possibly the most important piece of the panoply.[1] The principal structural component of the human head is the cranium. This is composed of numerous fused bones with a mean thickness of only 2.94mm at the frontal bone.[2] The cranium is not protected by deep tissues, and is relatively exposed. The principal function of the cranium is to protect the brain, but it also houses some of the body's major sensory organs such as the eyes and ears.[3] The brain is highly sensitive to damage, while injury to the other sensory organs can have serious consequences, and reduce effectiveness of a soldier both in the short and long term. Moreover, the mouth is essential for communication in battle. Nowhere in the human body are so many important organs found in such close proximity. Seneca's *De Beneficiis* (5: 24) gives some indication of the terrible punishment that armour and men could sustain in battle. A veteran soldier pleading before Julius Caesar explains why he was not recognised:

> 'you do not recognize me, Caesar; for when that happened I was whole. Afterwards, at Munda[4] my eye was gouged out, and my skull smashed in. Nor would you recognize that helmet if you saw it: it was split by a Hispanian sword.'

Significantly in this instance the helmet had served its purpose. Although cleaved by the Iberian *falcata*[5] it had obviously protected the veteran sufficiently for him to stand before Caesar years later.

Aside from protection, the helmet can have a number of secondary functions:

Homogenization

As helmets began to cover more of the head and face they served to dehumanize the wearer. Individual traits such as hair colour and facial features would have been obscured and the helmet would have become the identifier. There are numerous references in the literature to the effect of helmets concealing identity.[6] For example, the following incident occurred at the Battle of Ruspina in 46 BC when the armies of Caesar met those of Pompey.[7] During the battle the Pompeian commander Titus Labienus:

> 'was riding up and down the front line bareheaded, cheering on his own men as he did so, and occasionally addressing Caesar's legionaries'

An argument ensued between Labienus and with a veteran of Caesar's tenth legion. This soldier then:

> 'threw off his helmet, so that he could be recognized by Labienus, then aimed his javelin at him and flung it with all his might.'

Both Labienus and the veteran had to remove their helmets so that they could be recognised (*BAf.* 16).

In battle standardized helmets can help reduce individuality which would serve to enhance unit cohesion. Roman authors refer to the superiority of Roman tactics, resulting from the cohesion of the unit, compared to the individualistic orientation of many of the barbarian tribes. However, this does not preclude the helmet from becoming a platform for personal adornment and display (see the decorative red enamel studs on the first century AD Imperial Gallic C iron helmet used on the cover). This individual expression differs from the official insignias of rank.

Identification of rank

Helmets provide a platform that allows the insignia of rank to be displayed. For example, Vegetius (2: 16) notes that:

> 'centurions had complete cuirasses, shields and helmets of iron, the crests of which, placed transversely thereon, were ornamented with silver that they might be more easily distinguished by their respective soldiers.'

In battle with the facial features obscured the helmet becomes a mechanism for rank to be displayed.

Intimidation

Head gear has long been used for intimidation. British grenadiers used their gear to enhance the appearance of their height. The use of plumes and crests would have had a similar function. The use of lateral helmet plumes (*geminae pinnae*) was a continuation of an ancient tradition of dedication to Mars. Polybius (vi: 23), writing in the mid-first century BC, describes how the *hastati* wear a:

> 'circle of feathers with three upright purple or black feathers about a cubit in height, the addition of which on the head surmounting their other arms is to make every man look twice his real height, and to give him a fine appearance, such as will strike terror into the enemy.'

Parts of the helmet

Bronze remained in use as a material for helmets and other armour long after it was replaced by iron for weapons (Blyth 1993). Furthermore, in the thousand years that the Roman army in the West was in existence there were considerable variations in helmet design. However, there are a number of elements which are commonplace. The helmet bowl is the principal component of the helmet assembly. Changes in fighting methods often bring about the need to redesign the different pieces of furniture that are attached to the bowl. By the later first century AD helmets had developed all the features necessary to provide the maximum protection to infantrymen, without restricting the wearer. Infantry helmets of this period had some or all of the following features:

Neck guard (lateral volutes)

The back of the neck was protected from blows from behind as well as from aerial projectiles falling from above, such as arrows or sling shots. Neck guards project horizontally or with a downward projection.[8] The projection would also deflect downward-falling missiles away from the upper shoulder region. It would also deflect blows arriving at any angle to this guard. In frontal attacks the energy would be deflected away from the wearer. Cavalry neck guards are, by necessity, much narrower than those of the infantry.

Brow guard

The brow guard deflected downward-slashing blows away from the eyes and face and reinforced the front of the helmet.

Cheek pieces (bucculae)

Cheek pieces gave protection to the face and jaw. They were formed in such a way as to give an unrestricted field of vision.[9] Normal binocular vision covers an angle of almost 180° (this can vary by 1–2° with individuals with pronounced cheekbones). When looking straight ahead binocular vision is 100°, although any movement in the peripheral field is registered. Close-quarter melee fighting had the potential for an attack to come from a multitude of directions. Under these conditions good all-round vision was essential. Restricting the field of vision is problematic as it will reduce the combat effectiveness of a soldier (see Figures 49–50). Cheek pieces make the compromise between more effective face protection and improved vision.

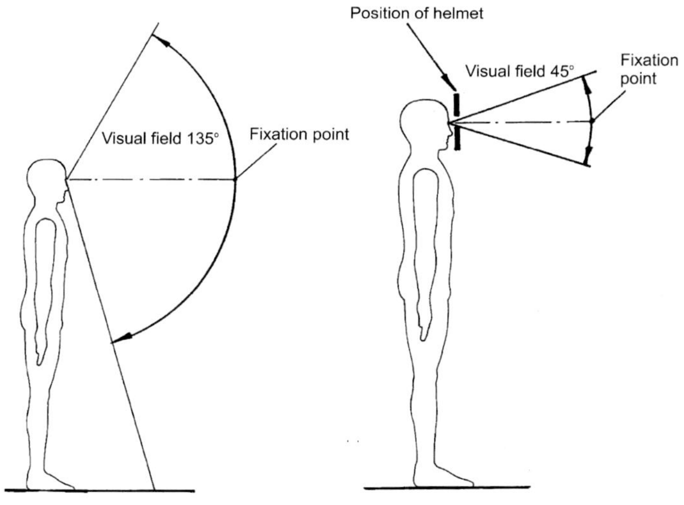

Figure 49: An unrestricted field of view in the transverse plane (left), compared to a restricted field of view caused by a visor in the transverse plane (right)

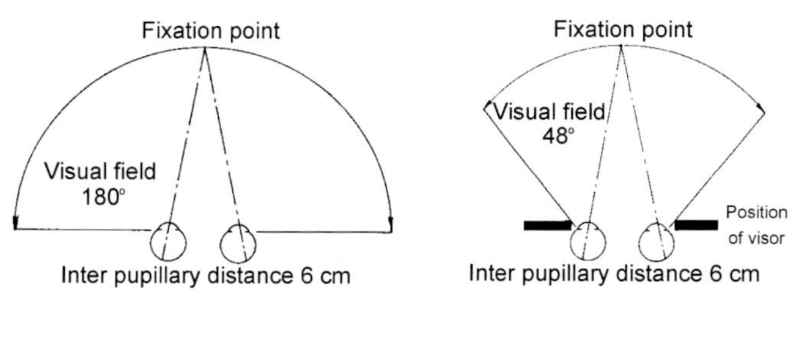

Figure 50: An unrestricted field of view in the median plane (left), compared to a restricted field of view in the median plane caused by a visor (right)

Ear guards/protectors

The more senses a soldier could rely on in hand-to-hand combat the more effective he would be. Hearing is just as important as sight – not only to hear orders but to hear the instructions of comrades and the sound of the surrounding battle in order to act accordingly.

Earlier helmets forms, including the Coolus, did not as a rule have cut-outs for ears. From the first century AD cut-outs and, subsequently, ear protectors became more commonplace. Ear protectors provided additional functionality beyond simple protection. Simply cutting a section out of the helmet rim for the ear would serve to weaken the rim. The addition of ear protectors not only provided protection for the ears but also provided additional strengthening. The guard would also serve to channel sound to a limited degree.

Crests, finials and plume holders

Crests came in a number of forms, for example, sometimes there was a central socket for a plume of horse hair or feathers (*crista*). Sockets for feathers on the sides of helmets originate earlier in southern and central Italy (Köhne and Ewigleben 2000, 37). Central crest boxes could use either horse hair or feathers (cf. Barber and Walker 1992). The only example of a crest so far is from Vindolanda and was made of the locally occurring hair-moss.

The crest could also signify rank as well as decoration. Furthermore, the crest acted to increase the perceived height of the wearer and so contributed to the intimidation inspired by the helmet.[10]

Carrying handles

Many helmets had carrying handles, although this was not a universal attribute. The helmet was usually only worn in times of combat and parades. At other times, when the soldier was on the move, it was probably carried on a line strung round the neck and attached to the carrying handle on the back peak of the helmet.

Methods of manufacture

During the first and second centuries AD the basic infantry helmet consisted of a helmet bowl with cheek pieces and a brow protector. Other furniture such as ear protectors, crests, finials, plume holders and carrying handles were applied according to the form of helmet and the requirements of the time (Table 10).

	Coolus	*Imperial Italic*	*Imperial Gallic*
Cheek pieces	Yes	Yes	Yes
Brow guard	Yes	Yes	Yes
Crests, finials, plume holders	Possibly	Possibly	Possibly
Ear protectors	No	Possibly	Possibly
Carrying handle	Possibly	Possibly	Possibly

Table 10: Furniture associated with different helmet forms in the first and second centuries AD

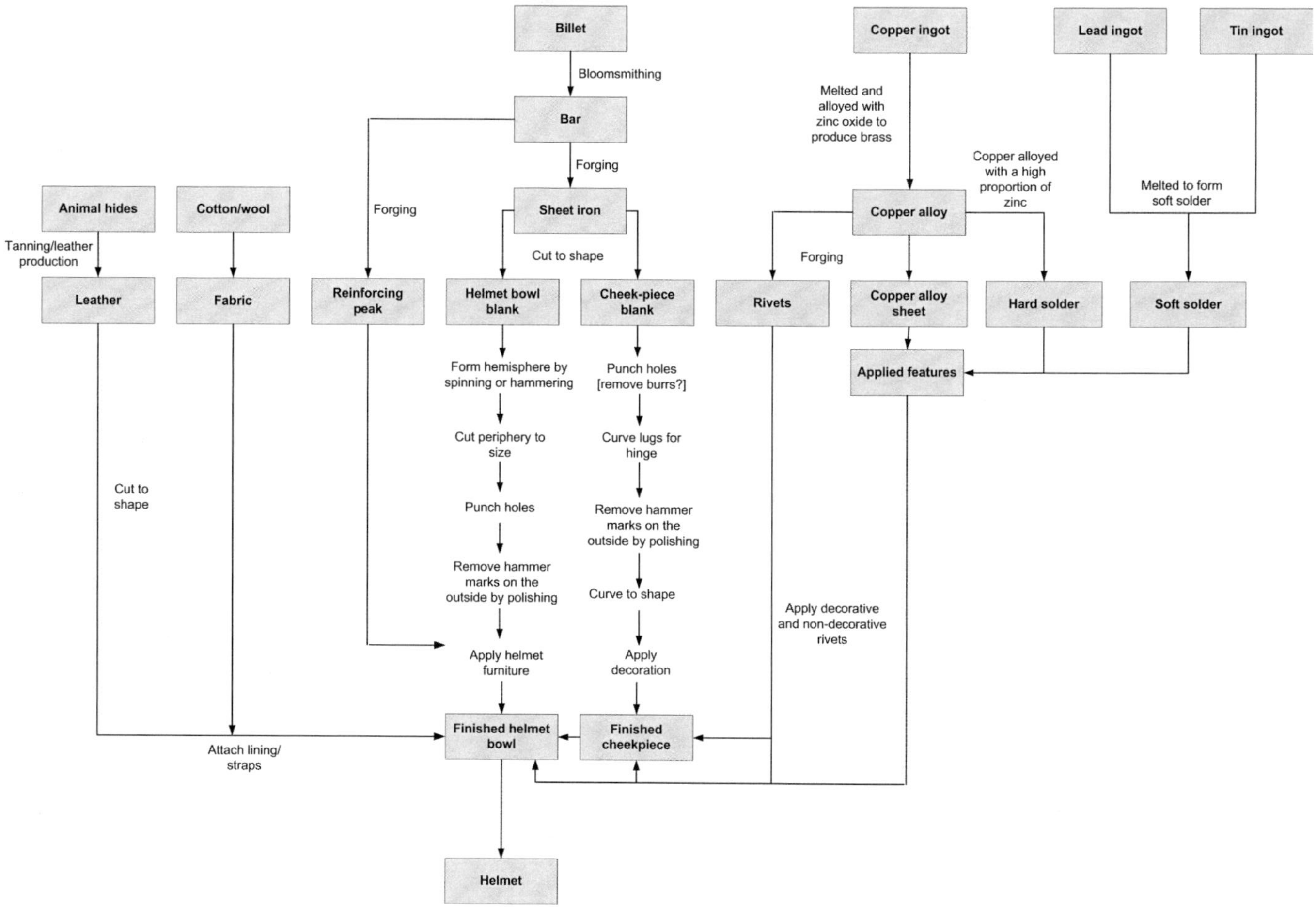

Figure 51: The processes required to produce a Roman military helmet

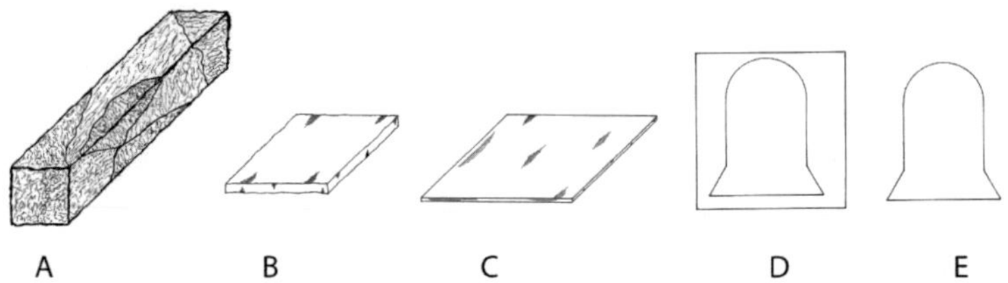

Figure 52: The production sequence for the manufacture of a helmet 'development'

Because of the variety of helmet furniture, the production process for a helmet could be complex. It is probable that the processes were divided up between specialist craftsmen. For example, the late second century *De rei militari* by Tarruntenus Paternus provides a list of military craftsmen including cheek piece makers (*buccularum structores*).[11] Such craft specialization is well attested in the ancient world; there is evidence for specialist Greek helmet makers (cf. Aristophanes *Peace*: 1250 ff.). The production sequences shown in Figure 51 give an indication of the basic operations required to produce the various components of a military helmet.

The helmet bowl

The helmet bowl and its associated neck guard formed the core of the helmet. All the other furniture was attached to this core. The earliest helmets were of copper alloy and were raised. There is evidence that, as early as the seventh century BC, helmet makers were aware of the need for repetitive cycles of annealing and hammering in order to harden copper alloy for battle conditions (Pantosa *et al.* 2005).[12]

The starting point for an iron helmet bowl was a billet of iron (see Figure 52: A). This was forged down into a rough square with parallel surfaces (Figure 52: B). As discussed in Chapter 5, a system of rollers was probably used to produce a sheet with unblemished faces and of uniform thickness (Figure 52: C). A template would have been used to draw the outline of the development on this sheet (Figure 52: D). This was then cut to shape, probably using sheers. The bowl could then be formed either by raising, using a doming block or spinning (see Chapter 3).

The apex of a helmet bowl (indeed, any hemispherical shape) has complex mechanical properties.[13] If the helmet has been formed by raising then the metal in the apex of the bowl will be thinner than the metal at the rim, because it has been stretched the most. The example shown in Figure 53 (left) is from a mid-first century AD copper-alloy Coolus helmet recovered from the River Thames, in London *c.* 1934.[14] In this example, the metal at the apex of the bowl is half the thickness of the material nearer the rim. The example shown in the same figure (right) is from a spun copper alloy Coolus from Chichester Harbour, West Sussex, also from the mid-first century AD. As would be expected, the thickness of the sheet metal is consistent at the crown and the rim. Thinning can be caused if the spinning is carried out without due care and attention, in the example shown the minor variations could also be due to corrosion after deposition.

The thinning of the metal caused during raising does not significantly reduce the

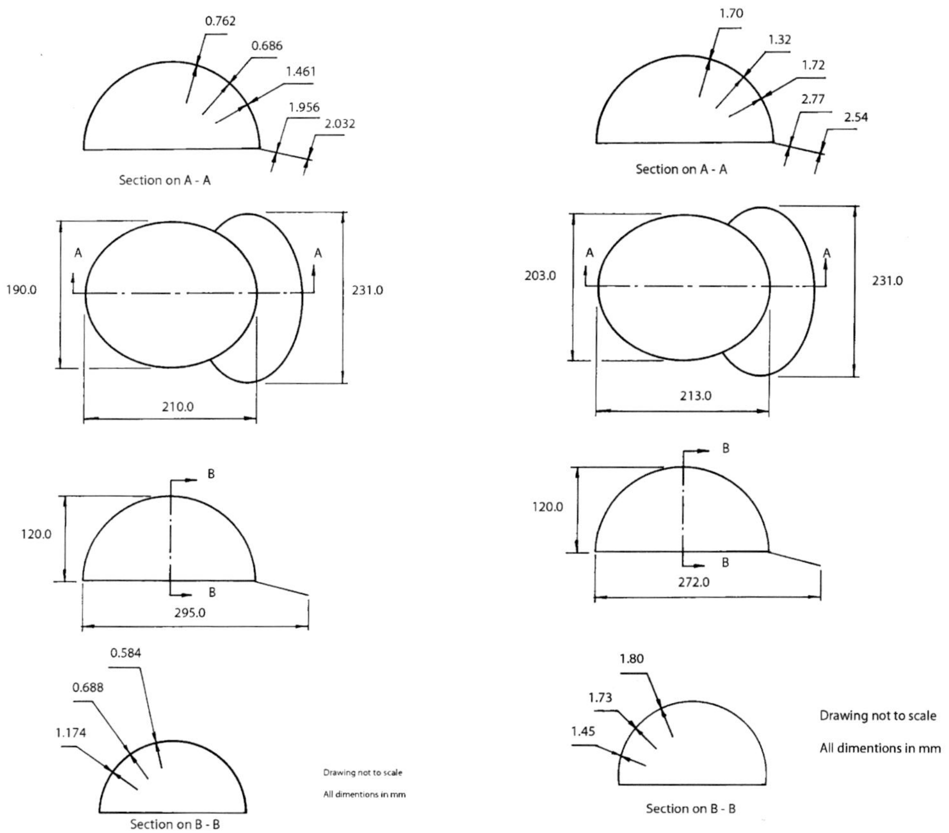

Figure 53: The comparative dimensions of raised (left) and spun (right) mid-first century AD copper alloy Coolus helmets, highlighting the thinning of the metal at the apex of the raised bowl. The raised helmet (left) is the Thames Coolus and the spun helmet (right) is the Chichester Coolus, both dating to the mid-first century AD

defensive properties of the helmet because the thinning is partially compensated for by the work hardening that takes place during the raising process. Furthermore, the hemispherical shape of the crown also confers additional strength.

It seems likely that spinning produced a true hemisphere and that the elliptical form was produced by cold hammering. This hammering gave rise to the variations in thickness around the rim (Figure 54). The elliptical form was produced during the raising process and the majority of hammering was away from the rim. This is why the dimensional variation at the rim is so small.

Evidence of working methods is usually gained from a study of the inside of the helmet. It was common practice during the Roman period not to remove any of the tool marks from the inside of the bowl. The inside of the helmet was usually rough. This conferred an additional benefit if the lining was attached using glue because the tool marks would

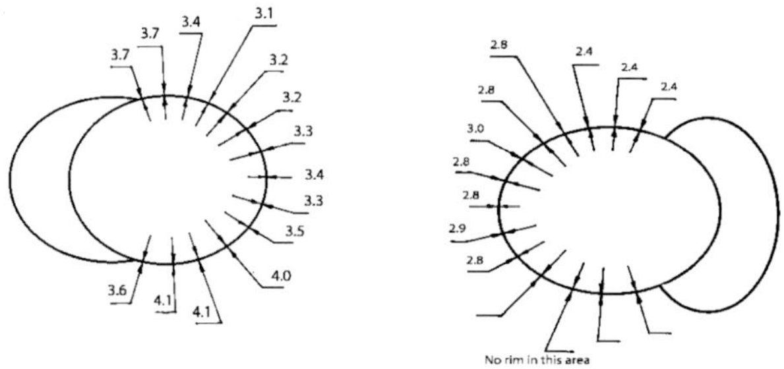

Figure 54: The rim thicknesses of a raised helmet (left) compared to a spun helmet (right). The raised helmet (left) is the Thames Coolus and the spun helmet (right) is the Chichester Coolus, both dating to the mid-first century AD

provide an excellent key. In contrast the outsides of the helmets usually have had all traces of any manufacturing process removed. It seems that the Romans were well aware that removing tool marks from the insides of helmets served no practical purpose whatsoever, while the outsides had to show a high quality of workmanship.

The neck guard

Joints can be an area of weakness in any structure. This potential weakness was widely avoided in Roman helmet manufacture by producing helmet bowls and neck guards that were formed from the same sheet of metal (development). The forming of the neck guard at around 90° to the body of the helmet adds significant strength to that area. It has the same effect as corrugations in iron sheet. [15]

It can be seen in Figure 53 that the neck guard is the thickest part of the helmet. This may be an indication that very little work was carried out on it after the initial forming of the bowl.

Tool marks that have been left on the underside of neck guards of many helmets (e.g. Kaminski and Sim 2007, 219) provide an indication of the types of tools that were used to form the guard and also provide valuable information concerning the sequence of operations. Figure 55 shows the remnant tool marks from the underside of the Chichester Harbour Coolus.[16] The elongated cross pein hammer marks on the inside curve were probably produced when the neck guard was bent out from the original form. The larger marks show that work was carried out in this area to remove any ripples caused during the bending operation. This also had the effect of work hardening it.

Cheek pieces (bucculae)

During the first and second centuries AD infantry helmets were provided with cheek pieces (*bucculae*). These were made of sheet metal, or in some cases leather, as seen in the Hadrianic statue of a deity from Rome who wears an Attic helmet, and possible finds from Vindonissa, Switzerland (D'Amato and Sumner 2009, 111).[17] Metal cheek pieces could be produced relatively simply from sheet metal.

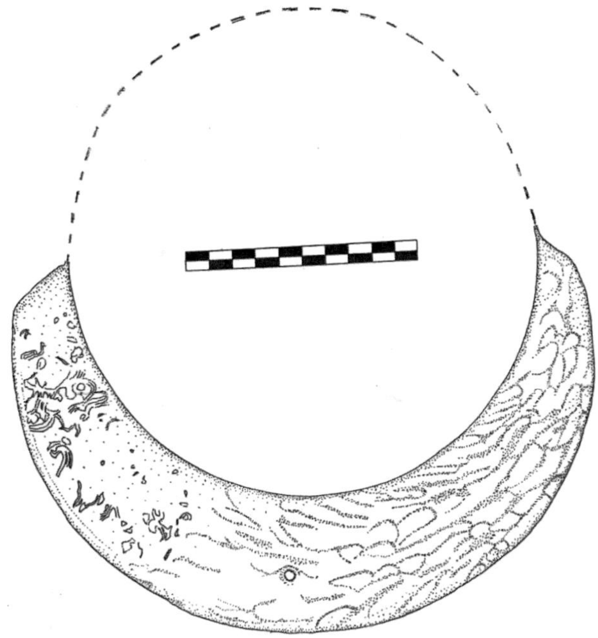

Figure 55: Preserved hammer marks from production on the underside of the neck guard of the Chichester Harbour Coolus, scale 10cm (Kaminski and Sim 2007: fig 2)

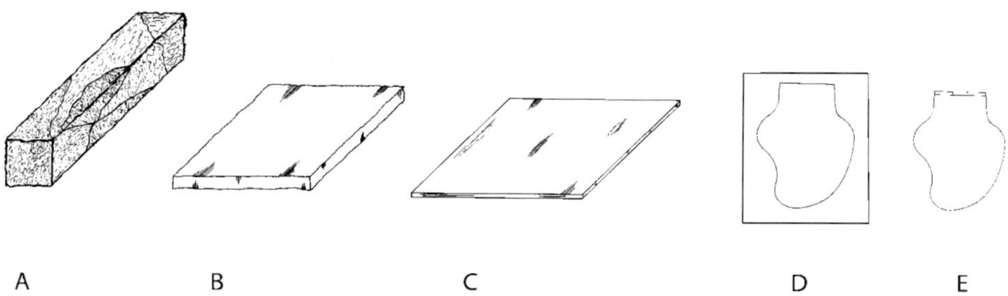

*Figure 56: The production sequence for the manufacture of cheek pieces (*bucculae*)*

For an iron cheek piece the starting point was a billet of iron (see Figure 56: A). This was forged down into a rough square with parallel surfaces (Figure 56: B). A system of rollers may have been used to produce a sheet with flat smooth sides of uniform thickness (Figure 56: C). A template would have been used to draw the outline of the cheek piece on this sheet (Figure 56: D). This was then cut to shape, possibly using sheers or chisels. The top edge was rolled to form the barrels for the hinge. It was then curved to follow the contours of a cheek and any decorative features were added. Finally it was attached to the body of the helmet. A strip of metal was bent to form a tube called a 'chenier'. This was then riveted, or less frequently, soldered to the helmet bowl.

Some cheek pieces were adorned with decorative rivets. For ease of manufacture these could have been attached before the cheek-piece was fitted to the helmet. The pair of second century cheek pieces shown in Plate 6b reveals evidence for mineralized leather around the rivets.[18] This highlights that, in some cases, decorative rivets were punched through the linings. Furthermore, the cross-hatched scoring of the interior surface is just visible on both cheek pieces and would have provided a key for the glue which would have further secured the lining. This provides a guide to the probable sequence of operations for the manufacture of this cheek piece. In this example, after the cheek piece was made, its inside surfaces would have been scored, glue applied and a leather lining attached. When this was dry a hole would have been punched in the cheek piece and the rivet passed through it and the leather lining, before being hammered over to secure the rivet to both the cheek piece and the lining.

There would have been subtle variations in the manufacturing process. For example, in some cheek pieces the exposed ends of decorative rivets were covered with the leather lining.

Finally the cheek piece could be attached to the helmet bowl. A joint pin, which was usually a piece of wire, could be inserted through the hinge (the *chenier*), thereby linking the cheek piece helmet. In use the cheek pieces hung vertically down from the bowl. As can be seen in Plate 6b, rings were attached to the lower part of the cheek piece. These would have been used for tying the cheek pieces by passing leather thongs or cord through them and securing under the chin.

Brow guard

Like the cheek pieces, the brow guard was universally provided on infantry helmets during the first and second centuries, highlighting the importance of reinforcing the front of the helmet and deflecting slashing blows away from the face. The production of brow guards relied on simple forge work. Their production started either with a billet of iron or non-ferrous metal. This was forged into a regular rectangular strip. Lugs were formed on each end and holes punched through the centre of the lugs. The strip was then bent into a curve, following the contour of the front of the helmet. Finally, it was attached to the helmet with rivets.

The properties of iron and copper alloy are different. This means that production of the brow guard has to be carried out in a manner specific to the properties of the metal. For example, it is possible to carry out considerably more cold work on copper alloy than on iron. When copper alloy has work hardened so it can no longer be formed it can be annealed readily by heating and quenching in cold water, returning it to its softest possible condition. It can then be further worked. Iron however, when it has become work hardened, requires a lengthy annealing process taking several hours to remove the work hardening.

As with many examples of armour the working marks were often left on the inner and undersides (Plate 3c). In this example, there are two distinct types of hammer mark. At the top of the picture shallow indentations made by the striking end of the hammer at the bottom of the picture elongated grooves produced by a cross pein hammer or a small fuller. In this case the probable sequence of operations is that the sheet was brought to the required dimensions by hammering. The cross pein hammer was then used on the inner edge in order to bend the sheet to the required curvature.

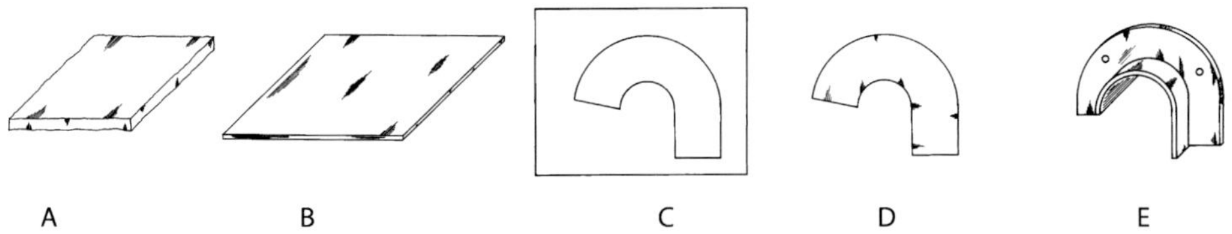

Figure 57: The production sequence for the manufacture of ear guards

Ear protectors

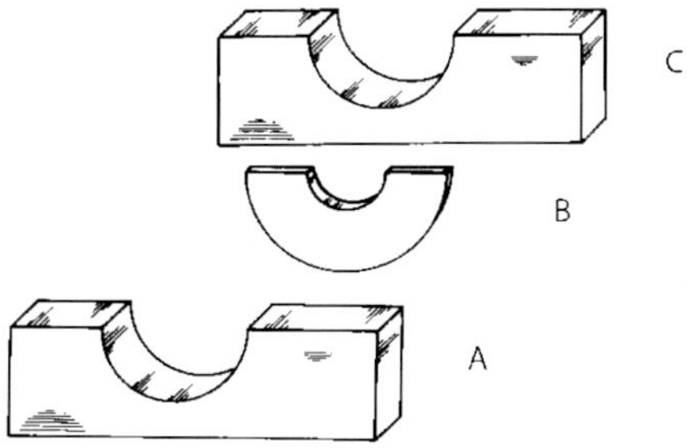

Figure 58: Shaping the ear protector (B) between a pair of formers (A and C)

Although some helmets had no accommodation for the ears, some had simple cut-outs to improve hearing; the more sophisticated forms had ear protectors. These would have been produced from sheet metal.

Ear guards were made from both ferrous and non-ferrous metals. The starting point was a block of metal; if it was to be made of iron, the initial stages are shown in the making of a helmet; if copper alloy, the starting point may have been a casting (Figure 57).

The second stage (Figure 57: B) was to produce a flat smooth sheet. It was essential to have a smooth sheet of metal at this point because removing imperfections from the surface was much more difficult when the piece had already been formed to shape. Forming it from smooth metal reduced production time later. This would have been best accomplished with rollers if available. The probable method of forming the ear protectors from this sheet was as follows.

A template was probably used to mark the profile of the ear guard onto the sheet. This was an item that was likely to have been produced in large numbers and production time would have been reduced by making a template to draw around as shown in Figure 57: C. It also would have ensured uniformity in the items produced.

The blank for the ear protector (Figure 58: B) would have been sandwiched between two formers (Figure 58: A and C) that were then clamped together. Its top edge would have been made level with the top edge of the formers and all three pieces clamped together. A round-headed hammer would have been used to bend over the section of blank left exposed between the formers (Figure 57: E). This amount of hammering would have produced significant work hardening in the metal, giving the ear protectors greater structural strength.

Ear protectors were generally riveted to the body of the helmet. This is because soldering is a much longer process than riveting – is more time consuming and less effective. A riveted joint can withstand a slashing blow whilst a soldered joint would fail more easily.

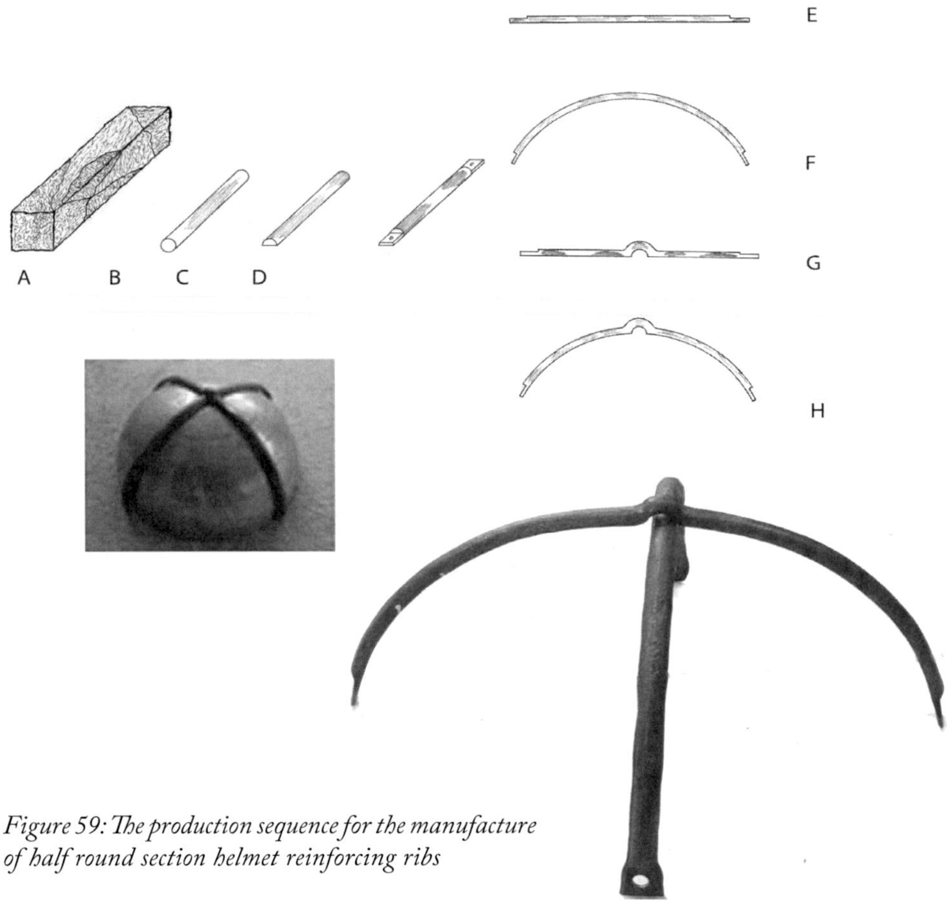

Figure 59: The production sequence for the manufacture of half round section helmet reinforcing ribs

Helmet bowl reinforcement

In battle the helmet bowl would have made an attractive target. Reinforcing ribs were added to some helmets to strengthen the bowl by increasing the thickness of the metal where it is generally thinnest at the apex of the helmet and deflecting blows sideways.

Reinforcing ribs were made of either iron or non-ferrous metal. The different types they fall loosely into two different forms: rectangular cross-section and half round cross-section. The rectangular cross-section forms are evident in both infantry and cavalry helmets, while those of the half round cross-section are more commonly found in infantry helmets. Both forms were usually attached using rivets.

Experiments by Sim (2002) have shown that these ribs can be produced through simple forge work (see Figure 59). Assuming a starting point of a billet of iron (Figure 59: A) reinforcing ribs of the half round cross-section could have been produced using the following sequence of operations.

The billet was forged into a round bar that was long enough to make both ribs; this was then forged into a half-round section using a bottom swage (Figure 59: B and C).

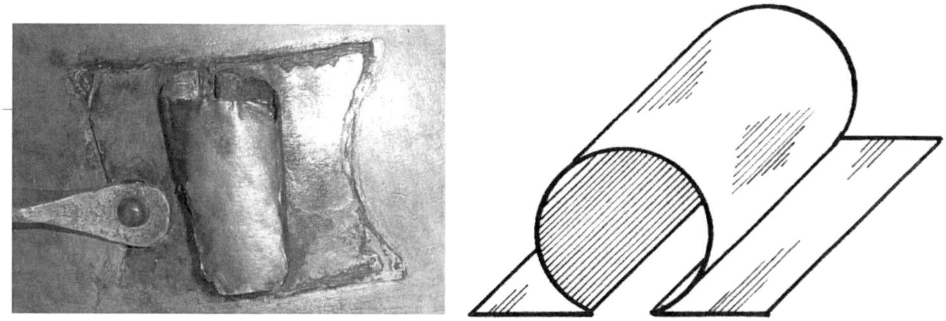

Figure 60: Detail of the plume holder from the Thames Coolus and a schematic plan view of its construction

The bar was cut into two lengths, each slightly shorter than the required finished length. A flat was forged at each end of the bar. This elongated the bar and brought it to the required finished length. A small hole for the rivet was punched in each flat (Figure 59: D). The resulting rib was then bent to fit the contour of the helmet. The top rib was forged as shown in Figure 59: F. A half loop was formed in the centre of the rib using a bottom swage and a top fuller (Figure 59: G). This top rib was then bent to fit over the bottom rib and to follow the curve of the helmet (Figure 59: H). The ribs were attached to the helmet using rivets made of softer iron than the helmet. If a riveted joint receives a heavy blow, softer rivets will fail before the metal of the helmet body.

Experimental work has revealed that approximately 40 minutes are required to produce and fit the half round reinforcing ribs using the above sequence of operations. This includes 20 minutes to forge the two ribs and a further 20 minutes to attach them to the helmet body (Sim 2002: 105).

Finials and crests (crista)

Crests were usually attached to helmets immediately prior to battle. As Caesar records in his *Bellum Gallicum* (II: 21) an attack by the Belgae caught his troops by surprise and so they were unable to attach their insignia to their helmets or remove their shield covers (see also *BAf.* 12). Crests could also be used as a means of identification for officers the *crista transversa* being the most obvious manifestation.[19] Vegetius records that the *crista transversa* could be silvered to further aid identification in battle. Crests could be located centrally at the apex of the helmet while plume holders can be found on the temples.

Although these crest boxes may not have been designed with defence in mind, their very presence would have had the effect of absorbing some of the energy from a blow. Similarly, finials were fitted at the apex of the crown and would have the effect of deflecting blows that arrived in this area. They were often attached by soft soldering which meant that much of the energy would have been dissipated in breaking the soft soldered joint. Such a joint would not require any hole to be made in the helmet that would weaken the helmet at an already vulnerable point.

The cylindrical plume holders from the Thames Coolus were made of sheet copper alloy only 0.4mm thick (Figure 60). This remarkably thin material emphasises that the plumes which they would have held would have been lightweight (feathers or horsehair).[20]

Helmet linings

The majority of military helmets were mass-produced and because of the sheer scale of production it is unlikely that they were made to fit individuals. It is more probable that each workshop produced helmets in a series of sizes. This makes production of helmets more manageable for the manufacturer.[21]

Of course, some individuals who could afford it would have had bespoke helmets made for them but most soldiers would have been given a helmet that was close to their head size. Any significant difference between the wearer's head size and the size of the helmet could have been compensated for by the use of extra padding and lining material.

The principal function of helmet linings would have been to separate the metal of the helmet from the wearer's head. This would lead to a number of benefits:

- *Fitting*: the lining and associated padding would have allowed manufacturers to fit standard sized helmets to individual's heads.
- *Comfort*: the lining would have made the helmet more comfortable to wear.
- *Protection*: the lining and its padding would have absorbed some of the energy of blows sustained during battle.
- *Insulation*: the lining would have helped shield the wearer from excessive heat and cold which would have made the helmet uncomfortable to wear in extremes of climate. It would also have absorbed sweat. It is possible that different types of lining were used in different climatic conditions.

Because helmet linings would have been made of organic materials, only a limited number of examples have survived. A fragment of leather was preserved under a rivet on the inside of the Newstead sports helmet; furthermore, the iron helmet from Newstead also retained a thick woollen padded lining on the inside of the helmet bowl and mask (Curle 1911, 166, 170; Robinson 1975, 144), and further leather helmet linings have been found in the waterlogged deposits at Vindonissa. The cheek pieces shown in Figure 71 also reveal the presence of mineralised leather. However, while leather does seem to be widely used, an Imperial Gallic helmet from Hod Hill, Dorset, retains fragments of a coarse fabric lining (Brailsford 1962, 5). The presence of both leather and fabric suggests that both materials were exploited for helmet linings.

Conclusions

Helmets are designed to give protection to the head. During the first and second centuries AD the Roman military used helmets made of both iron and copper alloy. By this time generations of improvements in infantry helmet morphology had led to the production of a piece of armour that gave very good protection but did not restrict vision and only slightly reduced hearing. The technology and design of Roman helmets had reached a pinnacle of sophistication.

Helmets were produced either by raising or spinning and were manufactured from either iron or copper alloy. Both of these methods were well established as ways of shaping metal. Both were in use before the foundation of the Empire, and they were used in tandem during the first and second centuries AD.

Helmets had certain characteristics. Cheek pieces and brow guards were widely fitted to protect the face from slashing blows. The back of the neck was protected by a rear peak that would have deflected downward blows from hand-held weapons or falling projectiles. Not all helmets were fitted with ear protectors but those that were defended the wearer from downward blows but, as the ear was not covered, hearing would not have been significantly impaired. Some helmets were fitted with cross-reinforcing ribs over the apex of the bowl to deflect downward blows away from the head.

Surface marks left by forming were removed on the outside by filing, scraping and polishing with various grades of abrasive. The marks left by the production process can often be seen on the insides of helmet bowls and the parts of helmet furniture that are not outwardly visible. This gives a clue to the philosophy of the helmet makers. Well-finished interiors do not improve the effectiveness of the helmet and also add to the time and cost of production; therefore those parts did not have production marks removed. Classical sources explain how specialists were employed to make certain parts of helmets such as the cheek piece (*bucculae*) and it can be inferred that specialists were responsible for the production of helmet furniture and that the various components were brought together for assembly. From this it is possible to suggest that helmets (as well as other types of armour) were made in huge quantities on a system of large batch production. The production of a helmet was a skilled process which was, nevertheless, highly repetitive. Once learnt, a worker could produce a steady flow of helmets when required.

The value of the materials used and the comparative complexity of manufacture of helmets mean that they often had a long lifespan in military service as attested by the multiple ownership marks on some helmets (Collingwood and Wright 1991).[22] It may be that older grades of equipment were relegated to lower grades of troops (Simkins 1990, 121).

Notes

1 The panoply is the complete set of armour. The word derives from the Greek meaning 'all arms'. So technically the panoply of Roman infantry soldier would include the shield, helmet, body armour and greaves, in conjunction with the sword and *pilum*.

2 The male frontal bone has a range between 1.0mm and 7.0mm in thickness. It should be noted that cranial total thickness is not statistically significantly associated with the sex, stature or weight of an individual (Lynnerup *et al.* 2005, table 1).

3 The design of Roman infantry helmets offered no protection to the eyes, and in some conflicts eye wounds were not uncommon (*B. Civ.* 2: 60; Seneca *De Beneficiis* 5: 24).

4 The Battle of Munda took place on 17 March 45 BC in the plains of Munda, modern southern Spain. This was the last battle of Julius Caesar's civil war.

5 The Hispanian saber (*machaera Hispana*) referred to by Seneca is generally thought to be the Iberian *falcata*.

6 Famously, Patroclus was killed by Hector as he led the Myrmidons and Achilles retainers because he was mistaken for Achilles during the siege of Troy (Homer, *Iliad* Bk 16). Obviously the considerable differences between Bronze Age Greek armour and Roman forms make a direct comparison problematic.

7 After defeating Pompey at Pharsalus, Caesar sailed to North Africa with five legions of raw recruits and the veteran V Alaudae to secure the territory from Pompeian control. The Pompeian forces were commanded by Titus Labienus and comprised many Numidian allies. Whilst foraging Caesar's soldiers were surprised and had to make a fighting retreat to his fortified camp at Ruspina. During the battle Caesar may have lost up to a third of his troops.

8 The neck guard was a common place for soldiers to inscribe their names. This highlights that soldiers did not ordinarily keep their armour with them, but that it was stored in *armamentaria* under the control of the *custos armorum* or the *armamentaria* (MacMullen 1960, 23).

9 Experimental work has shown that Roman cavalry and infantry helmets (without facemasks) do not restrict the field of vision. If comparison is made to some medieval helmets fitted with visors the field of view is restricted to 78°. A restricted of field of view like this makes the wearer of such a helmet vulnerable from attacks from the side.

10 The crest box could have conferred an incidental degree of protection from downward blows to the helmet.

11 This surviving fragment of Paternus's *de rei militari* is preserved in the sixth century *Digesta seu Pandectae* (Webster 1998, 119).

12 Neutron and synchrotron X-ray analytical techniques were used to characterize a seventh century BC Corinthian-type bronze helmet from Manchester Museum. The neutron data hinted at repetitive cycles of annealing and hammering in order to harden the alloy. The authors suggest that the helmet was probably cast as skull-cap, then beaten, heated and dressed down to its final thickness and shaped to fit the wearer's head. The final process was probably a hardening step. The orientation of grains, suggested hammering of the bronze sheet in one direction. It is evident that the maker made a considerable effort to harden the alloy (Pantosa *et al.* 2005).

13 If a hemisphere and a full sphere are loaded in the same way at their respective centres, then they behave in much the same manner. However, if the load on a hemisphere is applied closer to the rim, then there is a significant loss of resistance, because there is only half the structure compared to the centre. In the centre it is a 'dome' while on the edge it is more of a 'curved beam'. These have significant differences in their mechanical properties. The strength of the middle of the hemisphere may also be increased because of the 'membrane' behaviour, but this is dependent on thickness, diameter, etc.

14 The 'Thames' Coolus was purchased by the British Museum in July 1950. The helmet (1950,0706–1) is a well-preserved example of a mid-first century Coolus of Robinson's Type E (Robinson 1977, 32–3). Only the body of the helmet remains; unsurprisingly for a river find the cheek pieces, helmet finial and helmet loop attachments were not recovered. The helmet is made of copper alloy, and has a circumference of 647mm and weighs 1052.3g. Its overall dimensions are 295mm long, 231mm wide (at the widest point of the neckguard), and with a helmet dome 120mm high. The helmet has a hemispherical dome and broad neck guard. It has a separate brow protector, which was attached by a rivet at either side, and was originally secured to the helmet dome with solder. It has tubular plume holder attachment for cheek piece at each side. There is a hole for a carrying rivet in the neck guard. The neck guard also has four different punched ownership marks (Brailsford 1951, 18; RIB 2425.2).

15 There are some exceptions to this. For example, the auxiliary cavalry helmet from Guisborough has a welded neck guard, although this could have been a later repair. The Guisborough Helmet (British Museum Acc. No. 1878,0910.1) is bronze with engraved and embossed ornament. It was found in the bed of an old water course on Barnaby Grange Farm, Guisborough, Cleveland.

16 See also Figure 68 for similar working marks on the underside of the helmet's brow guard.

17 The use of leather *bucculae* could be one reason why so many helmets are found without cheek pieces, the other being the degradation of the securing wires on metal cheek pieces leading to their loss in the archaeological record.

18 Leather was not the only material used for lining cheek pieces, the examples from Hod Hill bear traces of what may have been a fabric lining (Russell Robinson 1975, 56).

19 The *crista transversa* was certainly used during the early imperial period but evidence for this identifier begins to diminish during the second century.

20 See for example the plumed helmet of Flavius at Hexham Abbey and the tombstone of Insus at Lancaster City Museum for plumed helmets in a cavalry context (Bull 2007).

21 Although it is tempting to use the measurement of helmet diameters to highlight the different 'standard' sizes, this is not possible. Because the helmets measured span centuries and geographical zones, there do not appear to be any standard sizes – however, it is probable that each workshop would have had its own standard sizes to which it worked.

22 For example, some helmets have as many of four ownership marks punched on them, including the Thames Coolus from London.

8. Scale Armour (*lorica squamata*)

Body armour

Armour can be separated into its principal components in relation to the parts of the body itself for which it gives protection. These are the head, the body, the arms and legs, and, finally, the non-specific protection provided by the shield.

The function of body armour is to protect the torso. Numerous organs are contained within this area. The heart and lungs, in the upper torso, are given some degree of protection by the rib cage, but the plethora of organs in the abdominal region including, the intestines, liver, kidneys, bladder, etc, have very little protection. Damage to any of these will at the very least incapacitate a soldier. It has been estimated that a 50mm deep wound to the thorax can be fatal (Jones 1984, 247).

Body armour therefore provides a mechanism to protect many of these important internal organs. Much Roman body armour provided all-round protection, surrounding both the back and front of the torso. This all-round defence means that the vulnerable organs in the lower back region, the kidneys and liver, were given some protection.

As with all armour, body armour attempts to mitigate blunt force trauma.[1] This is the amount of rearward deformation the body armour will receive when struck by an object. Although the weapon may not penetrate the body armour, the part of the body directly behind the point of impact usually receives a hammer-like blow as a consequence of the deformation of the armour as the velocity and energy of the impact are dissipated. Blunt force can lead to bruises and lacerations and, more seriously, it can produce damage to internal organs. The tissue damage caused by the transfer of kinetic energy can be fatal.

Lorica squamata

During the first and second centuries AD *lorica squamata* was one of four principal types of metal body armour in use by the Roman military. Additionally, segmented armour (*lorica segmentata*), mail armour (*lorica hamata*) and the muscle cuirass (*lorica musculata*) were being used simultaneously.[2] These different types of body armour provide different benefits and advantages (Table 11).

	Lorica squamata (scale)	*Lorica segmentata (segmented)*	*Lorica hamata (ring)*	*Lorica musculata (cuirass)*
Production time	High	Mid	Very high	Low
Material required	High	Moderate	Moderate	Low
Cost to produce	High	Mid	Very high	Low
Durability	Moderate	Moderate	Moderate	High
Level of protection	High	High	Moderate	Moderate

Table 11: A comparison of the four principal armour types used in the first and second centuries AD

Scale armour or *lorica squamata* is a type of body armour, which is known to have been in existence since at least the seventeenth century BC (Russell-Robinson 1975, 153). Scale armour works by initially dissipating the energy of a strike, then protects against any penetration to the soft tissues below and, finally, limits any damage to the area surrounding the impact. This is possible because the scales in *lorica squamata* spread the blunt trauma across the surface of the body armour so that the impact is not too great in any one area.

Scale armour was imbricated like fish scales or roof tiles, as can be seen in the reconstruction of part of a scale collar from Carlisle, Cumbria, shown in Figure 86. This type of armour was strengthened by connecting the scales into rows with links of copper alloy or iron wire or strip, which passed through the pairs of holes in the sides of each scale (see Plate 5c). Depending on how the scales are joined (wire or thread) then the armour is more or less flexible. *Squamae* joined with wire are semi-rigid.

Typology of *lorica squamata*

The typology shown in Figure 61 provides an extensible mechanism for classifying scales. Although there are numerous variations, the basic outline of the scales can be divided into the following forms: rectangular (A), lancet arch (B), radiused (C), minor radius (D), clipped rectangular (E) and triangular (F). In addition to the surface plane, scales also differ according to their cross-section, including flat (i), curved (ii), v-section (iii), single ridged (iv) and double ridged (v). Scales are also composed of either iron or copper alloy. The combination of material, profile and cross-section allows scales to be easily categorized. This typology is extensible; if different profiles or cross-sections are recovered in the archaeological record they can be added to the matrix. Other typologies such as Von Groller's classification of first century armour scales classifies *squamae* according to the location of attachment holes.[3] While this is instructive, providing information regarding the mechanism of linking scale and even their relative position, the morphology of scales can provide considerable additional information.

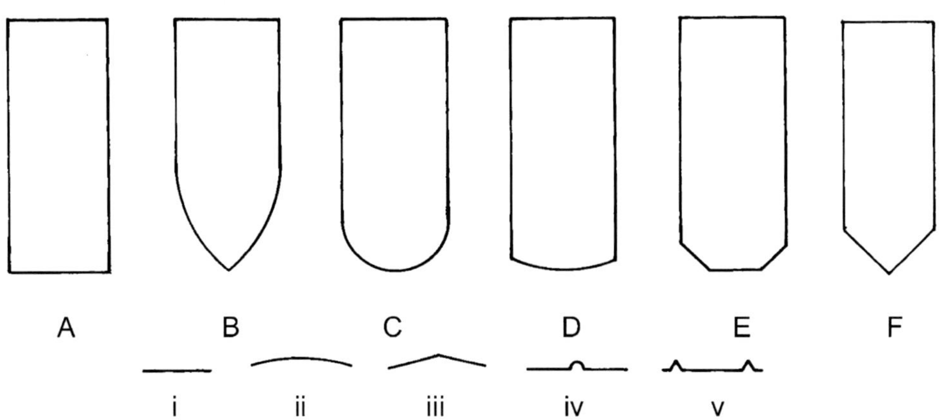

Figure 61: An extensible typology of lorica squamata *forms*

Cross-section

The most commonly found scales in the archaeological record are those with a flat cross-section. Rigidity of flat sheet can be significantly improved by the addition of corrugations, as seen in corrugated iron sheets and in corrugated paper. Rigidity can also be increased by changing the cross-section of a sheet from a flat section to a curve.

The bending stiffness of a flat sheet is proportional to the cube of the thickness, so by doubling the thickness, the stiffness is increased by a factor of eight. The rigidity is increased by moving as much material as possible from the central plane (the neutral axis).[4] By corrugating a scale the depth is increased because there is more material at a distance from the central plane. This has a dramatic effect upon the stiffness provided that the bending stresses are aligned across the ridges. If bent along the ridges, the scale will be even more flexible than a flat scale, because the beam length is effectively increased.

It is unclear if there were regional or military unit styles for *squamae*. The more work that was carried out on each scale increased the cost of the overall armour and this would have influenced the purchaser, whether an individual or the army.

Experimental evidence for scale rigidity

Three-point bend tests[5] were conducted on replicas of some of the most commonly found *squamata* forms.[6] The experimental results showed that changing the cross-section of sheet material affects the rigidity of the individual *squamata* (see Figure 62). The tests reveal that the strongest structure is the scale with a central ridge. It is evident that bronze and steel have a similar rigidity, whereas brass is considerably weaker. Interestingly, a *squamata* with a double ridge was significantly weaker than one with a single ridge.[7]

Numerous examples of Roman scale have been recovered with ridges and curvatures in the cross-section (see typology). The inclusion of a ridge or the production of a curve in a flat *squamata* incurs an extra operation in the production process. There is some decorative effect to the inclusion of curves and ridges; it is, however, most likely that their inclusion was to improve the defensive properties of the scale. Modifying the profile of the cross-section adds only approximately 10 seconds to the production time of each scale but the benefits from changing a flat cross-section to a different geometry are obvious.

The nature of scale armour

In order to function effectively scale armour is composed of two principal structural components: the interlinked *squamae* and the material between this layer and the body. The inner layer(s) were essential. The compound shape of the *squamae* would be uncomfortable at best against the skin or over light clothing. Furthermore, if the *squamae* were connected using wire the cut ends of the wire would sink into the wearer's skin. Clearly this scale armour could not be worn against the skin without some form of protective padding. The presence of possible examples of mineralised leather on the inner surface of some of the scales recovered from Carlisle confirms that a significant layer of material would have to be placed between the armour and the wearer to prevent abrasion. The use of leather is further confirmed by the discovery of *lorica squamata* from Carnuntum, Germany, which retains fragments of both leather and coarse fabric backing (Robinson 1975, 156–7).

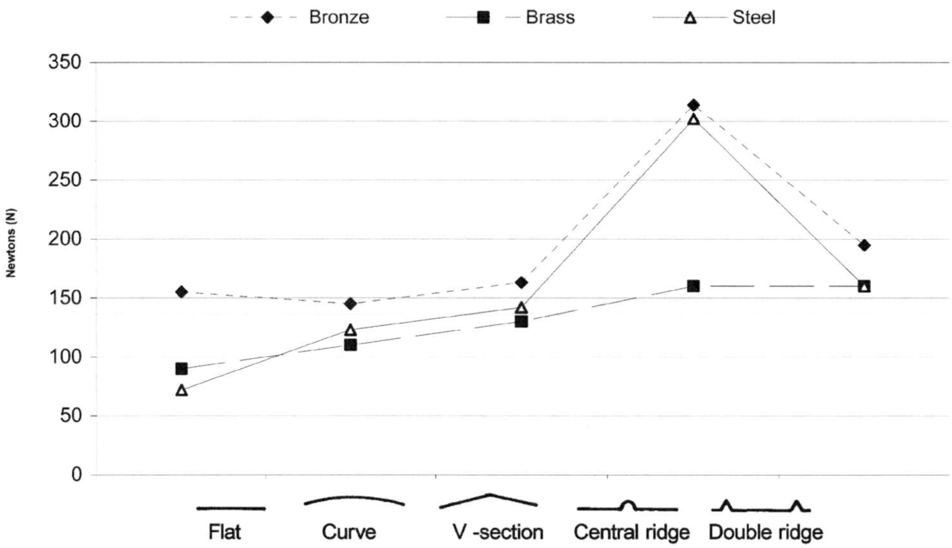

Figure 62: Three-point bend tests showing the comparative rigidity of common scale cross-sections

Another, well preserved, example of *squamata* from the *praetentura* of the Severan base at Carpow on the River Tay in Scotland retains both linen and leather. These rectangular scales with rounded lower corners were up to 16mm in length and 13mm wide. Ribbons up to 1.0mm wide tie the scales together in lateral rows using the side perforations. Cords were laid along the rows at the upper parts of the scales and were attached to linen backing with yarn through the upper pairs of scale perforations. Leather was also used as edgings, which was folded and attached with leather thongs (Coulston 1992, 21).

Testing of leather and fabric combinations with the scale armour revealed that the most effective and comfortable pairing was a single layer of linen against the skin surface, with a single thin layer of leather between the linen and the armour.

The effect of overlapping

Lorica squamata is formed of imbricated scales. This means that the thickness of the armour will vary according to how many layers of scales overlap.

One possible configuration is shown in Figure 63. Here each scale is linked in both rows and columns and so is overlapped on all four sides. In this configuration (Figure 64) there are areas that are one (11%), two (68%) and four scales thick (21%). This overlapping increases the defensive capacity of the armour considerably.

Clearly, these percentage figures are only true for scales of the geometry and dimensions shown in Figure 64. Changes in geometry will mean changes in percentage overlap, but these are likely to be quite small. Whatever the geometry or dimensions, imbricated scales will always have areas with single thickness of plate, double thickness, and areas with four thicknesses of armour. But most of each scale, in itself only 1mm thickness will have a

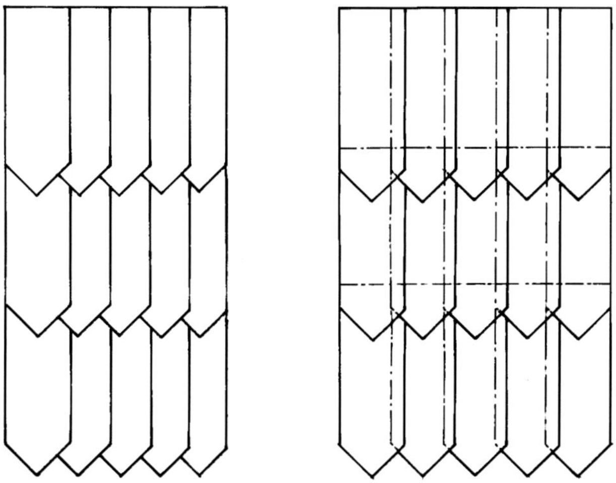

Figure 63: Overlapping scales (the chain dot line shows hidden detail)

depth of two or four thicknesses. It is possible to position the holes used for joining so that the scales overlap in such a way that there are no areas of a single thickness, though this also means that it would have taken more scales to cover a specific area which would have increased the weight of the armour.

It can be seen in Figure 65 that, at the point of impact where the blade strikes the scales, the energy is transferred through either four or two thicknesses of metal. At no point does the blade encounter only one thickness of scale because of the stepped effect of the imbrications.

The overlapping construction of the scales forms a series of steps. When the edge of a blade hits the armour it only contacts one point on each scale rather than running across the whole width of a single strip. This reduces the ability of a blade to cut through the scales. Because the armour is in the form of small scales, rather than a single piece, the energy of the blow is diffused between the scales.

Only 11% of this type of coat is a single thickness of scale. This single thickness area is protected by the step effect of imbrications and any slashing blow will not strike this area.

During a battle, it would have been unlikely that a projectile or blow from a slashing weapon would strike perpendicular to the surface of the armour. Any projectile arriving at exactly 90° would only have to penetrate the thickness of the scale. However, most blows would have arrived at an angle, and as such would travel through the metal of the scale at an angle and so have a longer traverse. This is known as obliquity (Figure 66).

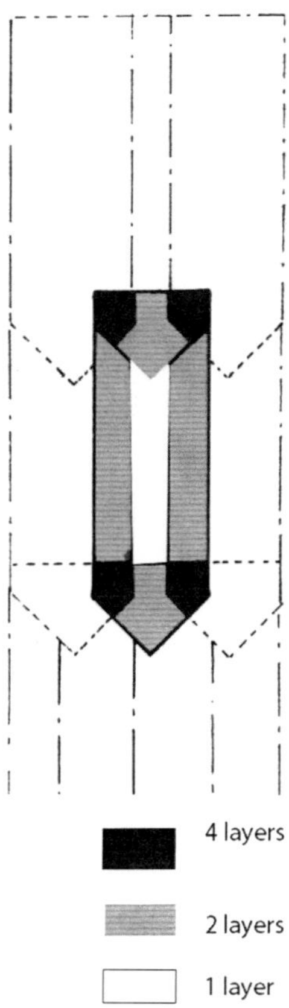

Figure 64: Schematic view of scale overlap

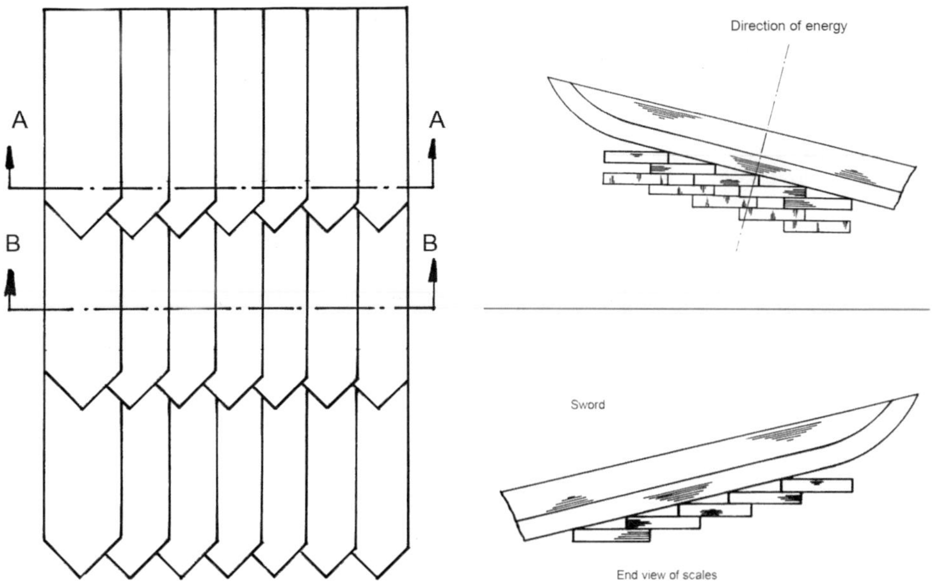

Figure 65: A blade striking squamata. *Line A–A shows where there are four layers of armour. Line B–B shows where there is only one thickness of armour*

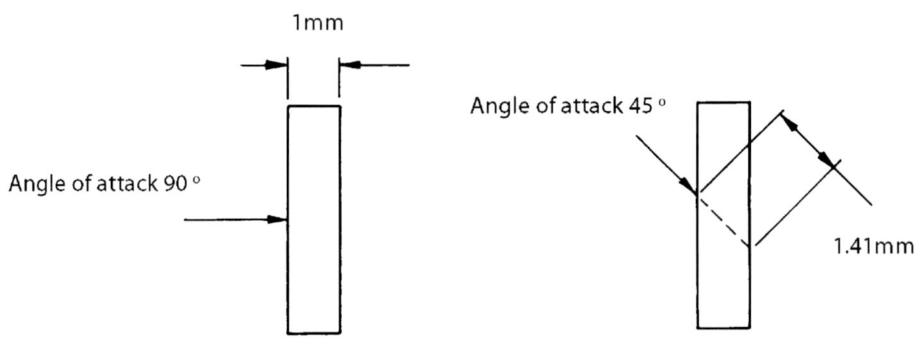

Figure 66: The effect of obliquity on the distance of travel through armour

Field repairs

Scales can sustain considerable damage during combat and still retain their functionality. Scales that buckled under impact could have been removed, straightened and reinserted and would still have given as much protection as before. Croom (2000, 130) has suggested that field repairs of *lorica squamata* were feasible. However, some scales would have been so badly damaged that they would have needed to be replaced.

It is not known if individual soldiers carried replacement scales with them, but they undoubtedly would have had easy access to them. It is highly probable that, occasionally, entire suits of scale were damaged to such an extent that they were used for spare parts – the scales were removed and reused for repairs. It is probable that the scales could have been repaired by non-specialists.

It was decided to conduct experiments to determine how difficult this would be with the absolute minimum of available tools and materials, as could be envisaged in the field. The production of a replacement scale in field conditions took only 9 minutes. It is possible that an infantry soldier may have carried small tools with them or had easy access to such tools, which would have made the process much simpler.

Case study: The Carlisle shoulder piece

Excavations at the Roman fort at Carlisle, Cumbria, produced a number of examples of articulated armour. These were recovered from the corner of a timber building on the north side of the *via principalis* and adjacent to the headquarters building (McCarthy *et al.* 2001). The armour fragments were recovered from timber-lined boxes in the floor of what has been tentatively identified as an armourer's workshop, dated to the first half of the second century AD. One find was of a fragment of *lorica squamata* belonging to the shoulder and held together by bronze wire (Plate 5e). Although a number of the scales were mineralized, a significant number were sufficiently well preserved to undertake metallographic examination. The results of the metallography provided sufficient data to attempt a reconstruction of the collar (Plate 4).

The individual iron scales measured 50 × 25mm, with a radius at the lower end (Form Fe:C.i and Cu: C.i). The scales from the body of the collar have four pairs of 2mm diameter holes on all four edges of the scale. The scales were joined with loops of copper alloy wire. Possible traces of mineralized leather were recorded on the back of some scales.

A similar collar has been recovered from Ham Hill, Dorset (Bishop and Coulston 1993: 88). In this example, three rows of scales from a collar were found. These scales, however, only have three sets of holes, so they are linked in rows, but are not linked in columns.

Metallography

Several *squamae* have been examined using metallographic techniques. These include a mid-second century scale (No. 3978) from the Carlisle hoard,[8] and a second/third century scale from the Balkans (Figure 67). Hardness tests were also conducted (Table 12).

Figure 67: Roman squamae *with wire attachments (Balkans second/ third century (private collection))*

Examination of the iron *squamae* from the Balkans revealed a laminted structure composed of three distinct pieces of metal separated by two parallel lines

Layer	*Grain structure*	*Carbon content (% approx.)*	*Mean Hardness (Hv)*	*Non-metallic inclusions*
1 (Outer)	Equi-axed ferrite grains (50μm) with small particles in the grains	0.6	266	Quite a few inclusions and slag stringer inclusions (3.3%)
2 (Middle)	Elongated ferrite grains (40μm) with small particles in the grains	0.4	217	Quite a few inclusions and slag stringer inclusions (4.0%)
3 (Inner)	Small elongated ferrite grains (25μm) with small particles in the grains	0.4	226	Quite a few inclusions and slag stringer inclusions (4.5%)

Table 12: Metallurgical analysis of Carlisle scale No. 3978

of slag (Figure 68). The lower section of the picture shows that this area has a higher carbon content than the rest of the sample. It is likely that this phenomenon is the result of the scale being carburised on one side only (the side that has been carburised is the outer side).

The scale from the Carlisle Hoard (no. 3978) comprises three layers of steel with a total thickness of 0.9mm. Each layer has different properties and the straight-line interfaces containing the slag inclusions indicate that the pieces were fire welded together (Figure 69).

The primary function of armour is to prevent injury to the wearer in combat; to do this it needs to be robust enough to take damage but still be effective in protection. The most efficient way of achieving this is to produce armour with a laminated structure. This is achieved in the Carlisle scales with an outer layer of high carbon steel overlaying two layers of tough lower carbon steel. This system of using different layers of metal with different properties is the basis for modern tank armour (Doig 2002, 62). Scales with an internal lamellar structure are also found in the natural world.[9]

One-sided carburization

Many items of Roman armour examined have been found to be made of several layers of ferrous metal, with differing carbon content. Scales subjected to metallographic examination from the Carlisle hoard revealed a laminated structure. The outer surface layer had a higher carbon content than that which backed it. This made it an ideal composition for armour in that its hard outside layer was supported by a tough back. It is possible that this structure was produced by carburizing only one side of the armour to raise its carbon content.[10]

Wire to join scales

Imbricated scale armour, such as can be seen in the collar from Carlisle shown in Plate 5e, was strengthened by connecting the scales into rows with links of copper alloy or iron wire/strip which passed through the pairs of holes in the sides of each scale (see also Figure 70).

There are several different types of material that could have been used for linking

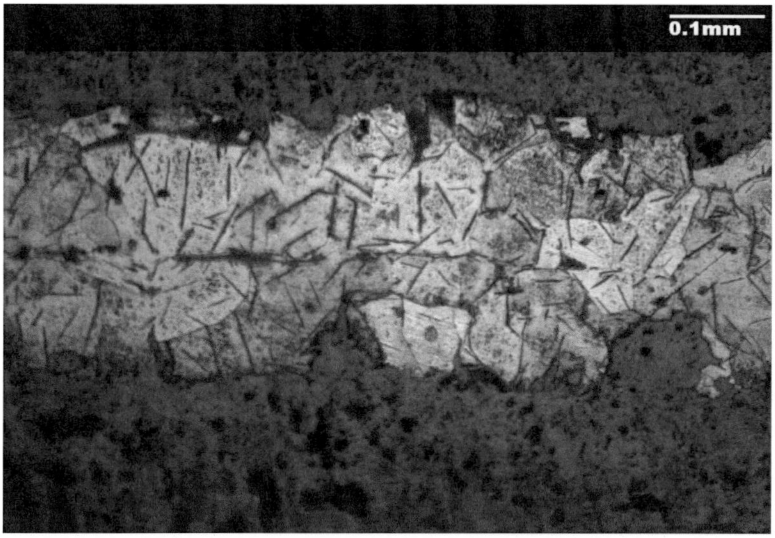

Figure 68: Microphotograph of Balkan scale armour shown in Plate 5f showing the ferrite structure with small amounts of slag inclusions (magnification ×200)

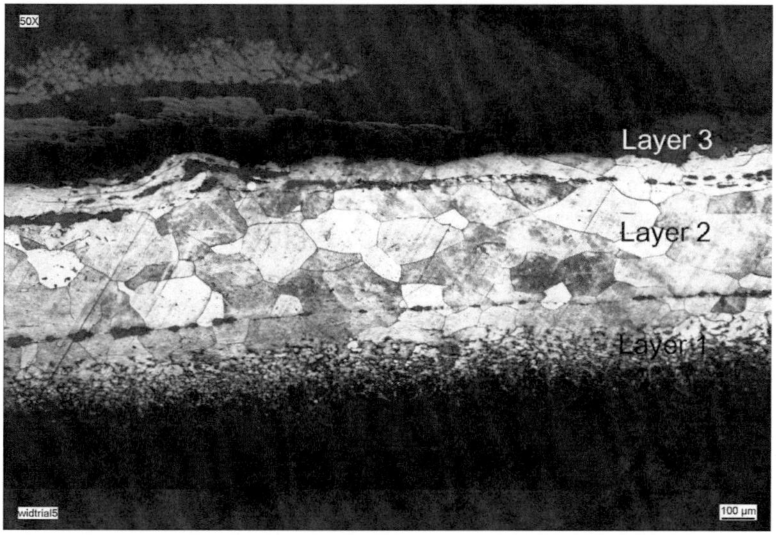

Figure 69: A cross-section of scale No. 3978 from the Carlisle Hoard showing the layered structure

individual *lorica squamata* scales together. These range from leather to metal. In antiquity only seven metals were available to metallurgists and smiths.[11] Of these gold and silver can be discounted for armour, leaving:

- Ferrous metal, iron and steel with low slag inclusions.
- Pure copper and copper alloy (the family of alloys known as brasses).[12]

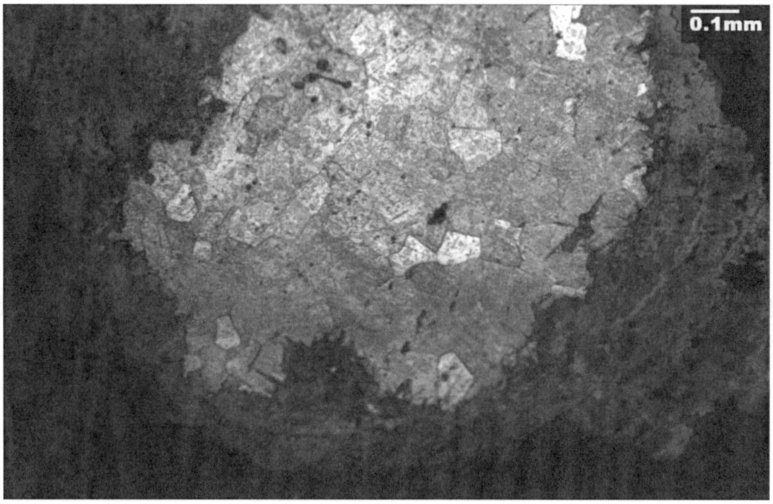

Figure 70: Microphotograph of the wire from the Balkan squamata *shown in Figure 67 showing a structure composed of equi-axed grains ferrite with small quantities of slag inclusions (magnification ×100)*

The production of wire from most metals by the use of draw plates (see Sim 1997a) was a simple task for Roman metal-workers. The sheer volume of wire required for ring mail and the joining wire for scale mail attests to the fact that wire was being produced in large quantities over most of the life of the Roman Empire. The reason for selecting a particular type of wire may be influenced by many factors including:

- *Appearance*: brass wire against blued steel will look striking.
- *Resources*: copper alloy requires less energy than iron to produce wire.
- *Cost*: ferrous metal is cheaper than copper alloy.

The wire is protected by the step effect of the individual scales overlapping each other (Figure 71). Provided that the height of the wire loop is level with or lower than the thickness of the *squamata,* then only the first loops at the start of the row are vulnerable. The remainder are protected from blows from edged weapons but not from direct attack from direct thrust or projectiles.

Replication of scale armour

The following sets of experiments were conducted in order to determine the time taken to manufacture a set of *lorica squamata* of the Fe.C.i. type found at Carlisle. The thickness of several scales from the Carlisle Hoard was measured. The average thickness was found to be 0.9mm, and the variation was only ±0.02mm. This level of accuracy has been observed in other types of Roman armour and has been seen as an indication of the use of a mechanical process such as rolling, or a controlled use of a trip hammer (see Chapter 5; Fulford *et al.* 2004). There is certainly an increasing body of archaeological evidence that suggests that such equipment was used during the Roman period (Lewis 1997, 111).

In order to produce the scales a billet has to be forged into material of a suitable thickness. This can be achieved by either producing sheet which is then cut into strip or producing strip directly from the bloom. Experiments conducted by the authors suggest that to produce such dimensionally similar scales could have been achievable more efficiently, by producing iron strip rather than producing iron sheet, and then cutting this to size. Therefore, for these experiments it was assumed that the billet was forged into strip.

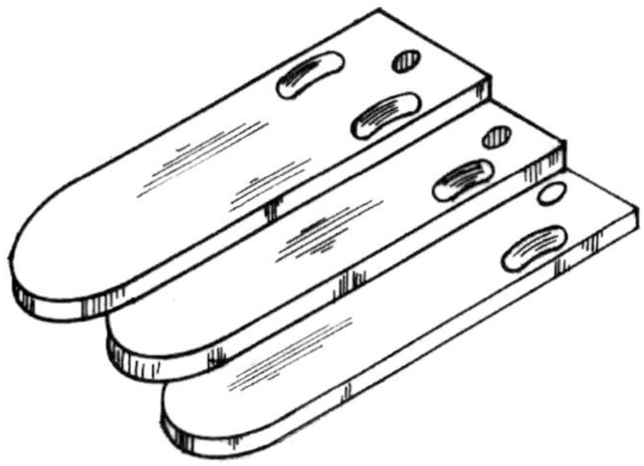

Figure 71: Showing the step effect protecting the wire loops

The starting point was a billet of iron (Figure 72: A). This was heated and forged into strip (Figure 72: B). The strip was cut to length (Figure 72: C). The radius was formed on one end of the strip (Figure 72: D). The holes were punched using a round tapered punch (Figure 72: E). The individual scales were wired together (Figure 72: F).

Most artefacts present the potential for a number of possible means of production. Therefore, in the reconstructions it was decided to select a number of possible production methods. This exercise was performed to determine the time required for mass production. The criteria for production were as follows:

- The scales must be produced in the shortest possible time with the minimum material loss.
- Only those tools known to be available in the Roman period to be used.

It is almost certain that any manufacturer making large quantities of a single item would invest in making special tools and templates to increase the speed of production. A reconstruction of the armour was attempted using the simplest technology available to the Roman blacksmiths (Figure 73).

The method of forging the billet into strip remained the same for all the experiments. The strip was cut into lengths using a pair of shears.

Experiment 1

A template was made and this was used to mark the radius and the position of the holes. The radius was roughly cut to shape (Figure 72: D), and then brought to a smooth radius using a file. The holes were punched with a tapering punch made from medium carbon steel that had been hardened and tempered (Pliny xxxiv: 146). The scale was placed on a lead block and the punch struck with a hammer (Table 13).

Experiment 2

A template was made and this was used to mark the radius and the position of the holes.

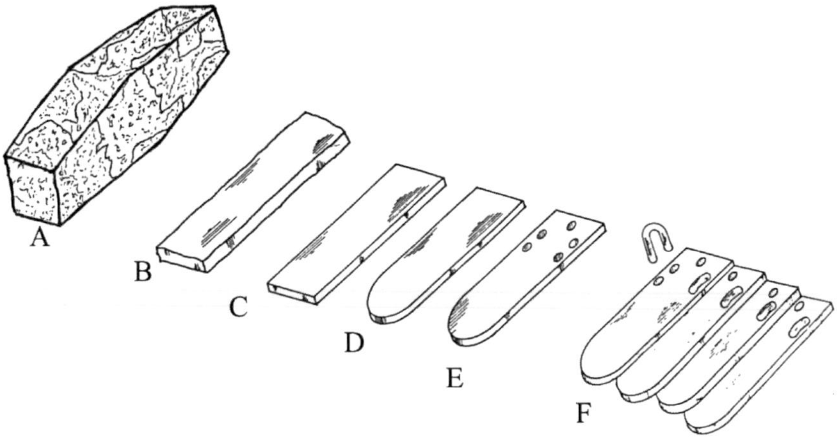

Figure 72: Production sequence for the manufacture of scale armour

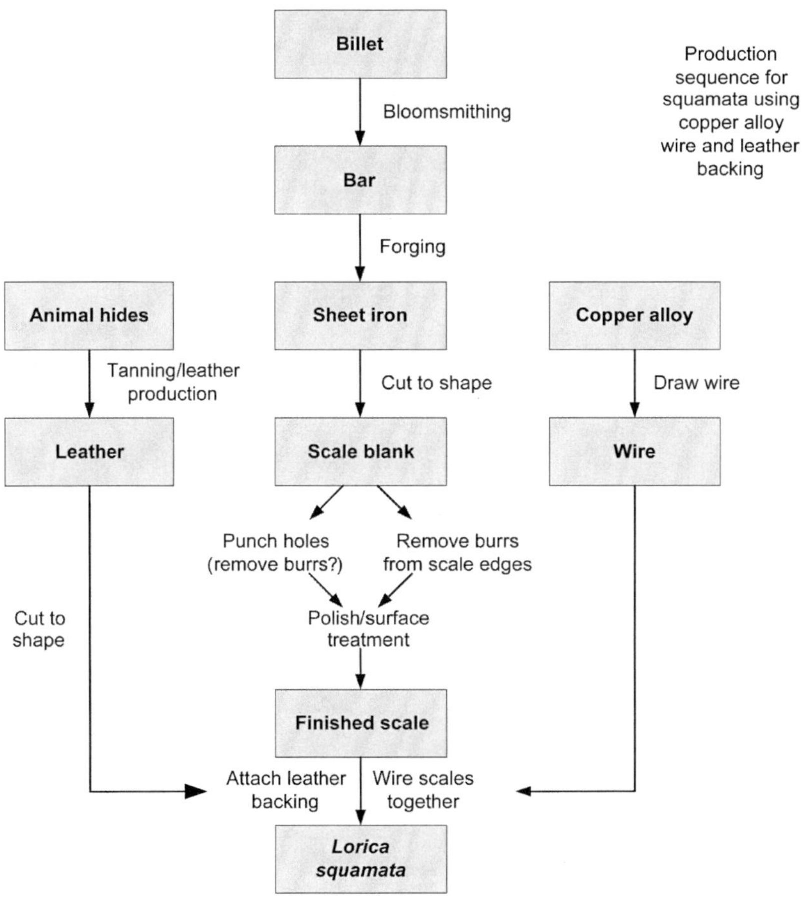

Figure 73: Flow diagram for the production of lorica squamata

Experiment 1	*Time*
Mark and cut to length	8 seconds
Mark radius and hole positions, shear radius to shape, file radius to shape, de-burr	1 min 56 seconds
Punch holes	25 seconds
De-burr edges with file	22 seconds
Inspect for flatness	5 seconds
Straighten buckled scales	10 seconds
Total	3 min 4 seconds

Table 13: Production times for Experiment 1

Experiment 2	*Time*
Mark and cut to length	8 seconds
Mark radius and hole positions, cut radius with cold chisel, file radius to shape, de-burr	2 min 15 seconds
Punch holes	25 seconds
De-burr edges with file	22 seconds
Inspect for flatness	5 seconds
Straighten buckled scales	10 seconds
Total	3 min 25 seconds

Table 14: Production times for Experiment 2

A cold chisel was used to rough shape the radius (Figure 72: D), which was then brought to a smooth radius using a file. The holes were punched as in the previous experiment (Table 14).

Experiment 3

A template was made and this was used to mark the radius and the position of the holes. A cold chisel with a curved edge was made and this was used to cut the shape of the radius with a single blow. The radius only needed a few strokes with a file to remove a very slight burr. The holes were punched as in the previous experiments (Table 15). It is clear from these experiments that this method was the most rapid (Table 16).

During the original manufacturing process, the punching of the holes threw up a burr on the back of the plate (Plate 5d). This burr can be seen on some of the original scales. It was assumed that these had not been removed on the originals in order to save time in the manufacturing processes. On the first set of experimental scales all the burrs were removed, but it was found that when the scales were wired together they became completely rigid. In contrast, when scales that had not had the burrs removed were wired together, these were found to be more flexible. In this context the burrs were acting as washers, slightly separating the plates and thereby allowing considerable movement and flexibility but without compromising the efficiency of the armour. When in contact with the scale underneath, the edges of the burr turn over, producing – as it were – a washer. This will slide more easily over the under plate. In this example the manufacturer is making use of the manufacturing process to maximise efficiency of the armour.

Experiment 3	*Time*
Mark and cut to length	8 seconds
Cut with curved chisel	20 seconds
Punch holes	25 seconds
De-bur edges with file	22 seconds
Inspect for flatness	5 seconds
Straighten buckled scales	10 seconds
Total	1 min 32 seconds

Table 15: Production times for Experiment 3

Experiment	*Time*
Experiment 1	3 min 04 seconds
Experiment 2	3 min 25 seconds
Experiment 3	1 min 32 seconds

Table 16: Summary of production times for Experiments 1–3

The future of scale armour

The principles and benefits of scale armour are still applicable in modern combat. For example, *Dragon Skin*™ body armour made by *Pinnacle Armor* in the USA, is made of 50mm wide circular discs which overlap and interconnect like scale armour. The discs are composed of a ceramic and titanium composite. The principle of *Dragon Skin* is similar to *lorica squamata* in which the blunt force trauma (impact) is dispersed over a wider area. The combination of energy dispersal and sophisticated armour composite material means that this scalar armour is capable of preventing the penetration of automatic, and even 'armour piercing' rounds.

Conclusions

It is evident that *lorica squamata* is a highly effective armour form. This is because:

- The imbricated structure results in varying thicknesses of *squamae.*
- Energy from impacts is diffused between these scales and the backing material.
- The imbricated structure of the scales results in a stepped structure which is effective at countering slashing blows.

Scale body armour was made from both ferrous and non-ferrous metal and there are examples of ferrous scales with copper alloy sheet overlaying them. There are also examples of a single coat being made of both ferrous and non-ferrous scales (McCarthy *et al.* 2001; Carlisle 2000). Some of the scales examined show that they had been made from steel. The structure of others has led to the conclusion that low carbon steel had been deliberately carburized on one side only. This would have been to produce a structure that had a steel exterior surface with a very low carbon back surface. This is the ideal structure for armour.

Scale armour was most likely worn over a *subarmale* possibly similar to the arming doublets of later periods. The overlapping scales, combined with a padded backing, create armour that will stop almost all hand-held weapons and projectiles. The protection comes at the price that this armour is 30–40% heavier than armour made from strips of iron. While the additional weight would have been sustainable to the Roman soldier, it does incur an opportunity cost by reducing the amount of additional equipment the soldier can carry.

Experiments have shown that people with no knowledge of metalwork can be taught to make scale armour in less than 2 hours, and can be fully competent to work alone after a single working day. Individual scales are very simple to make and require only the simplest of tools and moderate skill to produce. So although time consuming to make, the majority of processes associated with *lorica squamata* production could be relegated to semi-skilled or unskilled labour.

It may be concluded that scale armour was cheap and easy to make and lent itself to mass production. However, *lorica squamata* was a comparatively complex armour form. The large number of *squamae* in *lorica* provide a multitude of potential points of failure. While a *squamata* can be relatively easily replaced or repaired it is time consuming work because of the interlinked nature of the *squamae*.

Notes

1 Also known as the back face signature/back face deformation.

2 See for example, the Column of Marcus Aurelius, scene IX, which shows infantry soldiers in *lorica segmentata*, *lorica squamata* and *lorica hamata* (Ferris 2009, fig 26, 71) or the metopes at Adamklissi.

3 Similarly Reis's typology of Middle Byzantine lamellar armour uses the distribution of holes as the diagnostic indicator (Dawson 2002).

4 In addition to stiffening ribs this principal applies to I-beams, and honeycomb panels. But there must be good shear connection between layers for the system to act as an integrated beam.

5 The three-point bend test was conducted using an Instron 4206 tensile test machine. This test is carried out using a controlled load being applied at a uniform speed for a prescribed pre-set distance. The resulting figures give an indication of, amongst other things, the amount of force required to deform the specimen to a pre-set depth (in this case 8mm). The following specifications apply to the tests carried out: a load cell of 100KN was used, load range 5%, posfs 20, speed 5mm/sec, x = 0.5v/cm. Deflection 8mm, diameter of cylinders 10mm, distance between cylinders 50mm.

6 A set of five *squamata* was produced in 0.9mm thick iron, bronze and brass. Each set of *squamata* had five different cross-sections: flat, convex, pitched, convex with ridge, flat with two ridges (see Figure 4). The *squamata* sets were all cut from the same sheet of iron, bronze or brass respectively to reduce the likelihood of differences in the microstructures. The reconstructions were then subjected to three-point bend tests. It is expected that the most commonly used materials for *squamata* would be ferrous material and copper alloy. In order to make a comparison with another commonly used Roman metal, brass was included in this study. The frequency of use of brass armour is uncertain. The analysis does not take into account any form of backing material that would have been worn over the skin and underneath the armour. The three materials examined are probably those most commonly used for making scale armour. Undoubtedly there are other forms, in particular some iron scales are known to have been covered with a very thin layer of copper alloy material. Metallographic analysis of some of the scales has shown that they were constructed of a banded structure, containing different levels of carbon. It is not certain at this point what difference this makes to the defensive index of this type of armour.

7 The difference between, for example, the flat and the V-section in both steel and brass is 70 and 40 Newtons respectively. One Newton is the force required to cause a mass of 1kg to accelerate at a rate of 1m per second^2, in the absence of other force-producing effects. In general, force (F) in N, mass (m) in kg and acceleration (a) in m/second^2 are related by the formula: F = ma.

8 Archaeological excavations on the site of the Roman fort at Carlisle were carried out by the Carlisle Archaeological Unit between November 1998 and March 2001. The excavation of a probable workshop

from the second fort revealed an assemblage of Roman armour. It has been assumed that these items were sent to the workshop for repair, but were left behind when the second fort was abandoned in the mid-second century. The so-called Carlisle Hoard included protective arm guards, a helmet fragment, a greave, and a number of examples of segmented body armour (*lorica segmentata*). It also contained a group of 53 iron scales from the shoulder section of a *lorica squamata* collar.

9 For example, the scales of the African freshwater fish *Polypterus senegalus* possess a multi-layered structure. Each scale is composed of four different organic and inorganic layers. These are: 10μm of ganoine (a type of enamel) on the outside, to dentine (50μm), isopedine (40μm) and a 300μm thick basal plate of bone. This lamellar structure creates a highly effective armour for the fish (Bruet *et al.* 2008).

10 A series of experiments was conducted to determine a method that would produce one-sided carburization. A method that was found to work satisfactorily was to coat one side of two separate scales with clay, and to place those two coats together, effectively making a sandwich of two steel plates with a layer of clay between them. This was then placed in a container of powdered charcoal. The container was heated to 900°C and held at that temperature for six hours. On examination the carbon from the charcoal was found to have penetrated to the same depth as that seen on the Carlisle scale.

11 These are gold, silver, mercury, copper, iron, tin and lead. Because the focus of this book is mass-produced armour rather than bespoke pieces, the noble metals (gold and silver) are not considered here (although they are both easily drawn into wire), and, of course mercury is a liquid at room temperature and therefore is unsuitable for wire production. Lead and its alloys are malleable but not very ductile and are too soft to be used as wire for armour (Aitchison 1960).

12 Brass is an alloy of copper and zinc and was produced by a cementation process by heating powdered zinc with copper ore and charcoal. Metallic zinc was not produced until the sixteenth century and in the Roman period zinc was provided by the use of calamine (Burstall 1970, 71).

9. Ring Mail (*lorica hamata*)

Introduction

Ring mail or *lorica hamata* is a form of body armour made from interlocking rings of metal. Varro (*De lingua Latina* v: 116) attributes its origins to the Celts, from whom the Romans adopted it.[1] It was widely used in the Republican period and although other types of armour were introduced in different times, ring mail was in use throughout the Roman period by both infantry and cavalry (cf. Eadie 1967 and Figure 74).

Mail was the most time consuming (and therefore expensive) of the armour forms to produce. This is highlighted by the writings of Polybius[2] referring to the middle Republican period. He states how the soldiers rated at a property qualification above 10,000 *drachmae* wore a mail coat, while those below that rating wore a pectoral (Polybius vi: 24).

Provided ring mail is worn in a manner that allows it to hang loosely on the wearer and an adequate undergarment is worn underneath, ring mail will stop the penetration of most weapons and projectiles. The effect of the mail hanging loosely is exactly the same as a football net. The energy from the weapon is absorbed by the ring mail as it moves from its position in towards the body, thus dissipating the energy away from the point of impact.[3] This is similar to how *lorica squamata* functions; however, ring mail is considerably more flexible than *squamata* and has the potential to deform considerably. However, ring mail cannot 'give' too much, because the wearer might survive the penetration of the object, but suffer serious internal injuries resulting from blunt force trauma. Once again this highlights the importance of the backing garment in armour construction. It is the integration of the properties of the ring mail with the backing garment that make the armour effective.

An area of particular vulnerability was the shoulder, which was often exposed to downward slashing blows. This was mitigated by the use of shoulder doubling to protect this very vulnerable area.

Mail is the most flexible of the body armour forms. However, one disadvantage of mail is its weight. Well-made armour should be shaped to the wearer's body, and distribute weight as evenly as possible. This can be achieved with mail but generally it tends to hang down and benefits greatly from a belt to tie it in around the waist. Another issue with tight mail patterns can be trapped body heat making wearing mail for extended periods quite tiring.

Examination of original rings

The analysis of Roman ferrous ring mail rings presents many difficulties because of their generally poor condition. Although a huge quantity of mail was produced during the Roman period only a small quantity has been preserved in the archaeological record. It is also very difficult in some cases to be certain if the rings are of Roman manufacture or were made outside the Empire but copying Roman patterns.[4] In many cases the amount of information that can be determined is limited because the rings are fused together with iron oxide and, when examined, are often found to consist of a thin shell of iron with a hollow centre.[5]

Figure 74: Adamklissi metope showing three cornicen *wearing ring mail*

Many ring mail rings from the Roman period are fused together into solid lumps and it is not possible to detach single rings for examination (Plates 4a and 4b).[6]

Wire production

In this particular context wire is defined as metal of 4mm diameter or less that has been drawn. Material above that size is considered to be bar. Wire had many different applications in the production of armour. The two biggest uses were for the production of ring mail (*lorica hamata*) and for attaching individual scales together in scale armour (*lorica squamata*). However, wire was also used for the hinge-pins of helmet cheek pieces and also for the production of some types of rivets (for example, rivets of various materials were used for joining rings). It could also be applied as decoration to armour.

The earliest written reference for the production of wire comes from the Old Testament (Exodus 39: 3).

> 'And they did beat the gold into thin plates and cut into wires, to work it in the blue, and the purple, and in the scarlet and in the fine linen, with cunning work.'

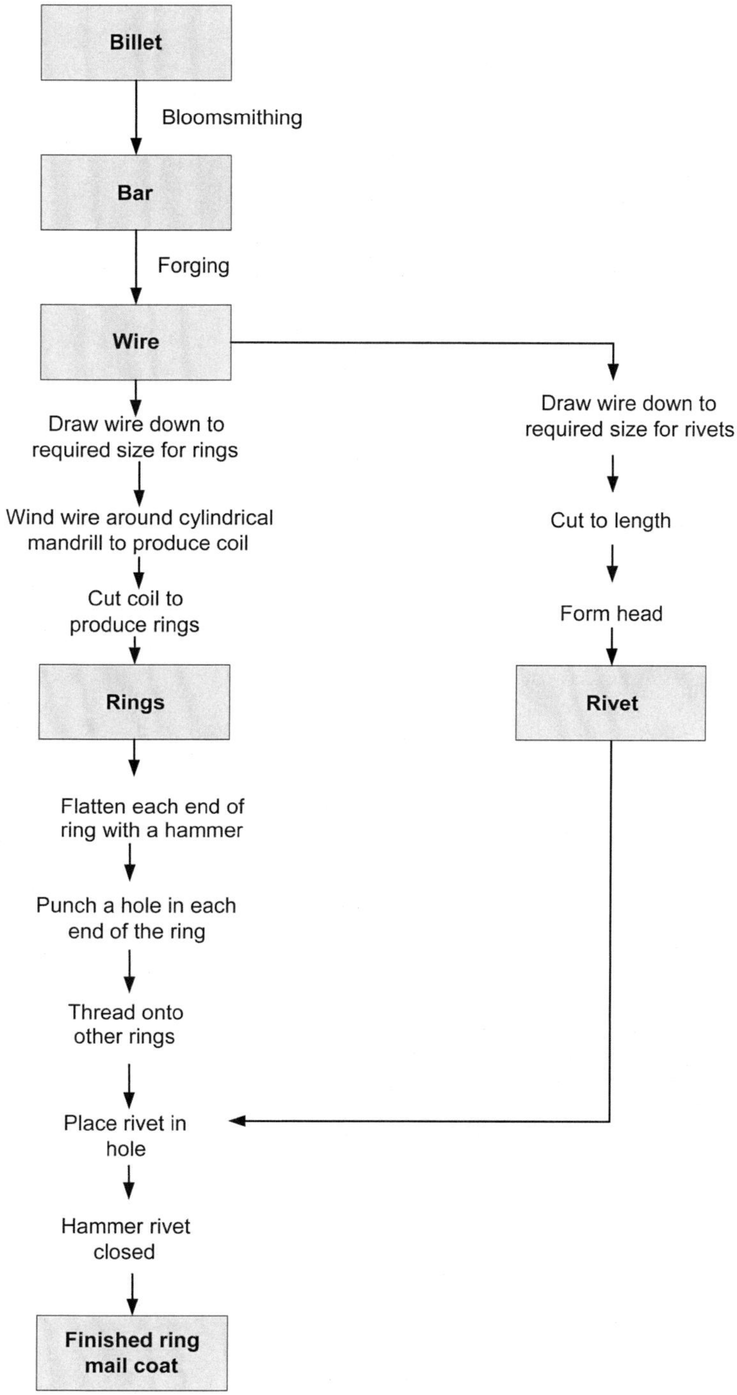

Figure 75: Production flow diagram for riveted ring mail armour

Ring no.	*Position*	*Mean size (mm)*	*Deviation from mean (mm)*
1	A	1.07	+ 0.03–0.07
	B	1.20	+ 0.00–0.00
2	A	1.00	+ 0.00–0.00
	B	0.89	+ 0.01–0.01
3	A	0.90	+ 0.10–0.02
	B	1.32	+ 0.08–0.04
4	A	1.06	+ 0.02–0.04
	B	1.29	+ 0.01–0.01
5	A	1.20	+ 0.00–0.00
	B	0.94	+ 0.02–0.04

Table 17: Riveted rings from Caerleon (dimension A is the width of the ring, and B its thickness)

Ring No.	*Position*	*Mean size (mm)*	*Deviation from mean (mm)*
1	A	1.04	+ 0.36–0.02
	B	1.92	+ 0.08–0.12
2	A	1.45	+ 0.15–0.17
	B	0.15	+ 0.06–0.04
3	A	1.25	+ 0.15–0.14
	B	1.80	+ 0.00–0.00
4	A	1.57	+ 0.10–0.05
	B	0.02	+ 0.02–0.00

Table 18: Riveted rings from Thorsberg (dimension A is the width of the ring, and B its thickness)

The inference is that gold was being made as fine as thread that is woven into the body of a fabric. Tables 17 and 18 show that the wire for the rings from Caerleon and Thorsberg was made to very tight tolerances. Different production methods were considered for the manufacture of the quality and quantity of iron wire needed for this application.

There are several methods of producing wire, but the two most likely methods are wire drawing and producing sheet, which is then cut into strips and hammered into either cylindrical or square cross-sectional wire. The production of wire from sheet was a resource-intensive, skilled operation.

Wire drawing

Wire is produced by pulling metal through a draw plate, which is a metal plate with a series of tapered holes that decrease in size (Figure 76). When metal is drawn the volume of the original piece remains the same. The cross-sectional area decreases and the length increases. No material is lost.

It is important that the holes in the draw plate diminish in size by approximately 10% of the diameter in order to allow the metal to be drawn into wire. This figure was never calculated and was arrived at by trial and error, indeed Leonardo da Vinci writes:

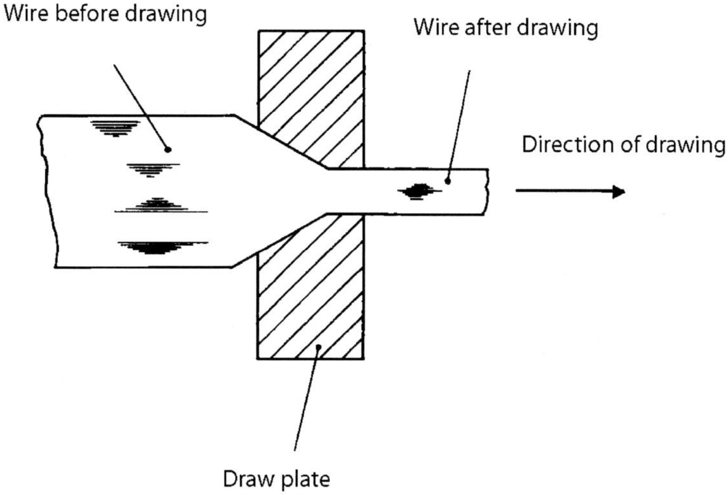

Figure 76: Schematic view of wire drawing

> 'The amount of force necessary to draw wire through a draw plate cannot be known except through experience'.

It would not be until the work of Erich Seibel, Anton Pomp and Werner Leug in the 1930s and 1940s that a theoretical framework to calculate the force needed for wire drawing was produced. They determined that the angle of the taper in the hole is not critical as long as it is less than 50° and greater than 2°. If either of these limits is exceeded than the wire will shave and not draw (Thomsen and Thomsen 1974). Given that the angle of the holes in a draw plate is so large, the making of a draw plate is a straightforward matter.

The quantity of wire that was needed to produce ring mail coats, the rivets for joining the rings and the wire for fixing together the individual scales in *Lorica Squamata* is staggering. For example, a coat of 40,000 6mm diameter rings contains approximately 760m of wire. It seems likely that during the Roman period this quantity of wire could only have been produced by drawing.

Roman draw plates from Germany and Britain

Thomsen and Thomsen (1976) have stated that non-ferrous wire from Persia of sixth–fifth century BC date could only have been made by drawing. Northover (1995) has argued that two bronze plates found at Iselham, Cambridgeshire, thought to belong to the Late Bronze Age, are draw plates. These draw plates are assumed to be for drawing non-ferrous metal. Thomsen and Thomsen (1974, 138) also describe a draw plate in the Burg Altena Museum in Altena (near Dusseldorf), Germany (Figure 77). This draw plate exists as a cast, the original having been lost. It has been dated to *c.* AD 45 and is thought to be of native/Roman origin, but no more details are available. The similarities with a second

Figure 77: Cast of a draw plate from Altena (207mm long, 31.5mm wide and 17mm thick)

draw plate from Vindolanda are apparent, not only in form but also in size. The main difference is that the Altena plate has a groove down the centre. The purpose of this is not certain but it could have been for holding a lubricant such as wax or animal fat.

Figure 78: Top, underside and side views of a draw plate from Vindolanda (length of plate 94mm)

The draw plate shown in Figure 78 was found at the Roman fort of Vindolanda. The general appearance of this object indicates that it was a well-made tool constructed from three layers of material that were fire-welded together.[7] There are no hammer marks visible and care has been taken to produce fairly flat and smooth surfaces. There is a small amount of corrosion inside some of the holes, but otherwise the draw plate is in excellent condition.

The plate is pierced by four holes and at the broken end there are the remains of a fifth. Figure 79 shows the sizes of the holes on both sides of the plate and inspection revealed that the holes taper. They are not perfectly circular but the deviation from true circularity is so small as to be negligible. The holes are fairly evenly spaced along the centre line of the plate. Microscopic examination reveals wear marks inside the smaller ends of the holes, although in two holes (diameters respectively 2.8mm and 3.2mm) some of the wear marks have been obliterated by corrosion.

Thomsen and Thomsen (1974) have shown that a draw plate can be made from the same material as the wire to be drawn through it. As long as the hardness of the draw plate is equal to or greater than the hardness of the wire to be drawn it can be made from any metal.

Type of metals used for wire

Both ferrous and non-ferrous metal can be drawn into wire. Figure 80 (1 and 2) show micrographs of a section through a mail ring from Stuttgart, Germany. The original wire

c

Plate 1:
a. Quenching in oil
b. Blue flame indicating the correct temperature for soldering has been achieved
c. The temper colours, oxides of different colours, formed by the application of heat

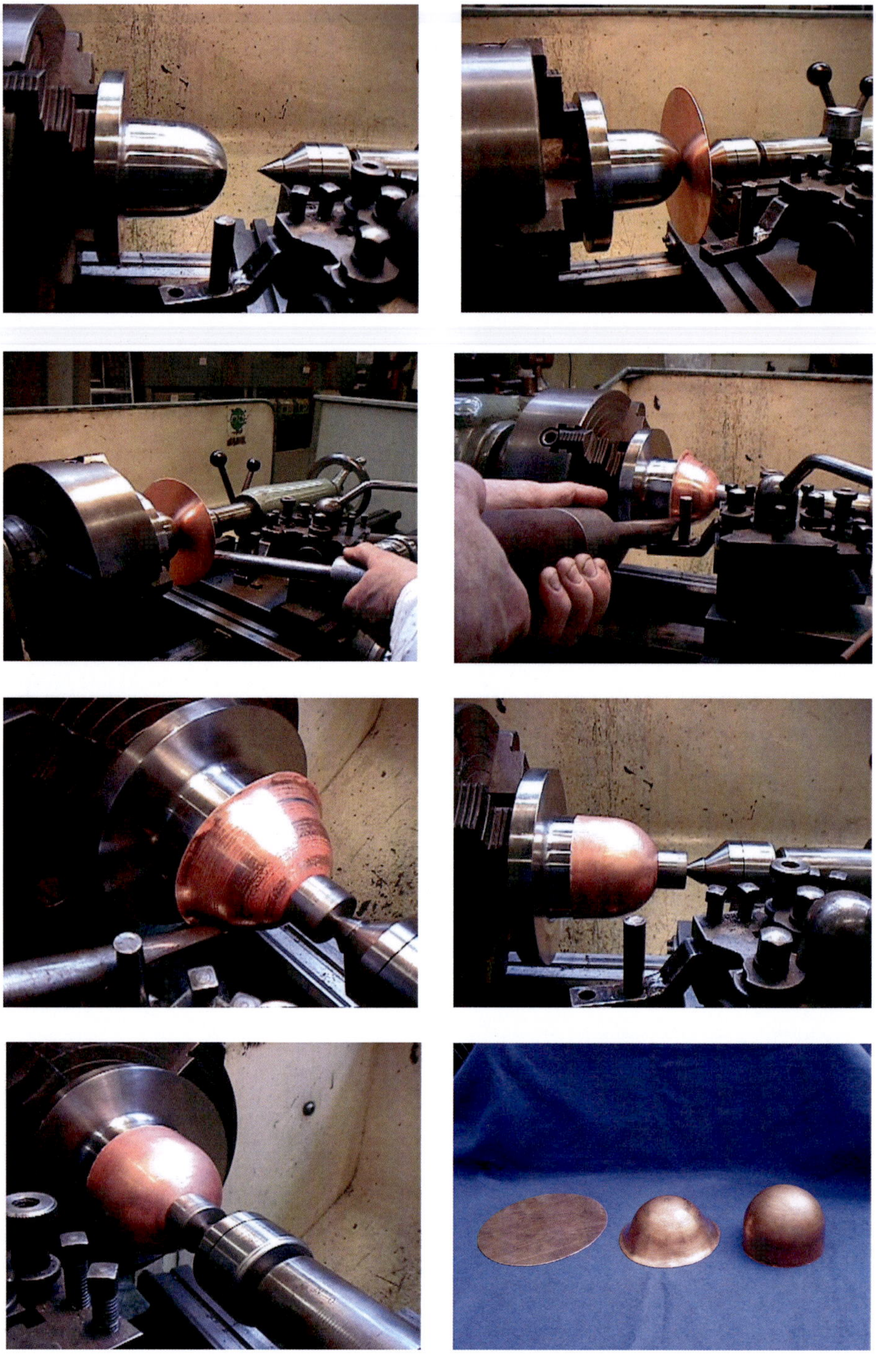

Plate 2: The spinning process in a contemporary workshop.

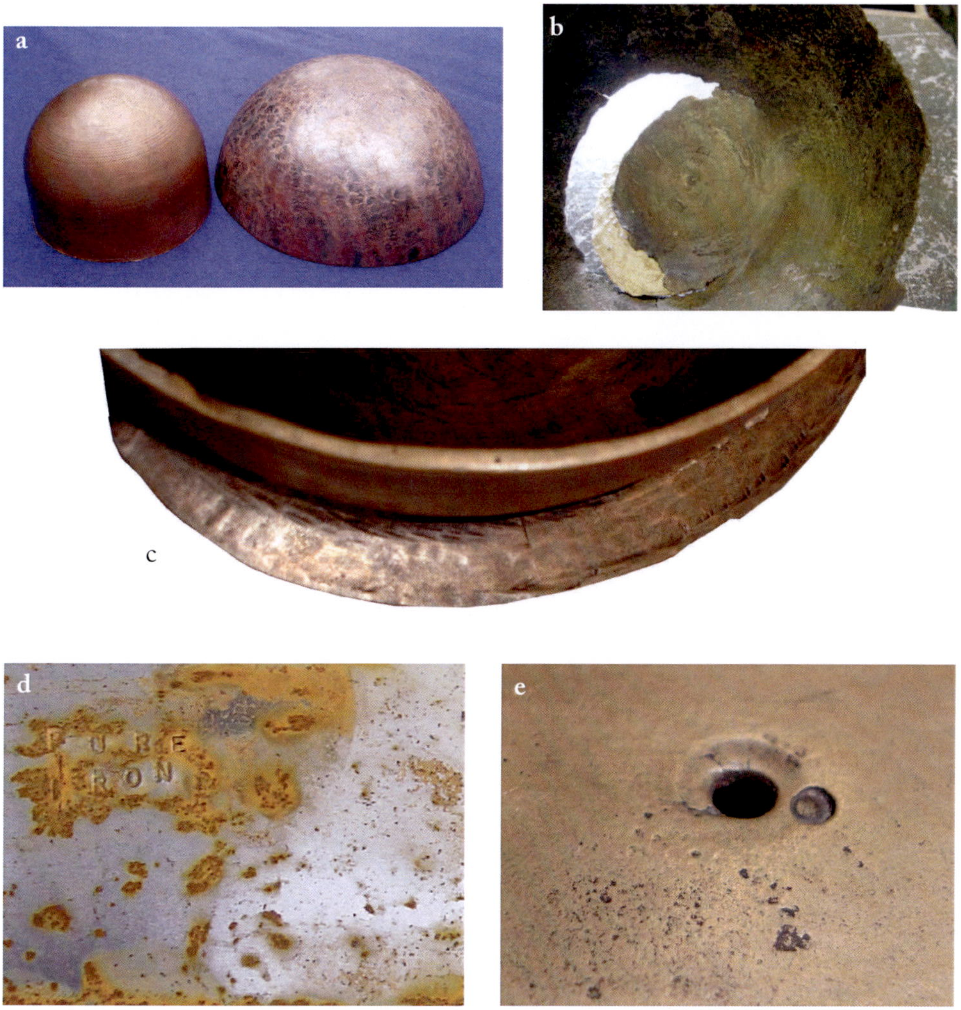

Plate 3:
a. The diagnostic marks left after spinning (left) and raising (right) reproduction bowls
b. Spinning marks on the inside of a mid-first century AD copper alloy Roman helmet recovered from Chichester Harbour (this helmet is currently housed in the Barbican House Museum, Lewes)
c. Detail of cross pein hammer marks on the underside of the brow guard of the Bosham Harbour Coolus
d. Pure iron after seven days exposure to the atmosphere
e. Detail of the toolmark left by a plug cutting punch on the upper surface of the neck guard of the Thames Coolus

Plate 4:
a. A concretion of Roman ring mail from Arbeia showing corrosion
b. Ring mail rings from Arbeia. Outside diameter of rings 7.50mm, thickness 1.3mm.
c. Solid and riveted rings from Leiden

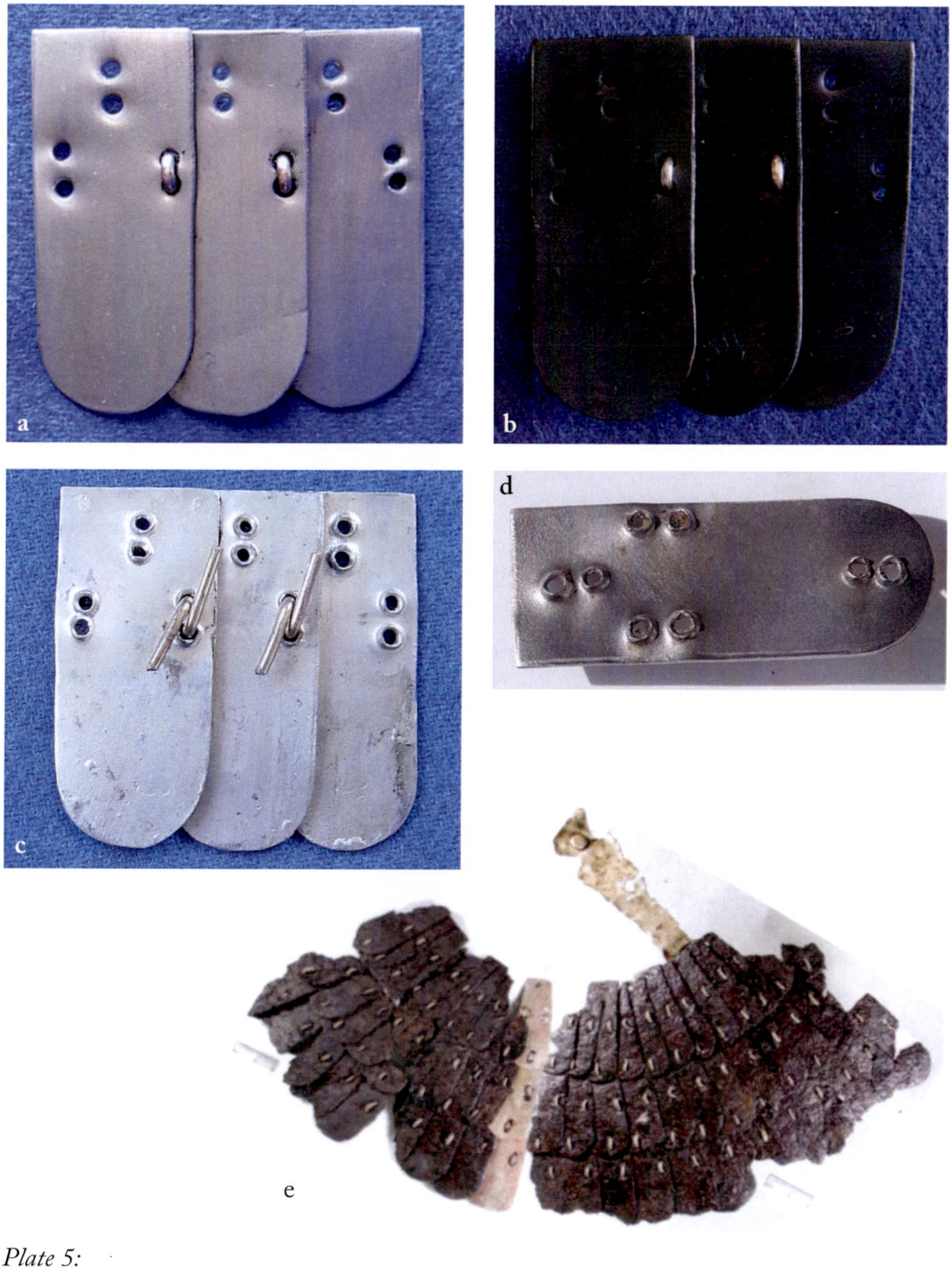

Plate 5:
a. Reproduction scales that have been 'blued'
b. Polished iron hot quenched in oil, giving rise to a smooth black surface finish
c. Reconstruction of tinned squamae joined by brass wire
d. Replica scale showing burrs on underside of holes
e. Replica of the Carlisle collar

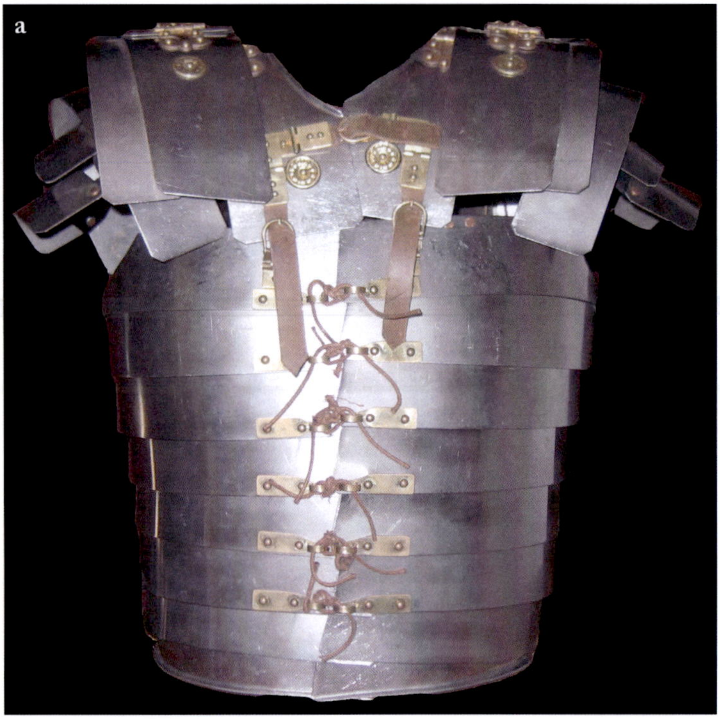

Plate 6:
a. Back-plate from Eining measuring 24.5cm × 18.0cm (Bishop 2002, fig. 6.4). By kind permission of M. C. Bishop
b .The interior of a set of second century copper alloy cheek pieces showing evidence of mineralised leather and scoring for gluing
c. First century AD. Weiler type cavalry helmet brass on iron core (private collection)

Plate 7:
a. A Chalcidian tinned bronze helmet, fifth–early fourth century BC (© Royal Athena Galleries). This is a rare variant of Pflug's Type V (Kunze-Group VII). Photograph provided courtesy Dr Jerome Isenberg of the Royal Athena Galleries. (Royal Athena Galleries 2007: 41)
b. An Imperial Gallic Type A tinned bronze helmet of the first century AD (courtesy of Christie's). The helmet was formerly in the Axel-Guttmann collection, Berlin (AG 292) and is of Weisenau/Nijmegan form. The cheek pieces are not original (Junkelmann 1999). Also note how regular cleaning of the helmet has worn through the tinned surface

a

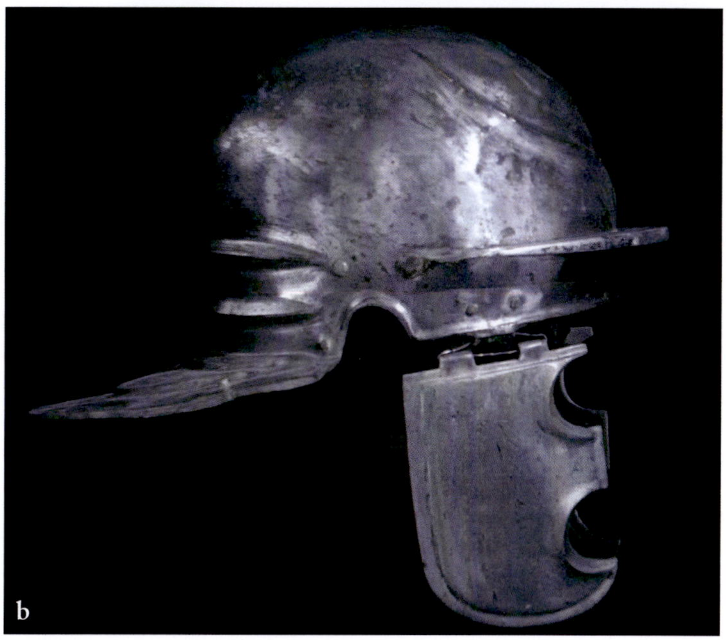
b

Plate 8:
a. Mosaic from Bignor Roman Villa, showing a winged cupid dressed as a secutor
b. Mosaic from Bignor Roman Villa showing combat between winged cupids dressed as a secutor and retarius
c. Diameter 21cm Trajanic period bronze tinned; battle damage is evident
d. Blacksmith and striker from The House of Vettii, Pompeii. This house was excavated between September 1894 and January 1896. The discovery of two seals has linked the building to the Vettii family, who are also recorded in election graffiti and are believed to be freedmen (Mouritsen 1988, 14). The frieze in which this scene is located can be found in one oecus of the house. In monochrome against black grounds, the freize shows show putti engaged in various trades, including wine-making, goldsmithing, perfume-pressing and smithing.

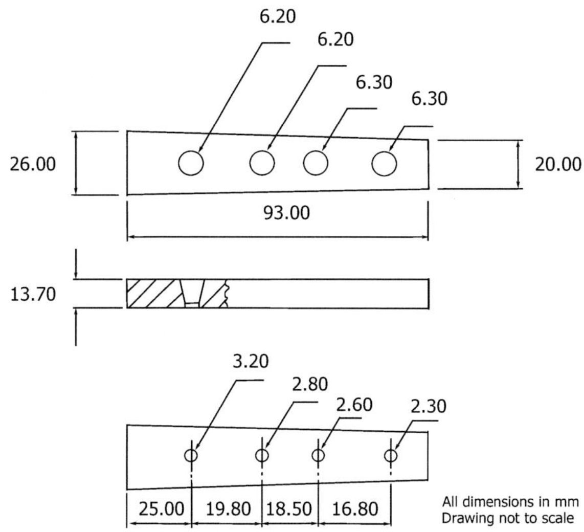

Figure 79: Schematic drawing of a draw plate from Vindolanda

is 1.2mm in diameter. It is iron that has been worked at a low temperature, possibly in the region of 500°C. It was probably worked with a small hammer. The hardness value was 180 VPN. The microstructure shows omni-directional, slightly elongated ferrite grains with small particles in the grains and in the grain boundaries. The central section shows fine equiaxed martensite grains. This area is martensite with some ferrite. There are quite a few slag inclusions and stringers.

Figure 80 (3 and4) show micrographs of a section through a mail ring from Nydam. The original wire is 1.2mm in diameter. Its hardness is 180 VPN. The structure shows omni-directional, slightly elongated ferrite grains with small particles in the grains and grain boundaries. It has not been possible to identify these particles. The area fraction of slag inclusions is 4.4%. The structure indicates this is iron that has been finished at a low temperature with a small hammer.

Figure 80 (5 and 6) show micrographs of a section through a mail ring from Stuttgart. The original wire is 0.95mm in diameter. The structure is composed of elongated ferrite grains with particles in the grains and grain boundaries. It has not been possible to identify these particles. There are quite a few slag inclusions and stringers, the area fraction of which is 4.4%. The structure indicates this is iron that has been finished at a low temperature with a small hammer.

Figure 80 (7 and 8) show micrographs of a section through a mail ring from Nydam. The original wire is 0.90mm in diameter. The structure is very fine equiaxed ferrite and lamellar pearlite grains with carbide particles in the grain boundaries. The area fraction of slag inclusions is 2.1%. This is a 0.6% carbon steel that has been warm worked, heated and air cooled.

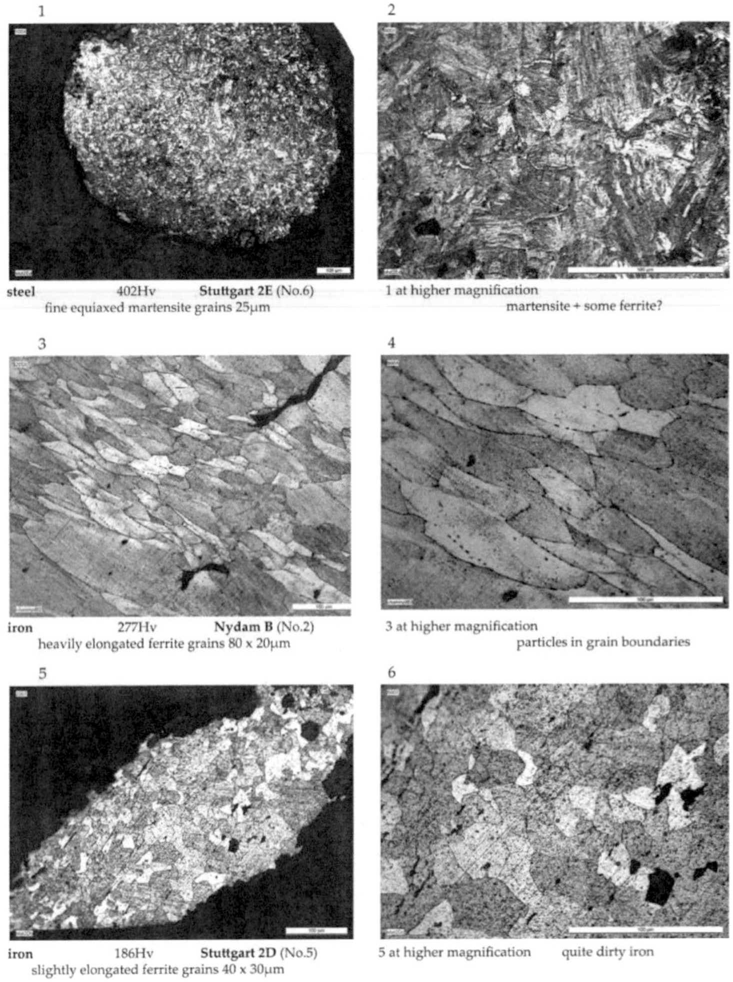

Figure 80: Optical micrographs of ring mail from Nydam and Stuttgart (after Fulford et al. *2004b)*

Experimental method for producing a draw plate

The following research adds to the experiments on wire drawing that have been published by Sim (1997a). Thomsen and Thomsen's (1974) research shows that a draw plate can be made from the same material as the wire to be drawn through it, and it was therefore decided to make a draw plate from a 0.3% plain carbon steel that was in the normalized condition prior to manufacture.

Before the advent of twist drills and powered drilling machines, drilling holes in hard metal such as iron and steel was a slow and time-consuming process. Consequently punching was the most common means of producing holes in iron. Material up to approximately 3mm in thickness could be cold punched, while material of greater thickness had to be heated and then punched. Experiments were conducted to form two different cross-sections of wire, round and square. Although superficially draw plates for round and square wire appear to be very similar, the methods of manufacture are different for each.

Draw plate for forming wire into a square cross-section

A length of 10mm diameter medium carbon steel was heated to dull red heat and forged into a tapering point (Figure 81). It was normalized (by burying in cold wood ash and leaving for 8 hours) and then hardened by heating to cherry red heat and quenching in olive oil. Although this punch was going to be used on hot metal which would draw the temper when they made contact, it was too brittle to be used in its hardened state. To remove some of the brittleness it was heated to a blue colour and again quenched in olive oil. The first hole was made by driving the punch through the heated plate until it reached the end of the taper. The second was driven in to approximately 1.0mm from the end of the taper and the process was repeated for 10 holes. This was all done by eye and the result appeared to be a set of holes of decreasing size from 2.0mm down to 0.9mm. A piece of copper wire 1.9mm in diameter was then successfully drawn through the first hole. It was then placed in the second hole but drawing was not possible. The punch was placed in the hole and given a light tap. The wire was presented again and did not draw. The punch was again placed in the hole and struck again. This was repeated until the wire could be drawn through the hole. It was repeated until all the holes could be used to draw wire. Some holes required less attention than others but this fine-tuning took 2 hours and 14 minutes. The extra punching that was needed during fine-tuning had the effect of smoothing the sides of the hole, thus giving a smoother surface finish to the wire. A series of tests was carried out to draw both copper and copper alloy wire. This established that this draw plate could be used to draw the copper alloys that were in use during the Roman period. The next step was to determine if it could be used to draw soft iron wire.

Figure 81: Square tapering punch

Previous experiments (Sim 1997a) have shown that drawing iron wire by hand was almost impossible and that a mechanical device was required. Therefore, the plate was clamped to a bench and a pair of tongs attached to a drum pulley system; this was then used to draw the wire through. This was found to work successfully. Soft iron wire of 2.0mm diameter was drawn down to 0.90mm in a series of five holes.

Figure 82: Round tapering punch

Draw plate for forming wire into a cylindrical cross-section

A length of 10mm diameter medium carbon steel was heated to dull red heat and forged into a tapering point (Figure 82). It was normalized (by burying in wood ash and leaving for 8 hours). In previous experiments the surface of the punch was left as forged, but it was found that any defects on the punch were transferred to the inside of the draw holes. When the wire was drawn through the holes, the marks on the inside of the draw hole left characteristic defects on the outside surface of the wire. These would have had to be removed by hand increasing the amount of work required to produce a good finish on the wire surface. In the second experiment the taper was filed to remove any marks left by forging and then polished with sand mixed with olive oil to act as a carrier. It was then hardened by heating to cherry red heat and quenched in olive oil. Although this punch was going to be used on hot metal which would draw the temper when they made contact it was too brittle to be used in its hardened state. To remove some of the brittleness it was heated to a blue colour and again quenched in olive oil.

The plate was heated to red heat and the first hole was made by driving the punch through the heated plate until it reached the end of the taper. The second was driven in to approximately 1.0mm from the end of the taper and the process was repeated for ten holes. This was all done by eye and the result appeared to be a set of holes of decreasing size from 2.0mm down to 0.9mm. A piece of copper wire 2.2mm in diameter was then successfully drawn through the first hole. It was then placed in the second hole but drawing was not possible. The punch was placed in the hole and given a light tap. The wire was presented again but unlike the experiments with the square punch, it did not draw. The punch was again placed in the hole and struck once more. This was repeated until the wire could be drawn through the hole. On inspection of the wire it was found to have marks on its surface.

It was decided to try a different approach to adjusting the size of the holes. An abrasive made from fine sand and olive oil was placed in the hole. The tapered punch was inserted into the hole and reciprocated by hand. After ten reciprocations the punch was moved through 90° and the process was repeated. This process was continued until the soft copper wire could be drawn through the hole. On inspection of the wire it was found that the lapping process had brought the hole to the right size for drawing and had also smoothed all the imperfections from the inside of the hole. The drawn wire had no blemishes that were visible to the naked eye. On very close inspection in daylight there were seen to be slight grooves running parallel to the long axis of the wire, but these were consistent with marks found on wire drawn through a commercially produced wire plate. It was repeated until all the holes could be used to draw wire. Some holes required less attention than others, but this fine-tuning took 1 hour and 19 minutes (Table 19). The production of draw plates for drawing wire is a straightforward piece of forge work that could be carried out by any competent blacksmith.

Operation	*Time (minutes)*
Forging the punch	11
File to shape	10
Polish on sandstone	15
Forge wrought iron 40 × 20mm down to 4 × 36mm	12
Punch 6 holes	21
Total time	1 hour 19 minutes

Table 19: Sequence of operations, and time for production of an iron draw plate

Wire drawing

Hole diam. (mm)	*Maximum load (N)*
2.0	1415
1.7	2094
1.4	2199
1.1	1146
0.9	1194

Table 20: Force required to draw wrought iron wire through a draw plate

The drawing of iron wire is more difficult than that of non-ferrous metals because the higher tensile strength of ferrous metals requires a much greater force to bring about drawing. Simple devices such as the capstan and forceps described by Landels (1978, 85) could easily have been used to supply the necessary force for drawing ferrous wire. In contrast drawing copper alloy wire can be achieved by manual means. However, drawing wire from ferrous material requires more energy than can be exerted by most men (see Table 20). Such forces would be almost at the limits of human strength and it is uncertain how long an individual could keep on exerting this sort of force. It is possible that in the Roman period a winding device could have been used to provide the power to draw iron wire. The force could easily have been supplied by the type of winch system used for drawing back the firing arms on ballistae (Marsden 1971).

Consequently mechanical means were most likely used. Devices for lifting large pieces of stone were employed during the Roman period and the principle of these devices is the same as that seen in medieval wire drawing devices; it is conceivable that the Romans used similar devices for drawing wire.[8] These would leave no diagnostic evidence in the archaeological record.

The effects of work hardening were understood by the Romans (cf. Philon of Byzantium *Artillery Manual* 72:11f). Laboratory experiments were conducted to determine the effects of work hardening on the wire used to make ring mail, and to establish if wire drawing increased the hardness of the original material. Wrought iron wire with a VPN hardness of 100 was drawn through five holes in a draw plate. Its hardness rose to 159 VPN.[9] It is possible that some work hardening will take place on the inside of the holes which will increase the working life of those holes. Annealing of the wire in between drawings would be necessary to reduce the power required for drawing. This would have been done for non-ferrous wire although it is not clear if this was done for drawing iron wire. Experimental evidence shows that iron wire can be drawn through a soft iron plate, providing the hardness of the plate is equal or slightly harder than the hardness of the wire being drawn.

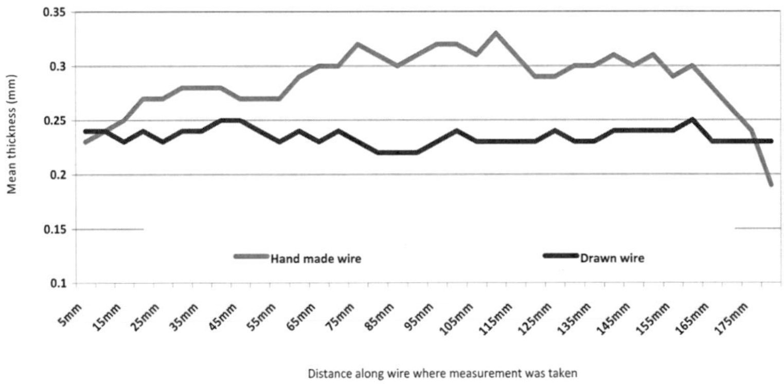

Figure 83: A comparison of the thickness of hand produced and drawn wire

Hand forging wire

It has been suggested (Singer *et al.* 1954, 74) that wire was produced by cutting sheet metal into strips and then forging these strips into wire. A series of experiments was conducted to examine this theory.

A sheet of wrought iron 4mm thick and 100mm wide was the starting point for this experiment. In the first experiment an attempt was made to cut the sheet using a pair of shears of a type known to have existed in the Roman period. This proved to be impossible. A second experiment used a cold chisel to cut a sliver off the edge of the sheet; the product of this experiment was a length of metal bevelled on one side with a very ragged edge that had to be removed with a file. These two operations took 34 minutes. In the third operation a sliver was cut by heating the metal to bright red and cutting with a hot set; this produced a piece of material with a bevelled edge but with no raggedness. This was then heated to red heat and forged into a length of round wire. This wire was bent round a cylindrical mandrel and cut along its long length to produce a series of individual rings. On inspection it was found that there was only enough material to make three rings and that the total production time was 3 hours and 21 minutes.

For making square wire using this method a sheet of wrought iron 4mm thick and 100mm wide was the starting point; it had already been established that cutting using shears and a cold chisel was ineffective. A sliver was cut by heating the metal to bright red and cutting with a hot set; this produced a piece of material with a bevelled edge but with no raggedness. This was then heated to red heat and forged into a length of square wire. This took only 15 minutes. The wire was bent round a cylindrical mandrel and cut along its long length to produce a series of individual rings. On inspection it was found that there was only enough material to make three rings and that the total production time was 2 hours and 30 minutes.

The round wire was measured every 120° around its circumference and at 5mm intervals along its length; the graph (Figure 83) shows these dimensions. When they are compared to wire that was produced using a draw plate the deviation is clearly visible.

Thomsen and Thomsen (1976) have shown that wire can be drawn through a plate made of the same metal as the wire to be drawn. They have drawn gold, silver, and copper wire through gold silver and copper draw plates. If this theory holds true for iron, then draw plates for drawing iron would not have to have been made from hardened steel. In another paper Thomsen and Thomsen (1974) have shown that if the hole in the die is in the form of a taper, drawing will take place if the draw angle is less than 2° and more than 50°. A series of tapering holes can easily be made in a piece of iron by making a tapering punch and driving it into the plate to different depths. This would be done as a forging operation.

In a ring mail coat there could have been as many as 20,000 riveted rings if the ring diameters were in the region of 12mm, and even more for smaller rings. Examination of Roman ring mail rings has shown that their dimensional accuracy is very close. Experiments by the authors show that making wire by hammering and filing is unlikely to be able to produce wire to the tolerances found in Roman ring mail coats or in the necessary quantities.

Ring types

There are many variations of ring design but they can be categorised into the following types.

1. *Butted*: An annulus with an open end (Figure 84).
2. *Riveted:* An annulus where the ends are overlapped and joined together with a rivet (see Figure 85). A description of the method of production of these rings can be found in Burgess (1953).
3. *Solid made by punching*: An annulus punched from sheet with no joints (Figure 86).[10]

Solid rings are used in conjunction with riveted or butted rings (Figure 87; Plate 4c).

Mail coat of solid and riveted rings

In the Roman period there were several methods of producing mail coats, for example: using only butted rings, all riveted rings, solid rings joined by riveted rings and solid rings joined by butted rings. The riveted rings are made from wire; the method of construction is shown in Drescher (1981); the solid rings have no joints or welds. A coat made of all butted rings will be the easiest to produce but will have the lowest defensive index, while mail coats made from riveted and solid rings will have the highest.

Consideration of solid rings

Rings that have no obvious method of jointing, such as welds or rivets, will be referred to as 'solid rings'. Such rings could easily be produced today using modern punch tools, whose manufacture requires precision machinery that is thought not to have existed in the Roman period. It is naturally assumed that precision punching was not the method used to produce solid rings. However, a high degree of precision can be achieved without the use of high-precision machines. The use of sharpened punches to produce solid rings was suggested as early as the 1960s by Biek (1963). A set of experiments was conducted to show that a punch and die can be made to a high degree of accuracy using only unsophisticated tools.

Figure 84: A modern reconstruction of butted mail

Figure 85: A modern reconstruction of riveted mail

Figure 86: A solid ring from Leiden

Figure 87: A schematic diagram of solid and riveted ring mail assembly (Sim 1995b, 211)

Table 24 shows that the variation in the dimension of the outside diameter of the Caerleon rings is very small – in the order of ±0.6mm as is the inside diameter. The consistency of these dimensions is all the more surprising, when the factors of wear and corrosion are considered. This suggests that the rings were made to a very high degree of accuracy/reproducibility. It follows from this that Roman tools could be made to a high degree of accuracy.

Justification for a two punch system

The rings from Thorsberg shown in Figure 88 show a perfectly circular inside diameter but the outside diameter has facets on it. This is consistent with a metal annulus being placed on a cylindrical tapering mandrel and the annulus being hammered on the outside

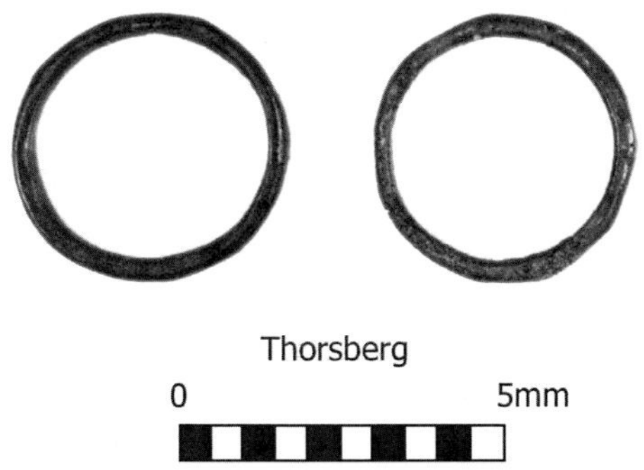

Figure 88: Two rings from Thorsberg showing facets on the outside diameter

Figure 89: An experimental ring

diameter. This produces the facets shown on the experimental ring on the right in Figure 89 and this corresponds with the facets shown on the Thorsberg rings in Figure 88.

When producing an annulus by punching, the wall width has to be sufficiently wide to support the metal while the punch passes through it, otherwise it will simply fold. The wall width of the Thorsberg example was found to be 0.9mm, which is not wide enough to have been produced by a single punch. It seems likely that the first stage of producing this ring was to make an annulus with a wall thickness wide enough to support the metal while it was being punched. It was then hammered on a tapering mandrel thus reducing its wall width and increasing its thickness, leaving behind a perfectly circular inside diameter with facets on the surface of the outside diameter as seen in Figure 89.

Producing a punch and die set

In order to test the hypothesis that solid rings were made by the method described above, an experiment was conducted to produce a punch and die set. It is suggested that such a set was made to cut the inside diameter first and then a separate set was used to cut the outside diameter.

In the current era, high-precision items are produced by high-precision machinery, which has led to the belief that in order to produce high-precision items, high-precision machinery has to be available. As no high-precision machines have been found from the Roman period, a false assumption has been made that high-precision tooling was not available at that time. However, the production of high-precision tools does not necessarily require the use of high-precision machinery. Indeed a skilled craftsman can produce precision items with simple tools; it is his skill and experience that makes this possible.

Using only the technology that was available in the Roman period a set of punch tools and dies was made to test this theory. The solid rings were made as follows: in order to make the punch and die to punch the inside diameter of the ring, a piece of medium carbon steel was forged into a rod using a pair of swages as shown in Figure 90. One end of the bar was then forged into a tapering point and the bar cut in half.

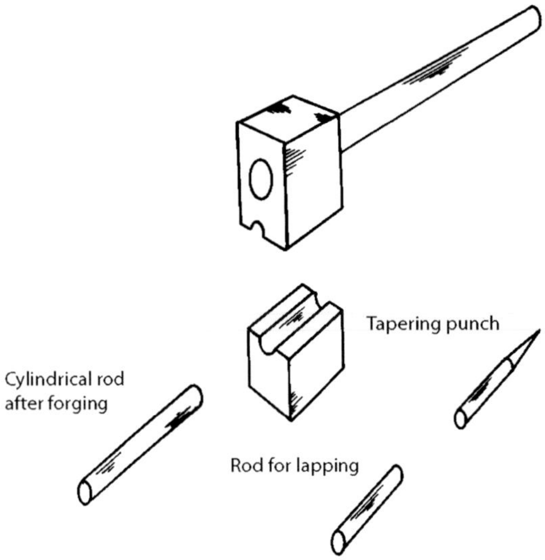

Figure 90: the production of a tapering punch using swages

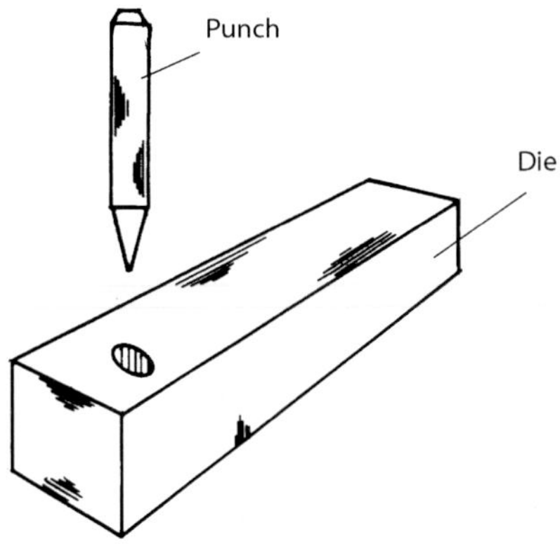

Figure 91: Tapered punch used to make a hole

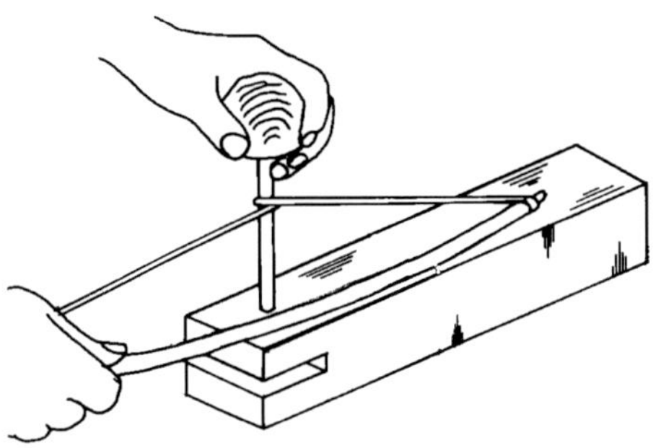

Figure 92: Use of a bow drill to lap the punch into the die

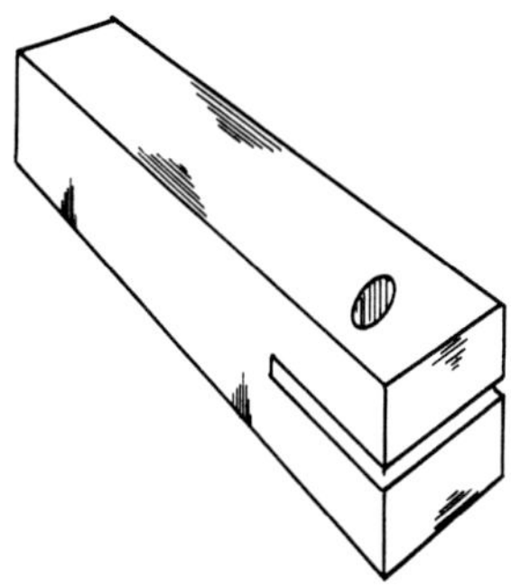

Figure 93: Completed die to produce inside diameter of rings

A block of iron 25mm square was heated to 950°C and a tapered punch was used to punch a hole through (Figure 91).

In the finished punch and die set the punch has to fit the die with a sliding fit. This means that there must be as little sideways movement as possible when the punch in the die. When the die cooled, the diameter of the hole shrank by 0.074mm which meant that the unused piece of bar was too large to fit in the hole. In order to make it fit the punch was lapped (see glossary) to fit into the die. The punch was the piece of rod that did not have a taper on it (see the rod for lapping in Figure 93).

The bar had to be made to fit the hole with the minimum of clearance between the two. The untapered bar was lapped to fit the hole. This was done by using a mixture of finely powdered glass mixed with olive oil which was used to make a grinding paste. The mixture was smeared on the punch; the bar was then put over the hole and a bow drill used to impart a reciprocating motion to the punch (see Figure 92). This caused the punch and die to be ground to fit each other. As the punch was hardened, it is likely that most of the metal removed came from the die.

Great care was taken to keep the punch vertical. A smooth sliding fit between die and punch was achieved in 12 minutes. A slot was then cut into the end of the bar as shown in Figure 93. The slot was made 0.5mm wider than the strip of iron that had been used to make the ring. This was to allow clearance between the slot and the strip. Figure 93 shows the punch and die with the strip in place. The strip was punched and produced a hole that would become the inside diameter of the ring. The die that was produced was used to cut the inside diameter of the rings.

Making punch and die to cut the outside diameter of the rings

In order to make the punch and die set to punch the outside diameter of the ring a pair of swages was used to produce a stepped punch with both parts concentric to the centre line of the bar. The larger diameter is equal to the outside diameter of the ring, the smaller to the inside (see Figure 95). The form of this punch is a tenon.[11]

To make the die for producing the finished ring a piece of bar was heated to 950°C and a hole was punched through it with the same punch as was used to produce the die. The stepped punch shown in Figure 95 was then used to make a stepped hole shown in Figure 96. The punch was lapped to fit the die by the use of a bow drill with finely powdered glass as an abrasive.

Figure 97 shows the punch and die in operation. The smaller diameter of the punch was located in the hole in the strip and then positioned in the small hole in the die. The punch was then struck with a hammer and the ring cut out (Figure 97). Figure 98 shows a cross-section of this operation. The punched ring was placed over a tapered mandrel, and the outside diameter of the ring was hammered as the mandrel was rotated (Figure 99).

In order to obtain a high degree of accuracy in the measurements of the rings, they were measured on a shadowgraph and the results are presented in Table 21. The Caerleon rings have no remaining external markings. Any such markings would probably have worn off during the use of the coat, so it is impossible to determine if any further work was carried out after punching.

In further tests, Vickers Hardness measurements were carried out on the rings from Thorsberg and Nydam and were compared with some of the experimentally produced rings. The results are shown in Table 22.

It can be seen that the experimental ring which was hammered on a mandrel after punching is harder than the ring that has only been punched, indicating that some work hardening has taken place. The experimental punched ring had a hardness value of 146 VPN, which is very close to the 149 VPN of the metal from the experimental ring. This indicates that punching did not produce any significant work hardening. The experimental ring that was hammered on a mandrel increased in hardness from 146 VPN to 210 VPN,

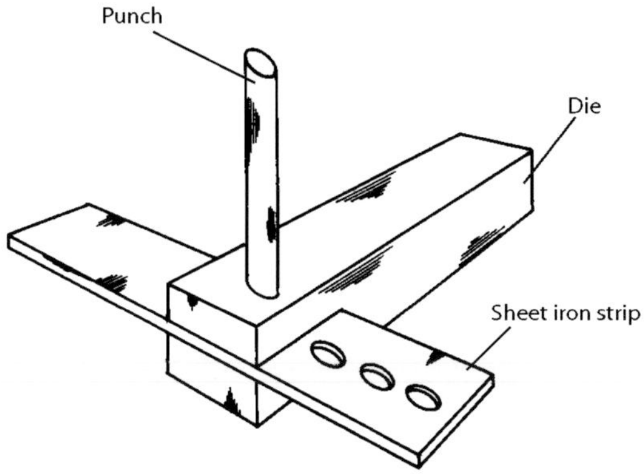

Figure 94: Showing the inside diameter of the washer being cut

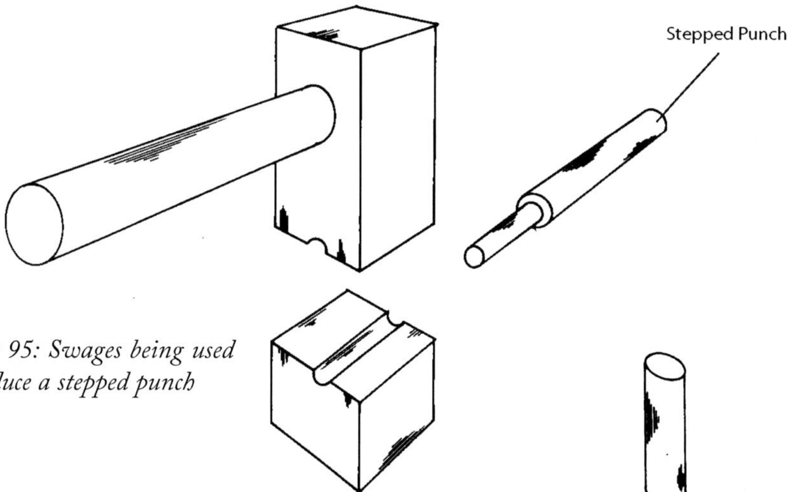

Figure 95: Swages being used to produce a stepped punch

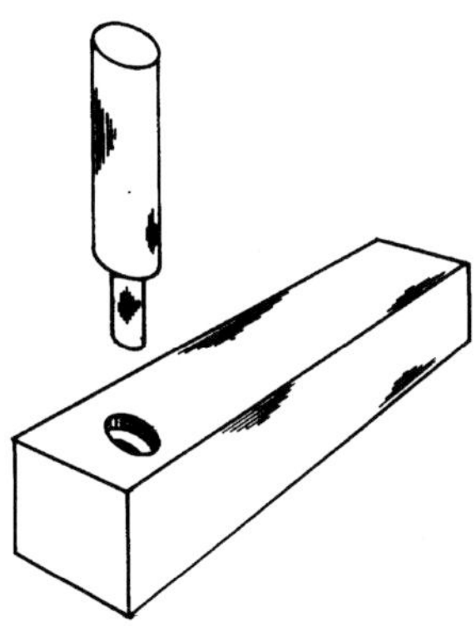

Figure 96: A stepped punch being used to produce a stepped hole in the die

which is in the same region of hardness as the Roman originals. The hammer marks together with the hardness of the rings suggest that work hardening was brought about by hammering. Thus hammering on a mandrel improves the hardness of the ring because of work hardening and also the appearance of poorly punched rings.

Metallography was carried out on the experimental rings and the specimens from Nydam and Thorsberg. This showed similar characteristics between the experimental rings and the originals. To produce one solid ring by punching took 21 seconds, while hammering it to shape on a taper mandrel initially took 50 seconds. With further practice the time was reduced to 32 seconds.

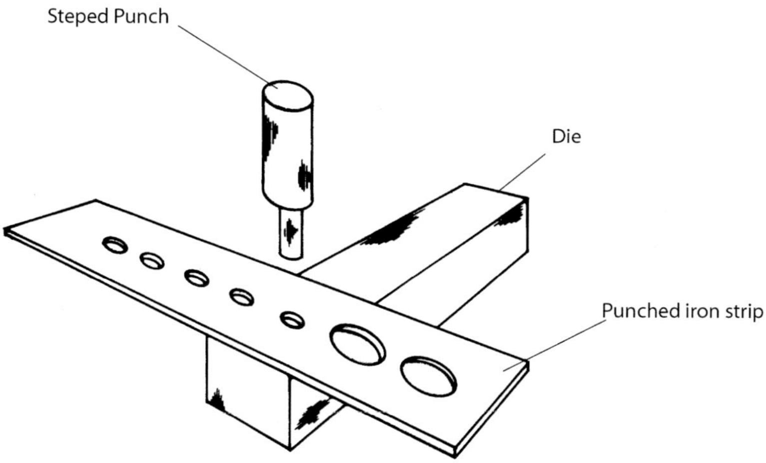

Figure 97: A stepped punch being used to produce the outside diameter of washers

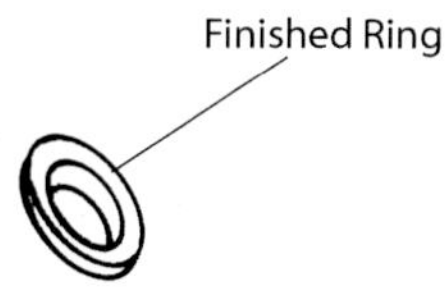

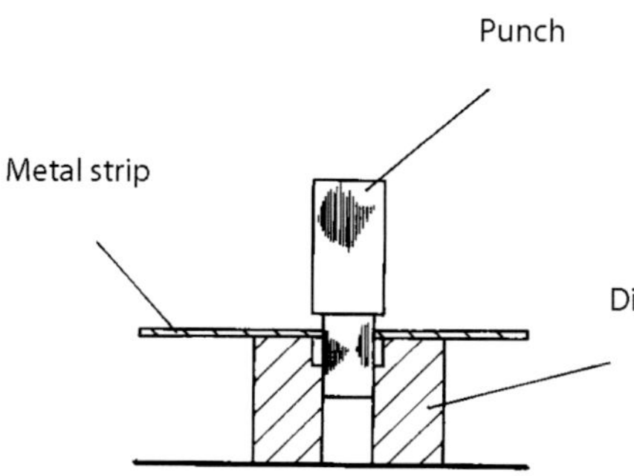

Figure 98: Section through punch and die in operation

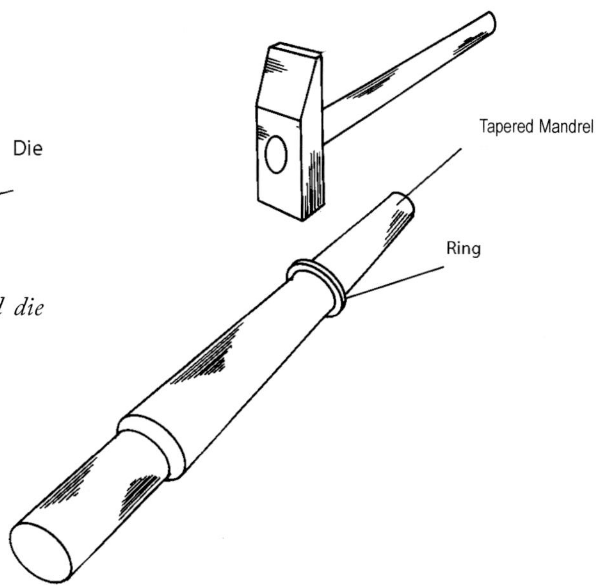

Figure 99: Tapered mandrel being used to finish the outside diameter of the ring

Ring no.	*Position*	*O/D mm*	*I/D mm*	*Thickness mm*
1	1	9.491	6.371	1.52
	2	9.000	6.402	1.59
2	1	9.557	6.360	1.51
	2	9.679	6.540	1.56
3	1	9.419	6.231	1.48
	2	9.322	6.474	1.49
4	1	9.750	6.294	1.52
	2	9.623	6.316	1.58
5	1	9.560	6.495	1.59
	2	9.625	6.288	1.61
6	1	9.524	6.315	1.46
	2	9.819	6.603	1.49
7	1	9.550	6.533	1.59
	2	9.389	6.277	1.49
8	1	9.464	6.291	1.47
	2	9.505	6.365	1.41
9	1	9.698	6.544	1.54
	2	9.551	6.382	1.55
10	1	9.610	6.405	1.51
	2	9.629	6.647	1.69

Table 21: Experimental rings (O/D = outer diameter; I/D = inner diameter)

Sample	*Vickers pyramid no. (VPN)*
Thorsberg ring	191
Nydam ring	187
Experimental ring punched then hammered on a mandrel	187

Table 22: Vickers hardness tests on solid rings

Non-ferrous rings

The non-ferrous rings from Leiden, The Netherlands, were assembled so that a single riveted ring had four solid rings inside it (Figure 100). Six solid rings were examined under a microscope and measured on a shadow graph (Table 23).

Figure 100: Solid and riveted rings from Leiden

The outside diameters of the solid rings measured 3mm. When examined under a microscope the shape of the solid rings showed that these rings were probably made by punching from a solid sheet. If the technology existed to punch small rings from non-ferrous metal then it is possible that the same technology was used to punch rings from

Ring no.	*Position*	*O/D*	*I/D*	*Thickness mm*
1	1	3.110	2.212	0.51
	2	3.147	2.123	0.58
2	1	3.057	2.209	0.61
	2	3.013	2.257	0.63
3	1	3.174	2.203	0.48
	2	3.062	2.212	0.52
4	1	3.147	2.129	0.54
	2	3.133	2.209	0.59
5	1	3.054	2.268	0.57
	2	3.100	2.257	0.57
6	1	3.197	2.213	0.61
	2	3.196	2.234	0.58

Table 23: Non-ferrous solid rings from Leiden, The Netherlands (O/D = outer diameter; I/D = inner diameter)

Ring no.	*Position*	*O/D mm*	*I/D mm*	*Thickness mm*
1	1	6.957	4.968	0.989
	2	6.990	4.869	0.948
2	1	6.761	4.865	0.852
	2	6.948	4.765	1.513
3	1	7.381	4.791	1.263
	2	7.344	4.909	1.177
4	1	7.401	5.169	1.119
	2	7.513	5.465	1.116
5	1	6.703	5.024	0.864
	2	6.945	5.006	0.929
6	1	7.087	4.827	1.071
	2	7.247	5.042	1.036
7	1	7.605	4.818	1.501
	2	7.503	4.761	1.431
8	1	6.645	4.413	1.126
	2	6.609	4.356	1.071
9	1	7.850	4.939	1.393
	2	7.736	4.820	1.441
10	1	6.871	4.567	1.239
	2	6.974	4.465	1.441

Table 24: Solid rings from Carleon (O/D= outer diameter; I/D = inner diameter)

sheet iron. Some solid ferrous rings from a second century context in the *Via Principalis* at Caerleon (Nash Williams 1932) were examined under a microscope and measured on a shadow graph. The results can be seen in Table 24.

Riveted rings

Riveted rings come in a variety of sizes and those shown in Figure 101 are some of the smallest non-ferrous rings. Experiments were successfully conducted to reproduce these rings using the same production method as described above. However, producing rivets to go through the holes proved impossible as the holes are 0.4mm in diameter. The punches required to form these rivet holes had to be produced to a very high degree of precision. Because there are no remaining rivets in this section of mail it is conceivable that the rings were secured by organic material such as horsehair.

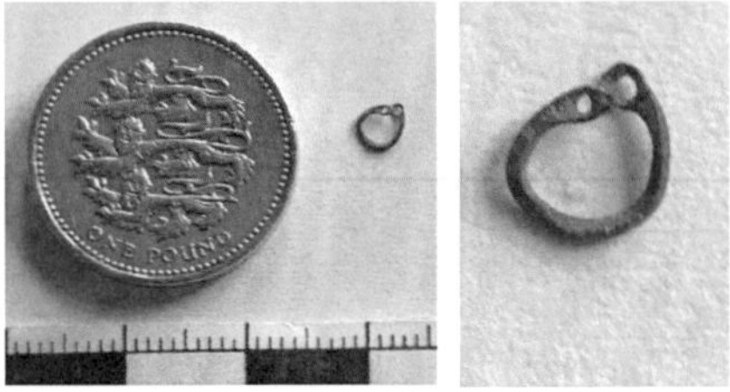

Figure 101: Non-ferrous riveted rings from Leiden (left), enlargement of ring (right)

Discussion

The size of the smallest rings (3mm diameter) and the intricacy of the work involved in punching the holes for riveting is more the type of work conducted by a jeweller rather than a blacksmith. It is not being suggested that jewellers carried out the making of ring mail but that the equipment and the fine nature of the work would have employed the skills and tools of a jeweller rather than those of a blacksmith.

In the example of a mail coat constructed from a series of solid rings, with four riveted rings passing through it where the rings are 6mm in diameter, then the whole coat, will require 40,000 rings. The production of the solid and riveted rings requires approximately 200 days work. The assembly of the coat requires up to 30 days, depending on the system of manufacture.

This is a staggering amount of time to invest in armour. It indicates that mail would probably have had a long field life and would have been repaired if damaged. Although it is unclear what the life expectancy of a mail coat was or what percentage of the military were using mail at any one time.

Conclusions

The experiments to make punches and dies using simple technology have shown that such tools can be made to a high degree of precision using the technology that would have been available in the Roman period. Such tools could be produced quickly and maintenance was quite simple. When a die wore out, a new die could have been made in less than 20 minutes.

The comparison of the sizes of the Roman rings with experimental rings shows that the size ranges and variations are within the same order. Thus, it is possible that Roman rings could have been made using punches and dies similar to those made experimentally.

The Roman rings that have facets on the outside diameter have a hardness that is almost the same as that of experimental rings made by punching and hammering on a mandrel.

The hardness of the ancient rings examined is higher than the hardness of wrought iron. This difference in hardness can be accounted for by the work hardening that takes place when the outside diameter of the ring is hammered.

It is suggested that the wire made for the production of ring mail coats was made by drawing wire through a draw plate. The solid rings were produced by a three stage process, the inside diameter was produced first, and then the outside diameter. The final process was to hammer the outside of the ring when it had been on a tapering mandrel.

The ring mail fragments examined display a high degree of dimensional accuracy in the individual rings. Experiments to produce rings by hand have failed to achieve the same degree of accuracy. It is suggested that in the case of solid rings, they were produced by punching from strips of iron using hardened punch tools. The difficulty of performing this operation by hand indicates that a punch tool was used. The rings made from riveted wire also show a high degree of accuracy in overall dimensions and cross-sectional dimensions. Producing wire to this degree of accuracy was not possible using traditional hand forging methods; this indicates that either a forming tool such as a pair of swages was used, or the wire was produced by drawing. In view of the number of mail coats produced and the considerable amount of time required to make wire by hand forging, there is a strong possibility that the wire was produced by drawing and the drawing was assisted by some mechanical means. Irrespective of the place of manufacture, the operations to produce the individual rings are not as complicated as would first appear; and it is possible to train an unskilled workforce, including children, to make the rings and assemble the coats. This is probable when one considers the time involved. A skilled craftsman would be wasted in making such a coat, when his services were necessary to produce items that could only be made by a skilled man.

Experiments have shown that:

1. Simple technology can be used to produce a punch and die that are capable of punching rings from sheet iron.
2. The die and punches can be made in 45–50 minutes.
3. Wear on the die can easily be rectified by putting the punch in the die and striking a single blow.
4. The die can be made from soft iron but the punch needs to be made from steel or case-hardened wrought iron.

When experimental rings were compared with originals the amount of deviation from the mean was similar in both cases. It is suggested that solid Roman rings were made by punching with a punch and die similar to that used in the experiments. These punching sets were easy to produce and required no precision machinery.

Two iron plates from the Roman period have been shown to exhibit all the characteristics of draw plates, but it cannot be proved that they were used to draw iron wire. However, experiments have shown that iron wire can be drawn through iron draw plates and that such draw plates are simple to produce. During experiments the force required to draw iron wire was between 1415 N and 2094 N; exerting this force by hand reaches the limits of human strength, but a simple system of pulleys would have been able to produce the necessary force.

The dimensional accuracy of the wire used to make Roman riveted rings was to a level that could not reproduce by forging and filing or by swaging. It is suggested that the accuracy of the rings and the time to produce the necessary quantities of iron wire for riveted rings means that the wire was probably made by drawing wire through draw plates. The apparent scarcity of equipment for drawing iron wire can perhaps be attributed to some draw plates having been misidentified as nail-heading tools, as well as the degradation of iron items in the archaeological record.

Experimental evidence has also shown that a draw plate for square wire and the tools to make it can be produced in 2 hours and 54 minutes, while a draw plate for cylindrical wire and the tools to make it can be produced in only 1 hour 19 minutes.

Notes

1 Although Scythian grave finds from the fifth century BC hint at an earlier origins it is unlikely that these nomads would have produced this armour themselves (Piggott 1965, 240; Russell-Robinson 1975, 164).

2 Born in Megalopolis in Arcadia, Polybius (*c.* 203–120 BC) was a Greek historian most famous for his *Histories* which cover the period of 220–146 BC. As such he is one of the earliest surviving historians of Roman history, along with Cato the Elder.

3 The principal behind ring mail is emulated in modern body armour forms such as Kevlar and other ballistic materials which use layers of ballistic fibre to match the energy of projectiles. The weave of the fabric acts like a net and gives, absorbing energy.

4 Iron rings from Thorsberg and Nydam, Denmark, were also examined (Engelhard 1866); Raddaz (1968) has proposed a date of AD 150–250 for these rings.

5 In a slightly acidic environment, iron will dissolve by atoms losing two electrons and form iron (II) ions. CO_2 can make rainwater slightly acidic (Fe -> Fe 2 + 2e). The ions are soluble and can move about in a watery medium. Where they go to will depend upon the circumstances of the burial and deposition, etc. Oxygen from the air will oxidize Fe2+ to Fe3+. The iron (III) ions may be precipitated as for example ferric hydroxide Fe(OH)3 which then can lose water to form rust (Fe(OH)3 --> Fe(OH)O + H2O). Although other products may be precipitated, the tubular appearance is due to the migration of iron (II) ions before oxidation (cf. Cronyn 2004, 185).

6 Some individual rings exist and were made available for examination. These include 20 fine gilded bronze rings from Leiden that were found in 1902 in Ouddorp, on the island of Goedereede, in the province of South Holland and are illustrated by Robinson (1975). The context is unclear but the armour was found beneath a layer of clay under Roman pottery. Iron rings from Caerleon (found in *Via Principalis* 207 phase 5B, second century) were also examined.

7 The carbon content and structure are unknown as no metallography was possible.

8 Compare the Roman crane shown by Singer *et al.* 1954 (fig. 602) with the wire drawing device shown by Biringuccio 1540 (Sim 1995b, fig. 4.71).

9 The first stage of preparing the wrought iron wire for drawing was to forge a length of wrought iron down to 3.5mm square and then anneal it by heating to red heat and burying it in wood ash. After annealing the hardness was 100 VPN. The wire was lubricated by wiping it with beeswax and drawn through the five holes on the draw plate using an INSTRON 4206 Universal Testing Machine. No annealing was conducted between each drawing and due to work hardening of the finished wire, the hardness had further increased in hardness to 159 VPN which is harder than the holes in the draw plate which was 127 VPN.

10 Solid welded rings are attested during the medieval period. These are solid rings where the ends are overlapped (scarfed) and fire welded together (see glossary). It is possible that these were in use during the Roman period. However, no examples have been examined by the authors. The existence of this type of solid ring warrants further investigation.

11 This is an operation frequently carried out by blacksmiths.

10. Segmented Body Armour (*lorica segmentata*)

Introduction

The earliest forms of metal *lorica segmentata* date to around 9 BC. These early Kalkreise forms have been recovered from Dangestetten, Germany and Vindonissa, Switzerland; they had a complicated system of joints and buckles. Over time the complexity of the system used for connecting sections was simplified (Bishop 2002; Bishop and Coulston 2006, 95).

By the last quarter of the first century AD the earlier *segmentata* forms were beginning to be replaced by Corbridge and Carnuntum types with A, B and C variants. The 40 articulated segments were riveted to three leather straps. The latest incarnation was the Newstead type (AD 164–80) based around 48 articulated parts but showing a further simplification compared to the Corbridge types.

The articulated *lorica segmentata* conferred a number of advantages to the wearer. It was relatively flexible and was highly effective in preventing penetrating blows. But its greatest advantage came with its comparatively rapid production time. With the exception of *lorica musculata* the alternative body armour forms (*squamata* and *hamata*) were far more time consuming to produce. *Segmentata* was based on relatively simple sheet metal work. The laminated strips could easily be produced and then rapidly formed into shape. Furthermore with many more components *squamata* and *hamata* armour forms were more problematic to maintain.

The length of operational use of this armour indicates that *segmentata* was effective body armour. It was made of strips of ferrous metal joined by various forms of fastening that simplified as time passed. It provided protection for the torso and shoulders and in combination with segmented arm armour gave good protection to the wearer.

However, it did not give any protection to the groin or buttocks – both vulnerable areas. It is unlikely that these areas were left unprotected. *Lorica segmentata* was made from separate pieces of ferrous metal and this made it easy to manufacture and to repair by soldiers in the field, or by the armourer while in camp.

Lorica segmentata was made from sheet iron and sheet steel. Steel gives a higher defensive index than iron allowing thinner sheet to give the same defensive capacity as a thicker sheet of iron.[1] A fragment of *lorica segmentata* thought to be of second century AD date from the frontier fort at Risstissen was found to be steel that had not been hardened (Williams 1977).[2] Two pieces of *lorica segmentata* from Vindolanda show evidence of a multi-layered structure. In one sample (5767) the strip is divided into two layers; the outer layer consists of pearlite corresponding to a carbon content of 0.3% and the inner band is ferrite with some slag inclusions. This layer is steel in the normalized condition. The second fragment (2199) is again composed of two layers, the outer containing pearlite giving a carbon content of slightly less than 0.1% (Sim 1998d).

Roman smiths were aware of the benefits of producing sheet with different properties on each side. This laminated structure can be achieved by either welding sheets of metal with different properties together or by treating the metal using different methods on each side.

The first century AD iron shield boss from Melrose, Scotland shown in Figure 116 is composed of two layers of steel, which were welded to a layer of iron, with an outer layer of high-carbon (harder) steel (see Figure 117). Roman smiths clearly understood that a laminated structure would produce armour that was hard on the outside and tough at the back. The hard surface provided resistance to penetration and the tough back absorbed the energy of the impact.

Shoulder protection

The area from the neck to the edge of the shoulder was also a very vulnerable part of the body. The collar bone could be broken by a strong blow and this would render the arm useless, and as legionaries carried a shield in one hand and a sword in the other, having either arm out of use would have been a considerable disadvantage.

It is evident from archaeological evidence that the vulnerability of this area was clearly understood, because there is often a double layer of armour on the shoulders (Bishop 2002, 73–4).

In the case of shoulder armour being made from plates, as shown in Figure 102, the plates are overlapping; this would have provided some areas with a double thickness of armour and also would have deflected downwards blows away from the neck.

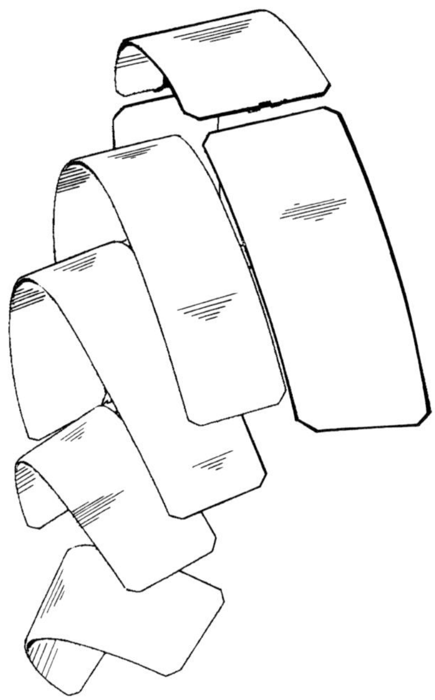

Figure 102: Schematic view of the arrangements of shoulder armour plates

Figure 103 shows the various components and techniques necessary to make both body and arm armour of strip iron. It is evident that the production of body armour required more than just metal working. Leather production and working was also required to furnish the straps and backings for armour such *lorica segmentata*.

Some examples, such as the *segmentata* fragments from Verulamium (Niblett 2001/2002) have mineralised leather adhering where straps used to be.

Maintenance

Every type of armour that is made from a number of strips of metal has a huge advantage over plate armour, when repairs are necessary. Muscled cuirasses made from a single piece of metal are rendered useless if they are heavily damaged, because the whole piece

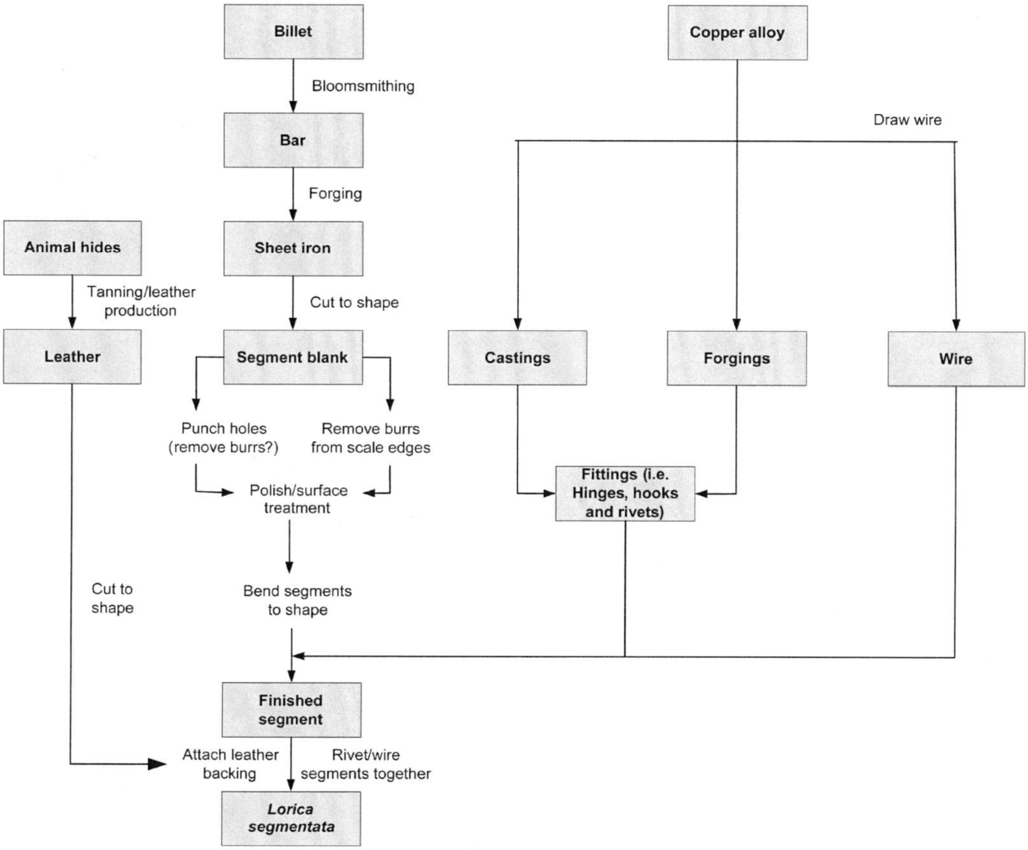

Figure 103: Flow diagram for the production of lorica segmentata *and* manica

has to be discarded and a new one made. With segmented armour, only the damaged component(s) need to be replaced; this makes it more economical. The metal thickness means that it can easily be cut to shape using shears and the various holes used for fixing can be made by punching. Both are simple operations and require only a basic knowledge of metal work to carry out. *Lorica segmentata* is more wasteful of metal when seriously damaged, but is as easy to repair in the field as *lorica squamata* (Table 25).

Conclusions

Compared to scale and mail *lorica segmentata* is flexible, lightweight armour. It is made of overlapping strips of iron that are joined by various methods such as leather straps and metal hinges. The manufacturing methods used to make sheet iron in such large quantities were likely to have been based on the use of mechanical hammers and rollers to produce sheet of such uniform thickness. The armour would have been effective enough

	Material required	*Time to manufacture*	*Weight for wearer*	*Maintenance*	*Ease of field repairs*	*Protective index*
Squamata	More	More	More	More	Easier	Higher
Segmentata	Less	Less	Less	Less	More difficult	Lower

Table 25: A comparison of lorica segmentata *and* squamata *(for a specific area, e.g. back plate)*

to protect the wearer from serious harm from hand held weapons and all projectiles, with the exception of those fired from a ballista. If a strip were damaged beyond repair, then it would have been necessary to replace the whole strip, which would have made it expensive to repair. The overlapping structure means that in many parts of the armour there are two thicknesses of armour, which increases its defensive index.

However, it is evident from both monumental and the limited archaeological evidence that *lorica segmentata* only came down as far as the waist, leaving the groin region unprotected. In contrast both *squamata* and *hamata* armour could extend down as far as the mid-calf. This difference in the potential area of torso protection is fundamental in understanding the different forms of body armour.

Notes

1. For example, *lorica segmentata* is approximately half the thickness of high medieval plate armour, but was just as effective as a method of defence. Being comparatively thin, it allowed the wearer considerable flexibility in combat and was much less fatiguing when it had to be worn for long periods, such as on a march or in extended battles.
2. R.66/39 Wurttemberg Landesmuseum.

11. Leg and Arm Armour

Arm armour

In antiquity many armies made use of the spear as their principal weapon of attack, but the Roman heavy infantry made use of the sword in addition to spears and javelins. A common tactic was for legionaries to discharge their *pila*, draw their swords to attack and defend themselves with their shields. During hand-to-hand combat the most exposed point on an infantry soldier for the enemy to attack was his sword arm because in the stabbing action the arm can be extended beyond the protective sphere of the shield. Such an unprotected arm is vulnerable and a blow even from a blunt weapon could cause the sword holder to drop his sword. If the blow was from an edged weapon, the effect would be to disarm; the wrist and arm carry several arteries which are close to the surface with little fleshy protection. A cut severing the ulnar and/or radial arteries in the wrist and forearm, or the *interosseous* artery inside of the elbow, could easily cause death by exsanguination. Furthermore, muscles in the forearm such as the *teres major* and *minor*, the *lumbodorsal fascia*, the *serratus anterior, latissimus dorsi, extensor* and *triceps* are all exposed. Even minor damage to these would, at best, debilitate the sword arm.

The principal attack weapon of the heavy infantry soldier was the short sword, the *gladius*. As a swordsman, he would know that his sword arm was his principal means of attack and he would also know the disadvantage he would be at with no protection for his sword arm. Even in contemporary fencing equipment it is apparent that fencers wear gloves on their sword arms, and those who use sabres have extra protection on their wrists. The Roman military used the *manica* as a mechanism for protecting the sword arm. The known examples are formed of a flexible, laminated structure. Figure 105 from Adamklissi, Romania, shows a heavily armoured infantry soldier in a classic fighting pose engaging two warriors. He wears a knee-length *lorica squamata* tunic, with a segmented *manica*.

Metallic laminated armour was first referred to in Xenophon's *Art of Horsemanship* (xi13–xi15) and subsequently used in gladiatorial contests. A graffito from Dura Europos, Syria, shows a heavily armoured mounted soldier with just such laminated limb (and abdominal) defences (Robinson 1975, fig. 190).

Once thought to have been designed to mitigate the slashing *falx* during Trajan's Dacian campaigns (cf. Richmond 1982, 49–50; Robinson 1975, 186) it is now apparent that *manica* were far more widely used (McCarthy *et al.* 2001) by the infantry and cavalry. Recent discoveries of at least three sets of crushed but complete segmented arm defences from the 'armour's workshop' in Carlisle complement fragments of *manica* recovered from Vindolanda, Newstead (Curle 1911, pl. xxiii) and Richborough in Kent.

A mosaic from the Bignor Roman Villa, Sussex, includes a long panel filled with cupids dressed as gladiators. The example shown in Plate 8a shows a winged cupid dressed as a *secutor* with *scuta*, *gladius* and visored helmet and leg guards tied to the leg. At least four straps are used to attach the protector to the leg. The sword arm is protected by what appears to be a metallic laminated *manica* (Figure 104). The mosaic shown in Plate 8b shows combat between winged cupids dressed as a *secutor* and *retarius*. Clearer images of apparently metal laminated *manica* can be found on the Zliten mosaic from Leptis

Figure 104: Heavily corroded manica *fragment from Vindolanda (Acc. no. 2199)*

Figure 105: Detail from the monument at Adamklissi showing an infantry soldier wearing arm armour

Magna, Libya, dating to AD 80–100. Gladiatorial armour was often a reflection of the armour worn by the military, and therefore it is conceivable that armour of a similar nature was used in combat.

It is possible that there were many different types of arm protection, such as padded sleeves or scale armour over padding, but no complete sets of such arm protection have so far come to light. The fighting style of many of Rome's enemies was the use of unarmoured, lightly armed warriors, who relied on speed and manoeuvrability. They made use of swords, but had no defensive armour on their sword arms.

Reconstruction of arm armour

The method of reconstruction followed the general principle that the metal must be as near to the original as possible; it must be made using only the tools and equipment known to have existed at that period.

The starting point was a billet of iron. This was forged down into strips of the required thickness, in this case 0.9mm. Because a human an arm is not a uniform size throughout its length, the strips have to vary in size to account for this. They had to be individually measured and then were cut to size using shears. Holes were punched for the rivets. The burrs were left on the inside of the hole to act as spacers between the strips.

The individual strips were riveted to strips of leather on the inside of the armour. The rivets were approximately 0.5mm smaller than the hole in the armour to allow the strips to move relative to each other. This combined with the spacers provided by burrs left on the holes make the arm armour (*manica*) highly flexible.

The metal *lamellae* in a *manica* overlap. In practical terms this overlap results in two layers of metal over much of the area of the armour, which improves its defensive capacity. This is also borne out by a copy made of the segmented armour found at Newstead, Scotland.

It is not usual for armour made from strips to have the strips butting against each other. If this were done then the jointing positions would be a weakness, where a blow could penetrate the armour.

The strips overlap such that if the overlaps are considered to be steps, then the steps ascend from the wrist to the elbow. Any blow arriving from a pointed weapon would slide up and over the scales; if the overlap were in the opposite direction, then the point could slide between the strips. The strips are held in place by being riveted to leather straps that run the length of the armour. There are three or four strips depending on the armour; if any two rivets were dislodged in battle the armour would stay intact and still provide good defence.

Padding under armour

Arm armour had to fulfil two functions as a protective device:

- To stop penetration by weapons.
- To protect the arm from blunt force trauma.

The thickness of the metal and the overlaps prevented penetration. It is not a realistic proposition that any armour was worn next to the skin. Metal items placed next to unprotected skin will, in a very short time, cause severe pain. Experimental testing by the authors has shown that, when properly constructed, armour can stop the penetration of most hand-held weapons. Nevertheless, in some cases such as the *falx* (Sim 2000) the blunt force trauma will still be fatal to a body that has no material between the armour and the skin. However, blunt force trauma will be reduced by the addition of a form of padding between the armour and the arm.

Weight

It was necessary to protect the sword arm but allow it to be flexible and manoeuvrable as possible. The weight of any arm armour had to strike a balance between protection and weight. If the armour were heavy it would encumber the movements of the sword arm, thus negating the effect of the protection given by the armour. The infantry *gladius* was predominately an offensive weapon; it was not a weapon that could be easily used to parry blows, although in extremis anyone will defend themselves with whatever comes to hand. Indeed blows were parried with the shield. So a legionary did not need the flexibility in his sword arm that a modern fencer needs. The reconstructions of arm armour made by the authors were tested by a number of volunteers, who all reported that there was enough flexibility to allow easy movement and allow for sufficient bending of the arm at the elbow.

Greaves (*Ocrea*)

The principal purpose of a greave was to protect the tibia or shin.[1] Triangular in section, the tibia is the strongest weight-bearing bone in the body and articulates with the femur and talus. The anterior crest and medial surface of the tibia are unprotected by muscle which makes the shin vulnerable to blows.[2] Some indication of just how vulnerable this

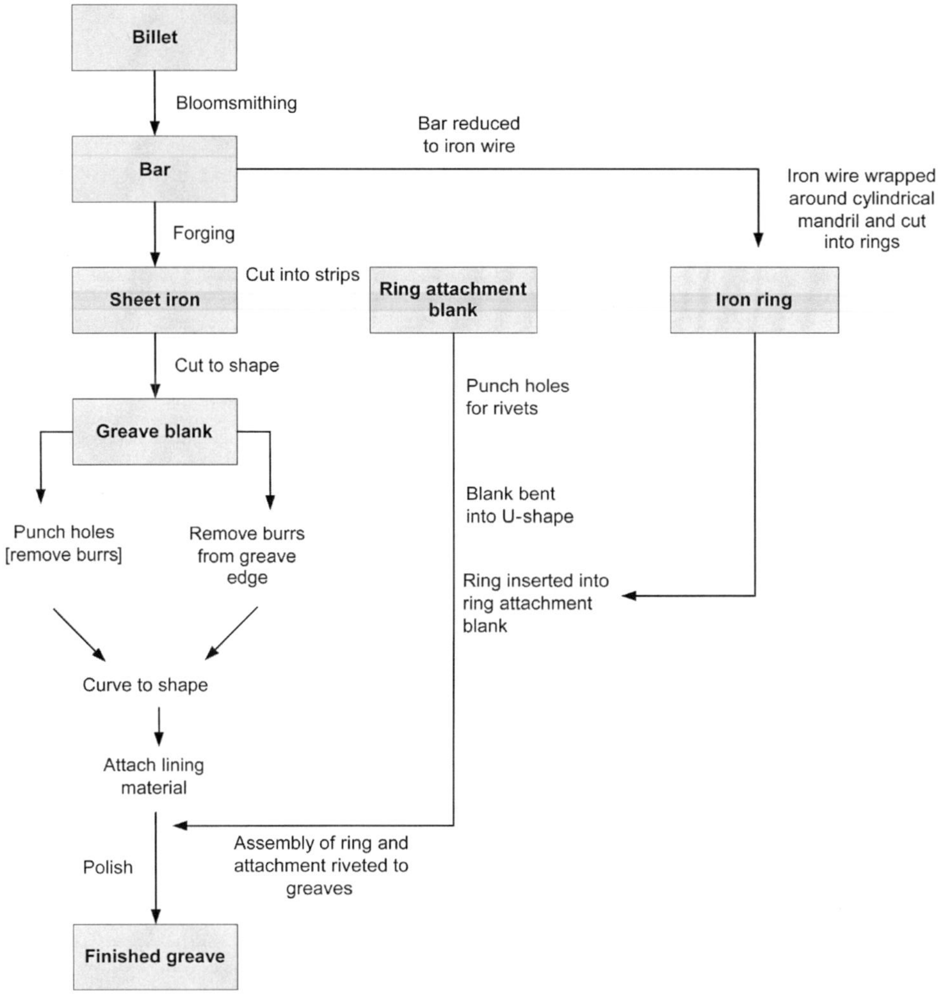

Figure 106: Flow diagram for the production of greaves

area is can be gauged from this description of a kick to the shin described in a book on unarmed combat first published in 1942 for the home guard:

> 'Kick him with the inside of the foot and aim at a point about a foot behind his instep. Make contact a few inches below the knee and scrape downward, putting all the weight into the finish across his ankle joint. This has the effect of scraping all the skin off his shin and smashes all the small bones on the top of his foot, a very tender and unprotected part of the body it renders the foot completely useless'
> (Hartley Leather 1950).

The round Roman shield affords some protection to the upper body but can leave the lower body exposed.[3] Although attacks to the lower body are not common (cf. Ström 1992) because they can leave the attacker potentially disadvantaged, it is evident that in combat attackers will probe and exploit any weakness that is evident. This is clearly seen in the wound distribution from the Battle of Visby fought in 1361 on the island of Gotland, between the forces of the Danish king Valdemar and peasants from Gotland.[4] A large number of clinically evident wounds were sustained by the peasants on their lower legs (39.9%) indicating the Danish army was exploiting the vulnerability and lack of protection underneath the shield of the poorly armed peasants.[5] The same would be applicable to fighting in the ancient world. In hand-to-hand fighting the shin and knee would be vulnerable to attack if they had no form of defence, especially if the attacker were armed with a spear or other weapon with a long reach.

It is apparent that an infantry soldier with no protection for his shin and with no body length *scutum* would be at a potential disadvantage in hand-to-hand combat. The greave only gave protection to the front and side of the shin and in some cases the knee, but it did not protect the back of the leg. This would not be too much of a disadvantage, as most combat was conducted face-to-face. The great danger was when a soldier was attacked from the back; where he was essentially unarmoured from the lower back to the ankle.

Method of manufacture

Across the Greek world greaves (*ocrea*) were recorded as being produced from a variety of metals ranging from copper alloy (Hesiod *Schield of Heracles,* 122), tin (Homer *Iliad* xviii: 612, xxi: 592), and gold and silver (Virgil *Aeneid* vii: 634, viii: 624, xi: 488). The classical sources are less informative about the lining material but it may have been felt, cloth or leather.

A pair of greaves was one of the six elements which formed the complete equipment of a first rate Greek or Etruscan warrior, and later the early Roman soldier from the time of Servius Tullius (Livy *History of Rome* I: 43).[6] Polybius (vi: 23) tells us of *hastati* wearing greaves and Vegetius records that 'infantry were made to wear an iron greave on the right leg' (1: 20) and marines also wore greaves (4: 44). During the imperial period greaves were still being used (Aelius Lampridius *Severus*: 40).[7] The evidence for the use of greaves is far wider than has been supposed (Stephenson 1999, 45).

The basic greave is made from a single piece of metal. The starting point for production would be a billet of copper alloy that was then formed into a sheet. As greaves were made in large numbers it is likely that a template was made to draw the shape on a sheet of metal. This template would be a 'development' of the shape, as greaves are curved. The use of developments of curved shapes was clearly understood at this time. The shape may have been cut using a pair of shears, which are well attested in the Roman period. The forming of the curved profile of a greave is simple panel beating, and requires the level of skill possessed by any competent metal worker.

As with all Roman armour, greaves were probably made in large numbers (see Figure 106). Bishop and Coulston (2006, 64) cite presses that were used to form greaves, implying mass production. The press tools themselves would be easy to make from wood. Beam presses are well attested from the Roman period for pressing olives – there is no reason

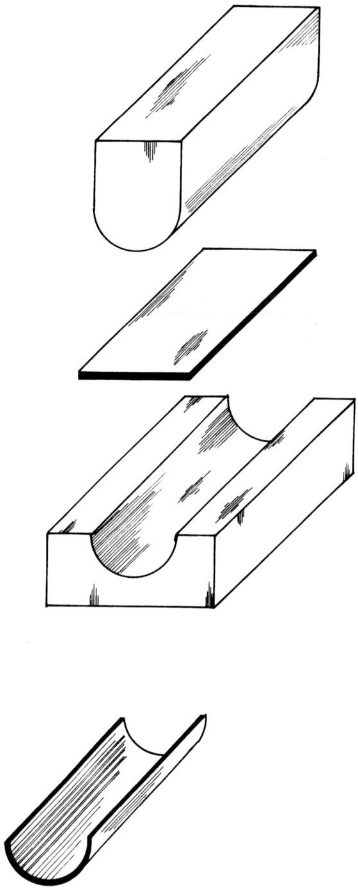

Figure 107: Schematic view of greave press tools

to suppose that this technology could not have been used in metalworking.

The press tools would be made from male and female matching cylinders. The difference in dimensions would be to allow the sheet of metal to fit between them. The top tool is then pressed into the bottom tool with the sheet of metal between them; the result is a curved sheet. An alternative method would be to make a bottom tool as shown in Figure 107 and hammer the sheet into it, using a wooden mallet.

The strength and rigidity of a greave made from thin sheet metal can be improved by introducing ribs into the surface; this acts in the same way as putting corrugations in a piece of paper. This can be achieved by using a punch with a convex shape on the end and hammering it into a lead block, thus producing the ridges seen on some greaves.

Whichever way they were made, either by hand or with the use of presses, they would have presented no technical obstacle to manufacture. Indeed a simple greave may have been no more than a sheet of metal curved into a gutter shape, worn over padding and attached to the leg with straps. The straps were attached to rings, and attached to the body of the greave by rivets. The greave was most commonly attached to the leg by leather cords (Plate 8a).

The need for padding behind a greave was even more important because the shin bone is so close to the skin. A greave worn without padding was of limited use because the kinetic energy of a blow would have been transmitted directly through the metal into the shinbone.

There is an example in the Vindonissa Museum (Bishop and Coulston 2006, 100) of padding for greaves possibly made from leather or other organic material. There is also a fragment of a copper alloy greave with a lining from Dura Europos.

The poor visibility of simple greaves in the archaeological record may be because they represented a good piece of metal for recycling.

Conclusion

The heavy infantry soldier had much of his body shielded by the *scutum*. However his limbs were sometimes exposed. The sword arm was exposed in combat while the shins and feet were exposed beneath the *scutum*.

The Roman army fought at close quarters in hand-to-hand combat. The sword was the principal weapon of the infantry and as such the sword arm was the closest point to the enemy. If left unprotected, it made the infantryman vulnerable to being disarmed. Segmented arm protection is now being found in larger numbers in various parts of the Empire, indicating that its use was wide spread. This makes sense as any soldier will always protect parts that are vulnerable. The weight of the arm armour was important and must not be so heavy as to restrict the arm, but strong enough to give protection. The legionary did not use the *gladius* to fence with; it was a weapon used for a thrusting attack, and so some restriction in arm movement was permissible.

The shin is another vulnerable part of the body. It is evident that greaves were worn by the infantry, cavalry and the marines. Greaves were relatively easy to make in during the Roman period, and required only basic sheet metal working skills to manufacture. They could have been mass-produced with only basic equipment such as press tools.

Notes

1 A few rare examples of greaves have been recovered with a hinged knee protector.

2 Hence, the reason modern sports such as football and cricket use shin pads to protect this region of the leg.

3 The full body *scutum* reduces this vulnerability.

4 The Danes landed on the west coast of Gotland, on 22 July overwhelming the farmer's attempts to block the landing. On the second day a battle at Fjäle Myr led to the death of a further 800–1000 farmers. On 27 July a final battle outside walls of Visby saw the death of 1800 more of the poorly armed and protected peasants. The discovery of three mass graves from this final battle between 1905 and 1928 has allowed osteoarchaeologists to study wound distribution (Blackburn *et al.* 2000, 1264).

5 16.6% were evident on the right tibia, 23.3% on the left, 3.5 on the right femur and 5.0 on the left, indicating that the peasants were victim to slashing blows from the left (Mays 1998, 179–181).

6 This early panoply consisted of a helmet, round shield, greaves, and mail coat, all of copper alloy, with a spear and sword as offensive weapons.

7 It was not just the military that benefited from leg protection; their use was evident in other walks of Roman life. For example protective leather leggings were worn by agricultural labourers (Pliny xix: 7; Palladius *de Re Rustica* I: 43) and by huntsmen (Horace *Satires* II: 3.234).

12. The Shield and Boss (*umbo*)

Introduction

The Roman shield included a number of metal parts. The most obvious and visible was the boss or *umbo*. Other metal components visible from the front of the shield included the edging strip or guttering found on some early imperial shields. These functional elements were sometimes complemented by decorative metal appliqués.

These highly visible, outward facing elements were sometimes complemented by less evident structural metal components such as reinforcing bars, and nails for attaching elements such as the *umbo*, guttering and appliqués. The shield was supported on the left arm through the use of a handgrip (*ansa*), and provided protection for the left shoulder. The most detailed description of a shield is provided by Polybius (vi: 23) during the mid-first century BC.

> 'The Roman panoply consists firstly of a shield, the convex surface of which measures two and a half feet in width and four feet in length, the thickness at the rim being a palm's breath. It is made of two planks glued together, the outer surface being then covered first with canvas and then with calf-skin. Its upper and lower rims are strengthened by an iron edging which protects it both from the cutting stokes of swords and from wear when resting on the ground. In the centre is fixed an iron boss, which turns aside the heavy impact of stones, spears and weighty missiles in general.'[1]

Polybius (vi: 21) records that their dimensions were 4ft by 2½ft. *Scuta* are sometimes referred to as *scuta longa* (Virgil *Aeneid* viii: 662; Josephus viii: 7.2).

The shield had a number of functions.

Defence

The primary function of a shield was defence. The *scutum* was adapted to the form of the human body, by being made oval, hexagonal or rectangular. It was curved so as to provide better protection by encircling the body. By increasing the size of the shield the Roman military was able to protect its infantry with comparatively light armour. The size and encircling nature of the Roman *scutum* may also have instilled confidence in the troops. Certainly during the Punic Wars Polybius considered that size of the *scutum* gave Roman soldiers a psychological advantage over the Carthaginians: 'Their arms also give the men both protection and confidence owing to the size of the shield'.

However, it should be noted that a *scutum* held in the defensive position close to the body severely restricts the arc of vision. A Roman soldier fighting at close quarters was unable to see the area below an opponent's chest, making him vulnerable to attacks to the feet and ankles. This was mitigated to some extent by the overall length of the *scuta*.

Offence

Of course, a shield could also be used as a weapon; if the shield was used to strike an opponent with a punching action then the protruding boss became an effective weapon that could overbalance him. *Suetonius* records just such an application of the shield at the Battle of Dyrrachium on 10 July 48 BC.[2] In this instance one of Caesar's badly wounded centurions Cassius Scaeva: 'boarded the ship and drove the enemy before him with the boss of his shield.'

Furthermore, the edge of the shield could also be used to drive up under the chin of an opponent, or down when he was on the ground. Metal guttering on the shield edge would increase the effect of this kind of blow.

Intimidation

The shield was also a tool of intimidation. The shield wall was an overwhelming obstacle. Furthermore, as Dio (Cassius Dio *Roman History* bk 15. IX.5) records, that during the capture of Syracuse the *scutum* was used as a means to instil psychological terror into the besieged city. At a given signal at the close of the siege the legionaries:

> 'raised a shout and struck their spears upon their shields, and the trumpeters blew a blast, with the result that utter panic overwhelmed the Syracusans.'

Identification

Because the shield obscured much of the body, unit identification could be difficult. The shield was therefore an ideal mechanism to signal unit affiliations. The comparatively large size meant that these unit affiliations could be seen from a considerable distance, making the job of the commanders controlling the battlefield easier.

> 'To prevent soldiers straying from their comrades at any time in the confusion of battle they painted different signs for different cohorts on the shields, digmata as they call themselves ... also the name of each soldier was inscribed in letters on the face of his shield, with a note of which cohort or century he was from.' (Vegetius 2: 18)

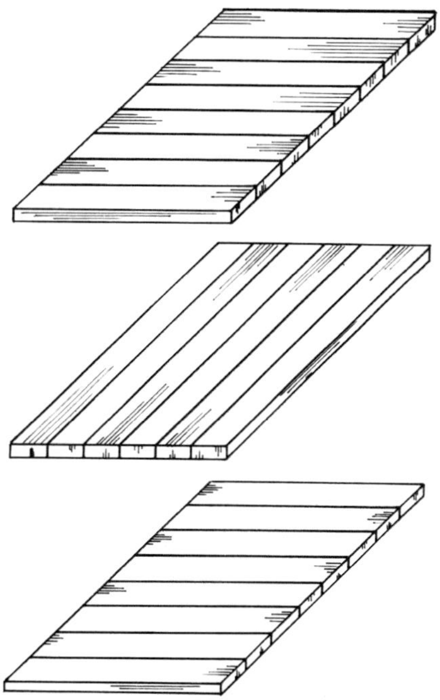

Figure 108: A schematic and simplified representation of triple layered Roman shield construction based on the example from Dura Europos

During the late first and early second centuries, Roman *scuta* took on the classic rectangular shape. Much of the technical knowledge of the construction of early Imperial *scuta* derives from the Dura Europos *scutum*. Although, this shield is securely dated to the mid-third century, it is likely that the method of construction parallels those of earlier periods. This shield was 106cm tall, 86cm wide around the curve, and 5–6mm thick. The shield was constructed of three layers of alternating horizontal and vertical birch strips (Figure 108). These strips would have been both light

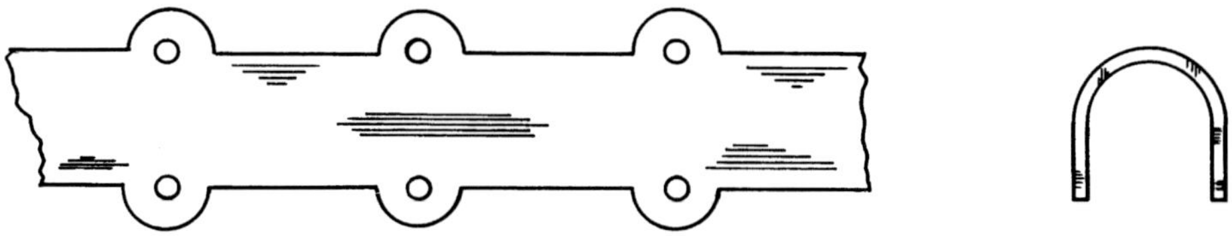

Figure 109: A schematic representation of 'tabbed' metal shield edging strip

and tough, an ideal construction for a shield, although not in themselves sufficient to prevent the shield being transfixed by some projectiles (see Vegetius 2: 15; and Arrian *Ars Tactica* 40: 6).

The type of glue used may have varied with different manufactures but the main types in use during this period were made from animal products (hide, bone and fish glues), casein, and those based on pitch and bitumen. The first two types are strong glues but are weakened when in contact with moisture and will eventually fail. Roman soldiers covered their shields with leather covers when not in action; it seems likely these covers were issued in order to keep shields dry.[3] In contrast pitch- and bitumen-based glues were waterproof. These glues were certainly used on Roman armour as attested by a first century BC helmet from Xanten. Analysis of glue traces revealed a product based on bitumen, bark pitch and animal grease.

Shield edging (guttering)

Some shields were provided with a metal edging strip. Such shield guttering appears to have had a variety of functions beyond the obvious protection of the edge from abrasion on the ground. The guttering would also have acted as an additional mechanism for the prevention of the entry of water and in conjunction with the nailing would have protected against delamination of the shield edge. The use of metal also makes the shield edge a more effective weapon.

Fragments of copper alloy edging strip have been recovered from Carnuntum, Austria (Bishop and Coulston 2006, 137) and Vindonissa in Switzerland. The edging strip could be either plain or tabbed. A schematic representation of the tabbed form can be seen in Figure 109. The strip was secured to the body of the shield by bending over the edge and nailing using the semi-circular tabs. Alternatively, plain edging strip was simply nailed through the guttering itself as in the case of the copper alloy shield edging from Sarmizegetusa, Romania, dating to the first half of the second century AD (D'Amato and Sumner 2009, 104). Such edging is represented in various monumental forms such as the Adamklissi metopes (see Figure 104) and Trajan's Column.

The construction typology of shield bosses

Roman shield bosses were constructed from either iron or copper alloy, with some hybrid forms combining both metals. The simplest in composition, and probably the earliest to produce, were made of a single sheet of either copper alloy or iron, formed into a

	Iron	*Copper alloy*	*Hybrid*
Single sheet	✓	✓	×
Double-skinned (loose)	✓	?	✓
Laminated (welded)	✓	×	×

Table 26: A comparison of shield boss typology with construction material

hemisphere with a flange. Holes in the flanges were punched to secure the boss to the body of the shield with nails.

Although superficially the *umbo* may appear to be one of the simpler components to construct, there may be greater complexity to the production of shield bosses than previously thought. Iron umbo can be made from single sheets or two seperate sheets loosely laminated together. In another form two sheets are welded together (Table 26).

Ferrous shield bosses

The simplest and most common form of *umbo* was the non-laminated variety composed of a single sheet of ferrous metal or copper alloy.

Figure 110 shows a flow diagram to produce a non-laminated shield boss using hand tools. It is seems likely that during the imperial period when large quantities of shield bosses were required, machinery such as drop hammers could have been used to increase the efficiency of production. To test this theory, a half-size drop hammer with a block and die was made specifically to produce shield bosses. The drop hammer has a (male) hemisphere in the hammer and a (female) hemisphere in the anvil. It was found that it was not possible to form a boss in a single strike; but if a set of collars were used, then the boss could be formed in three strikes with the metal cold and with no need for annealing. The resulting boss was ready for immediate use, and the work hardening of the operation had increased the hardness from100 VPN to 124 VPN.

If a hemisphere is made from sheet metal of uniform thickness, when the dome is formed the material will thin at the apex. If the hemisphere is made from sheet metal with a lens-shaped cross-section, then the thickness is likely to be uniform from the crown down to the edge. This is so when the forming is done by hand. The profile of a hemisphere will be uniform if it is made from material of the same thickness and produced by forming between a pair of dies.

There is no archaeological evidence of sheet metal with a lens-shaped cross-section, but the likelihood is that corrosion and cleaning when in service will have removed discrepancies in thickness.

Double-skinned ferrous shield bosses

Some shield bosses were constructed of not one but two layers of metal that were only connected by the rivets around the circumference. Two examples of these loose laminated shield bosses have been recovered from the fort at Vindolanda in the hinterland of Hadrian's Wall (accession numbers 6457 and 4656). The following iron example from Vindolanda (acc. no. 4656) although damaged, has a hemispherical dome with a hexagonal flange (Figure 111).

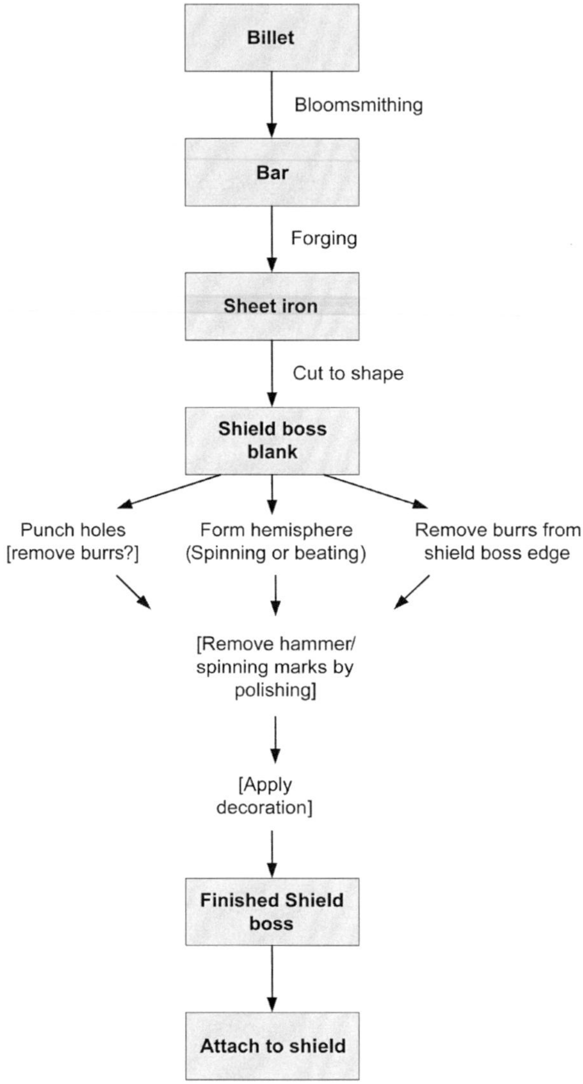

Figure 110: Flow diagram for the production of a non-laminated shield boss made from ferrous sheet

Although the domed hexagonal shape is a familiar Roman form, rather than being constructed from a single sheet of metal, the Vindolanda *umbo* has been assembled from two sheets of thin sheet iron which fit one inside the other, but are not welded together (Figure 112). The flange of the inner skin has been made larger than the outer, and has been folded over to pinch the outer skin, as can be seen in Figure 113.

The two *laminae* have been further secured by square rivets. The method of construction

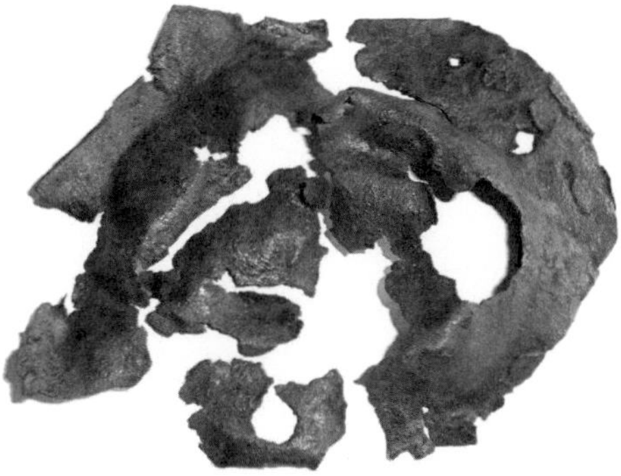

Figure 111: Fragments of a hexagonal laminated umbo *from Vindolanda (No. 4656)*

Figure 112: The laminated structure of the umbo

Figure 113: The folding of the outer edge as an additional mechanism to fasten together the two laminae

Figure 114: A bent rivet joining the two skins

is that both skins were held together and a square hole was punched through both skins (Figure 114). The metal from the outside layer was carried into the inner skin, locking them in place. A square tapering rivet or nail was put into the hole and then simply bent over. The burr on the inside of the punched hole opened out into four points, and the nail was folded between two of the points (Figure 114).

The outer skin is an average 0.78mm thick and the inner skin is 0.80mm. Substantial quantities of this sub-millimetre ferrous sheet would have been required for the production of shield bosses alone. At present no examples have been recovered of double-skinned shield bosses made from copper alloy, although there is no technological reason why loose double-skinned shield bosses could not have been so produced. A hypothetical production sequence for the manufacture of a double-skinned *umbo* is shown in Figure 115.

Roman smiths and artisans were familiar with riveting or welding sheets of metal together to form a single piece; examples are known from some cavalry parade face masks (Meijers and Weller 2007) and some scale armour. Double-skinned shield bosses conferred a number of benefits:

- Such thin metal could be easily formed to shape in a simple press using tools made from hard wood. This was unskilled work. The folding over of the edge to hold

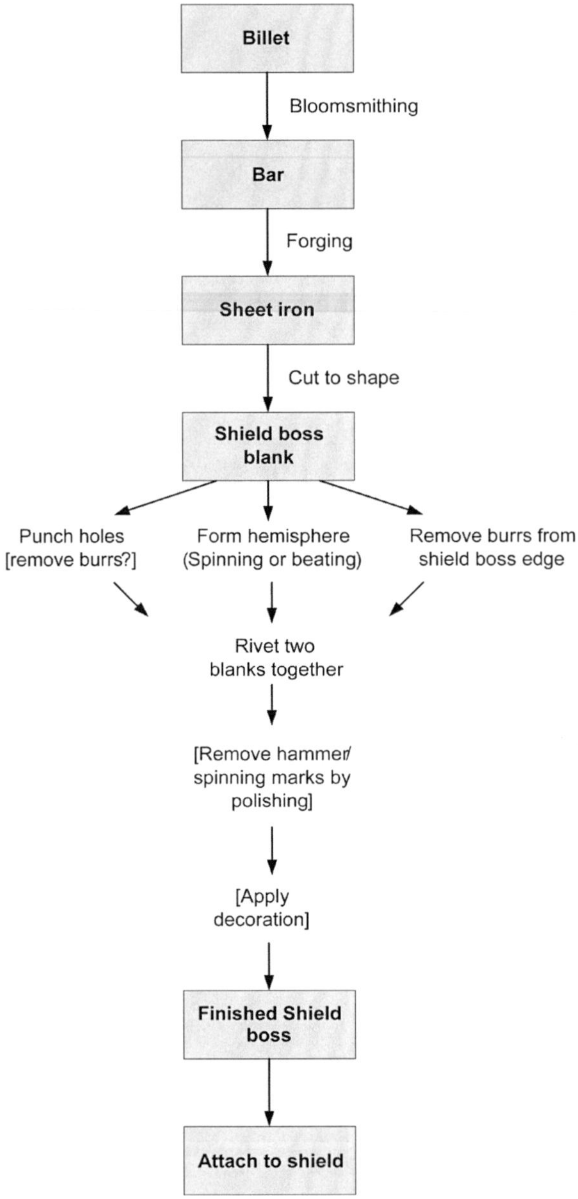

Figure 115: Flow diagram for the production of a double-skinned shield boss

the skins together made the punching of the rivet holes and the punching of the holes to fix the boss to the shield is very simple. The joining together of the skins using bent nails meant that the layers could easily be separated to effect repairs and required very little skill. These points provide a strong indication that laminated bosses were relatively cheap to make.

- A multi-layer structure may well have provided a greater degree of protection than a single layered metal structure by more effectively diffusing kinetic impact energy.

It is likely that these double-skinned shield bosses are under-represented in the archaeological record for a number of reasons. The loose layers can easily separate during burial or alternatively the skins could corrode together so superficially resembling a single piece. Furthermore, the structure may look superficially like the delamination of iron that takes place when the material is mineralized.

Laminated shield bosses (welded)

Another form of *umbo* was constructed of layers of metal that were welded together to form a highly resilient structure. The first century AD iron shield boss from Melrose shown in Figure 116 is composed of two layers of steel, which were welded to a layer of iron, with an outer layer of high-carbon (harder) steel (Figure 117).[4] The separate pieces show very few slag inclusions; the majority of inclusions are at what are thought to be the weld lines. The laminated structure would afford a construction that was both tough and flexible. Figures 118 and 119 show the same area of the sample, but at different magnifications. The outside was hard, while the back was tough; this was an ideal construction for armour. The hard surface provided resistance to penetration and the tough back absorbed the energy of the impact.

Figure 116: A first century AD shield boss from the legionary fortress at Melrose

Thickness measurements from the Melrose *umbo* are shown in Table 27. There is only a slight reduction in the thickness of the metal between the flange and the crown. From the table it can be seen that the last position measured is quite close to what would have been the apex of the boss. The grain size shows that the metal was heated and left to cool in air; this will have reduced the stresses set up during forging. This indicates that it is possible that the boss was formed hot between a pair of shaped dies. Cold worked steel shows more significant thinning compared to hot-worked steel.

Position	*Transect 1*	*Transect 2*	*Transect 3*	*Transect 4*	*Transect 5*
A (Crown)	0.96	0.78	0.91	0.85	0.94
B	0.83	0.77	0.86	0.87	0.96
C	0.93	0.77	0.78	0.89	0.89
D	0.57	0.85	0.98	0.94	0.76
E	0.96	0.80	0.70	0.95	0.96
F (Flange)	0.80	0.87	0.92	0.98	0.90
Average	0.75	0.81	0.86	0.91	0.90

Table 27: Thickness at different points across the first century AD Roman shield boss from Melrose. Measurements started at the flange and were taken in steps of 5mm. All dimensions are in millimetres

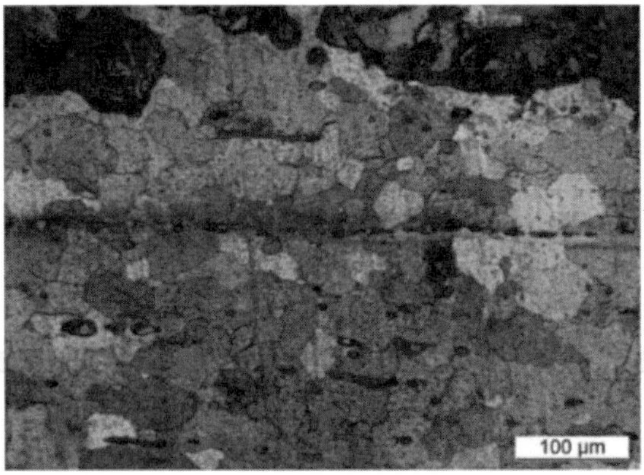

Figure 117: Micrograph of a first century AD shield boss from the legionary fortress at Melrose showing detail of slag inclusions at what is thought to be the weld lines (Magnification ×200)

Figure 118: Micrograph of a first century AD shield boss from the legionary fortress at Melrose showing the multi-layered structure (Magnification ×100)

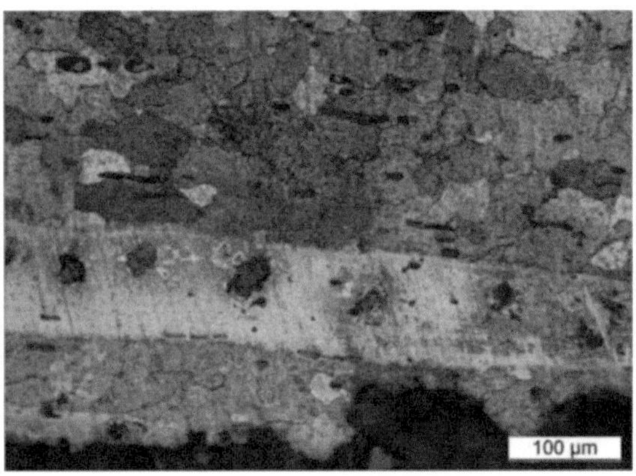

Figure 119: Micrograph of a first century AD shield boss from the legionary fortress at Melrose (Magnification ×200)

Figure 120: Diameter 21cm Trajanic period bronze tinned; battle damage is evident

Decoration

Shield bosses can be further divided into plain and decorated. The decorated bosses can also be divided into those that were solely for sports use and display and those that would have been used in combat but had been decorated either by their owner or by a specialist metalworker simply to enhance the soldier's appearance. Such decoration would be both visually appealing and would not interfere with the functionality of the shield boss. Many shield bosses had decoration produced by a combination of engraving and repousé. These would have been far too expensive to be subjected to the rigors of warfare. The shield boss shown in Figure 120, although highly decorated, has been damaged probably as a result of combat. The decoration on it is produced purely by engraving, and this has not lowered the defensive properties of the boss.

The shield boss is of bronze and is highly decorated. The standard of the workmanship indicates the work of a skilled professional metal-worker. The damage is most likely the result of battle damage. It shows that in this case decorated armour was used in battle. The quality of the decoration on the *umbo* is very high. The dedications in Latin using Greek letters record that the piece was dedicated by Flavius Volussinus to the memory of Marcus Ulpius, member of the *equites singulares*.[5] On the flange of the boss are numerous examples of armour such as crossed shields, greaves, *musculata*, helmets, and two victories holding *clipeii* with punched inscriptions. The *cuppa* has a central face of Medusa, surrounded by numerous Roman gods (Mars, Apollo, Jupiter, Hercules, Bacchus). Furthermore there is a Roman cavalry soldier riding down a barbarian. The disk-headed shield nails are decorated with Medusa heads. Figure 121 shows the production sequence for the manufacture of a boss.

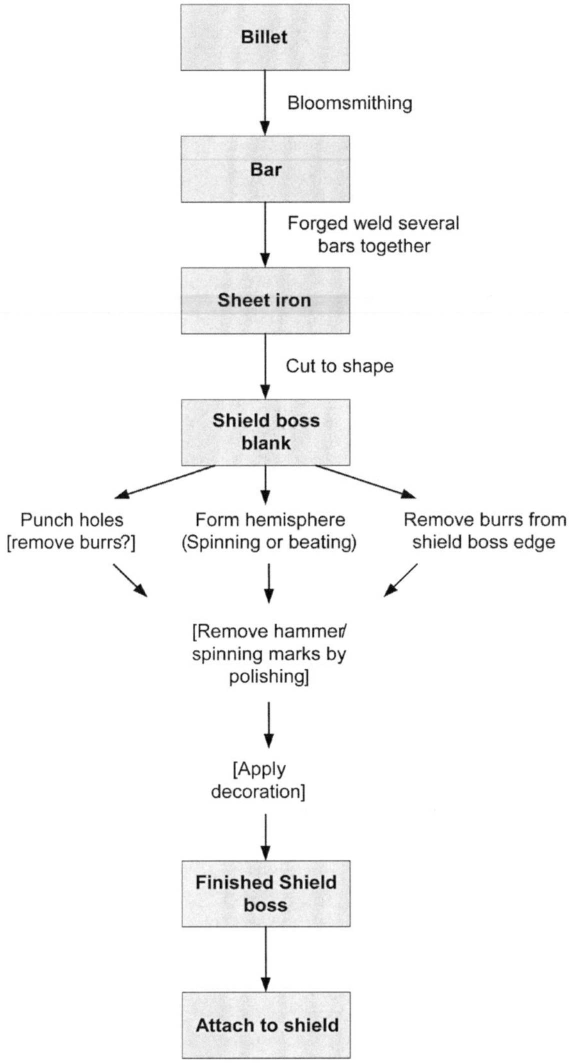

Figure 121: Flow diagram for the production of a laminated (welded) shield boss

Other materials

The *umbo* was only one component of the shield. Apart from the supply of iron and/or copper alloy for the metal components, wood and leather were required in large quantities for shield production (Polybius vi: 23).

Wood

The construction of the average Roman *scutum* required a considerable quantity of wood. Approximately 1m^2 of wood was needed for each sheet of laminate used. In addition to this plywood needed for the body of the shield, wood was also required in some cases for handles and reinforcing bars. Alternatively withies have been recorded as being used to form a wicker frame, upon which a leather cover was placed. Therefore, the military would have also been concerned with securing the supply of wood and withies.

Pliny in his *Natural History* (16: 209) notes that some woods are preferentially used for shield construction:

> 'The trees that have the coldest wood of all are all that grow in water; but the most flexible, and consequently the most suitable for making shields, are those in which an incision draws together at once and closes up its own wound, and which consequently is more obstinate in allowing steel to penetrate; this class contains the vine, agnus castus, willow, lime, birch, elder and both kinds of poplar.'

Leather

With a shield covering a surface area of approximately 1m^2, this required a significant proportion of a cowhide. Furthermore, there was also the shield cover which protected the shield when not in use (cf. Driel-Murray 1988). The Roman army was a prodigious user and consumer of leather – everything from tents, clothes, saddles, and armour lining required leather. Leather could have been secured as a by-product of feeding the troops. However, a complex supply network was required.

Conclusions

During the Imperial period the Roman *umbo* was made in a number of forms. Most commonly bosses were constructed using a single sheet of ferrous metal or copper alloy. Another group were of a double-skinned (loose) construction, and another group were laminated (welded). The use of laminated sheet joined together by welding presented an ideal form of armour, in that the outer layer was made from harder steel to deflect blows, whilst the backing layers were made from a tougher material, which would help to absorb energy. Each technique conferred a range of advantages and disadvantages and none can be considered superior to any of the others.

Notes

1 Treloar (1971) Argues that the translation does not indicate that the shield was a palm's breath (3in, *c.* 74mm) at the rim but that this was the depth of the curve of the shield.

2 The Battle of Dyrrachium (sometimes referred to as Dyrrhachium) took place during Caesar's civil war on 10 July 48 BC. In the battle in what is now Albania, Gnaeus Pompeius Magnus defeated Gaius Julius Caesar.

3 An experiment was conducted by the authors on a reconstruction of two Roman shields – one joined with fish glue and the other with casein. They were exposed to the elements during the summer months and examined every day. It rained twice during the first 5 days and by day 5 the strips of wood had become detached from each other by the action of moisture in the atmosphere.

4 The iron shield boss from Melrose (Edinburgh FRA 167) weighs 38g. Metallography reveals a banded structure comprising six bands. The first layer is steel (0.6% carbon from the pearlite to ferrite ratio). The second thin layer is decarburized steel – light etching due to a lower proportion of carbon containing pearlite grains. The third is steel of around 0.6% carbon. The fourth is composed of white etched ferrite grains (iron not steel), the black areas being penetrative rust. The fifth layer is steel with a carbon content

of 0.6–0.7% (from the ferrite to pearlite ratio) and of finer grain size (35μm mean diameter) than that of the third layer 50μm. The sixth layer is ferrite. These details suggest: layers 1 and 3 were steel pieces welded together – layer 2 being original surface decarburization. Steel piece 3 contains more slag inclusions than steel piece 1 and is therefore almost certainly a different piece of metal. Layer 4 is a piece of iron, being too thick to be decarburization of steel piece 3. Layer 5 is the outermost steel layer (and is different from the other pieces) with its decarburized surface as layer 6.

5 For further information see exhibition catalogue *Alles geritzt: Botschaften aus der antike* 69a, 40–1. Munich Archeological Museum (private collection).

13. Conclusions

The Roman army was composed of troops that fought in the field: infantry and cavalry; and those who fought on water: sailors and marines. At the period of history covered in this book the number of men under arms in the Roman army on both land and water was probably in the region of 300,000 to 400,000.

It was a time of considerable military activity in many parts of the Empire with constant conflict taking place. In time of war the losses of arms and armour were large. Equipment was lost in conflict and never recovered. Other equipment was damaged beyond repair and although it could be cannibalized to make other items the original had to be replaced. This meant that there was a constant need for new armour and arms. The Roman iron industry fulfilled that need. It was a huge industry comprising mining for ore, the production of charcoal for smelting and smithing and the acquisition of clay for building smelting furnaces. Examination of a large number of pieces of Roman armour has revealed much of it was made from a ferrous metal that has very low slag inclusions. In some cases there is no slag at all. This does not accord with the results known from the bloomery process where the bloom is a mass of slag and iron. Experiments have shown that repeated heating and hammering will not remove the slag. The conclusion is that in some instances the slag was not in the iron when the armour was made and that the iron was made by a hitherto unknown method of iron making that produced a liquid metal that was then processed into workable iron.

The industry employed a large number of skilled blacksmiths for forging armour and weapons and personnel to assemble coats of armour and finish them for use. It is almost impossible to give any figures for the size of the workforce employed in the iron making and armaments industries. It is obvious that at this time the Roman war machine gave employment to a huge number of people. When the call to arms is made an army cannot wait for its equipment to be produced before it goes to war; the equipment has to be to hand. This means that stockpiles of weapons had to be available to make the army ready for action. During a conflict there has to be a constantly replenished reserve of equipment. This constant need means that production has to be at a speed that can at least keep pace with demand but a better scenario is for supply to exceed demand. To accomplish this, production systems have to be as fast as possible. The production of armour is time consuming. Traditional methods of manufacture based on manpower alone will not be able to keep pace with demand. It is clear that supply did keep pace with demand and under these circumstances the most likely possibility is that manufacture was undertaken by a system that exploited both manpower and simple mechanical devices. There was a constant need for new iron to be produced. Some damaged items could be recycled but recycling will not meet demand because every time recycling takes place, significant amounts of metal is permanently lost, therefore the amount of metal in the recycling pool is constantly diminishing.

The question of the use of machines to aid the production of Roman armour has been highly contentious. Much is made of the fact that there is no literary evidence for the use of machines in armour production, nor is there pictorial or archaeological evidence. And yet archaeologists are confident that machines such as lathes were used in the production process of some helmet bowls. This is clearly evident because the diagnostic marks from the spinning process can be seen on these helmets. However, there is no literary evidence for helmet bowls being spun, neither is there pictorial nor archaeological evidence of lathes. It is the evidence from the object that tells archaeologists that lathes were used. The issue is that not all machines leave such clearly diagnostic evidence. Also where diagnostic evidence does exist it may be obliterated during later production processes. For example, a consistent thickness of sheet metal indicative of rolling could be obscured by later working of the metal or post-depositional processes such as corrosion.

Until well into the nineteenth century most machines were made of wood, which does not survive well in the archaeological record. As archaeologists have been taught that large machines were not in use in the Roman period they will not be on the look-out for them, yet large machines such a lifting cranes are shown on Trajan's Column.

The argument for machines is further strengthened by the dimensional accuracy exhibited by much Roman armour, both ferrous and non-ferrous. Experiments by the authors have shown that the degree of accuracy is not possible using hand-held hammers and even drop hammers would not produce the same results. The conclusion is that the strip metal for armour was often made using a system of rollers.

Pile drivers are known to have existed and it is quite reasonable to suggest that such heavier types of machines were used in the manufacture of armour and arms, as well as in the iron industry for processing iron ore through its various stages from ore to finished billet.

Supply on such a large scale cannot be conducted if the armour had to be made to fit individuals and it is most likely that they were made to a set design and in a limited number of sizes (e.g. small, medium, large). There is a standard at work here and although it was not to the exacting standards of modern manufacturing, the similarity of sizes seen in Roman armour and arms gives the notion of standards much creditability. Adjusting the thickness of the garment worn underneath the armour can do much to help armour fit an individual.

The under-garment plays a crucial role in the effectiveness of armour, because any armour system relies on a minimum of three components: the armour itself, the garment worn underneath the armour, and the body of the wearer. All these elements affect the way the armour behaves. The design of the armour has to fulfil many roles. It has to be effective at protecting the wearer. It has to comfortable, if not the soldier will not wear it. It has to have an appearance that will make the wearer feel empowered when he wears it, and it has to intimidate those who are going to attack it. Combat at this time was hand-to-hand and Rome's enemies would have seen armour at close quarters. Its appearance was very important because of the psychological effect, but also the finish will have a profound effect on the armour's life expectancy. Iron very quickly rusts; this diminishes its intimidatory effect, but it also will weaken the armour when the rust is cleaned off. Cleaning with abrasives removes a small amount of metal from the surface, and each time it is cleaned it becomes thinner, gradually reducing its effectiveness. This problem was clearly understood and many examples of different types of surface finish can be found on Roman armour. Such as the application of gold and silver leaf as well as tin that has been applied as a liquid (tinning).

The iron oxide formed in forging reduces corrosion, and when the hot forging is quenched in oil the protection is increased. This also produces a black shiny appearance to the armour that can have a similar psychological effect as polished armour.

It is likely that individual legionaries would have saved themselves much work by keeping their armour protected from rust by smearing it with animal fat or vegetable oil, of which there would have been large quantities in any camp. Armour even when given a protective coating needs to be polished from time to time and experiments by the authors have shown that easily available abrasives such as sand, wood ash, powdered pottery and powdered glass are very effective polishing agents, and when mixed with a small amount of carrier such as animal fat are easy to use.

During the time covered in this book the Roman army was using armour made from ferrous metal alongside that made from copper alloy. The fact that copper alloy was not used for the making of weapons of war clearly shows that the superiority of iron for weapons was understood. The techniques used for working iron are the same as those used for working bronze and it is likely that most metal-workers (blacksmiths) were proficient in working both metals using forging techniques. The most significant difference between the metals is that copper alloy can be cast at a temperature of around 1000°C (depending on the alloy) whereas iron requires temperatures in excess of 1200°C. In the case of copper alloy helmets there are examples of manufacture taking place using two completely different methods of production – raising and spinning – and it seems likely the same types of production systems were used to make iron helmets. Given that copper alloys are considerably more expensive than iron to produce and that they potentially offer a lower defensive index for armour than iron, the question arises, why were the two metals used side by side for the manufacture of armour? With the current state of knowledge this is a question that needs considerably more research to be conducted before a satisfactory answer can be reached.

With any form of armour there is always some form of trade off between protecting the wearer from harm and the restrictions the armour imposes. An un-armoured man has ease of bodily movement, clear visibility and hearing, but no form of protection. Considerable thought was exercised in the design of Roman armour to minimise the restrictions of armour. Helmets were made to protect the head from blows coming from every direction. Ears were protected but the ear was still exposed enough to not impede hearing. Cheek pieces protected the face but did not restrict vision and the other furniture provided re-enforcing at vulnerable places such as the crown on the helmet bowl.

Scale armour (*lorica squamata*) provided protection that would stop most weapons. Because the scales are imbricated most areas on the coat have at least two thickness of metal. The disadvantage was that it was heavy, and with many seperate components it could incur high maintenance costs. The weight of armour is a factor that would slow the wearer down but in the Roman army the ordinary legionary was extremely fit and trained in his armour. Constant use combined with a very fit man is a good indication that once the wearer was used to the armour he would be able to overcome the restrictions imposed by its weight. This type of armour was quick and easy to make, was robust and easy to repair both in the workshop and, more importantly, in the field.

Armour made from strip (*lorica segmentata*) was light and easy to produce. Its main disadvantage was that if a strip was damaged it would be necessary to replace the whole strip, although the damaged portion could be reused for other items. From the surviving example and the figures shown on various Roman reliefs it appears that this type of armour only extended as far as the waist of the wearer leaving the groin unprotected. It is unlikely that this was so but at the time of writing the nature of the groin protection is still a matter of debate.

The Roman army used the sword as its major weapon for close quarter fighting, whereas the spear was used by most other nations. Therefore amour for the sword arm was essential. There are examples of arm armour made from strips of iron overlapping each other. It is quite possible that other types of armour were used to protect the arm. The legionaries also carried a shield and the hand holding it was protected by a shield boss often made of iron, but there are also many surviving examples of bosses made from copper alloy. The shield itself protected most of the body but it was a heavy item and when the shield bearer took cover behind it he was protected but then had no visibility. To see he would have to put his head at least to the level of his nose above the top of the shield.

The shin is a vulnerable part on the body with little tissue covering the shin bone on the front of the leg. Protection was afforded by a greave or, most probably, a pair of greaves. These would have been worn over a thick padding to absorb the energy from blows. Examples of greaves made from both iron and copper alloy can be found.

Some Roman iron armour was made from metal that had little or in some cases no slag in it at all. It was made to such a high degree of accuracy the only likely method of production was rollers. The amount of armour produced would have needed the use of machines to meet demand.

The Roman legionary was the best trained fighting man of his day, equipped as he was with armour of such a high degree of sophistication it is little wonder the Roman army of the Early Empire was viewed with so much fear by its enemies.

Appendix 1
The Survival of Ancient Machines

The manufacture of machines made entirely from metal was not widespread until the nineteenth century. Until that time the principle material for the manufacture of machines was wood. Other materials such as metal comprised only a small percentage of the machine, such as cutting components, bearings, hinges or bolts. Wood was usually more plentiful and cheaper to acquire than metals. In the case of the military ballista, siege towers and battering rams, etc, were mostly composed of wood.

Such machinery need not have been sophisticated to function correctly. The example shown in Figure 122 is a simple wooden machine used for raising water. It is all wood and animal powered. Mechanically it is low in efficiency but this is not a concern because it fulfils the need to raise water, and as long as it does that, the efficiency is a low consideration to the people who use it.

Figure 123 shows a crude bearing composed of three pieces of wood roughly attached to each other. By modern standards it is crude but this type of bearing fulfils its task and when any part wears out it can easily be replaced.

In the hands of a skilled workman a very crude and simple machine (such as a pole lathe) can be used to produce very precise work. Machines are made to fulfil a special need as long as the need is met then the efficiency of the machine takes second place.

Figure 122: A machine made of wood and driven using animal power, from Luxor, Egypt (2007)

Figure 123: A simple wooden machine from Luxor, Egypt (2007)

The earliest steam engines were about only 2% efficient but they were viable because the work they did (pumping out water from mines) was virtually impossible without them.

After the machine had fulfilled its function the wood and timber could be recycled, or alternatively used as fuel. This was the fate of many of the wooden machines that had been used in Luxor, Egypt, until recently. When they were replaced with modern machines inhabitants used them for firewood. Even if wooden machinery was to survive the depredations of scavengers the wood would be highly unlikely to survive in the archaeological record. The preservation of isolated items of machinery such as the water raising wheel from Dolaucothi, Wales, or the two water lifting devices from London[1] are a function of the exceptional preservational environment. The use of several water powered mills from the Roman period can be seen at Barbegal, France (Hodge 1990).

A machine is a mechanical device that will aid and/or speed up production and lessen the amount of physical effort that has to be applied to a particular task. Many of these machines would have been composed primarily of wood and so have a low archaeological visibility.

Appendix 2
One-sided Carburization

Many items of Roman armour examined have been found to be made of several layers of ferrous metal with differing carbon content. Scales subjected to metallographic examination from the Carlisle Hoard revealed a laminated structure. The outer surface layer has a higher carbon content than that which backs it. This is an ideal composition for armour in that it has a hard outside layer supported by a tough back.

It is not clear how this layering was achieved. It is possible that it was a product of smithing a bloom with areas of high and low carbon content but this is unlikely, because it would be impossible to determine where in the structure the layers were positioned. A more realistic proposition is that carburizing (also called case hardening) only one side of the armour to raise its carbon content produced this structure. A series of experiments was conducted to determine a method that would produce one-sided carburization.

Carburization

Low carbon steel or iron items were placed in contact with carbon rich material inside a container that was then sealed. The container was then heated to a temperature between 900°C and 950°C and held at this temperature for several hours (the duration of this heating is dependent on the depth of case required). This causes carbon to be absorbed into the outside of the iron and converts it to steel.

Experiments to produce single sided carburisation

The objective of these experiments was to reproduce the structure found in the scale armour found at Carlisle.[2] This scale has a layer of high carbon steel backed by a layer of low carbon iron. It appears to have been case hardened. The containers were made from clay that had been baked to remove all moisture but they were not fired. The carbon rich material was course powdered charcoal. The samples were copies of the Carlisle scales with the holes punched and the burrs left in place. They were all cut from the same sheet of mild steel 0.9mm thick.

Experiment 1

Two samples were laid on a bed of sand inside a baked clay tray. It was pressed into the sand so that only one-third of the sample remained above the level of the sand. The samples were covered with powdered charcoal. A lid was placed on top of the tray and sealed with wet clay. The wet clay seal was left for 24 hours to allow it to become dry. The whole tray was then placed inside a furnace that was already heated to 950°C for three hours. The tray was removed and allowed to cool in air. A sample was prepared for metallographic examination and etched. The structure revealed that the sample had carburized completely. This is clearly not the method used for one-sided carburization.

Experiment 2

Two pieces of 1.5mm thick mild steel were wired together face to face were put into finely powdered charcoal in a clay container with the lid sealed with clay. They were heated to 925°C for three hours. The structure was found to be almost fully carburized.

Experiment 3

It was observed that when the scales were placed with the inner surfaces face-to-face the burr acted as spacers and there was a gap between them. Two scales were placed with the inside surfaces face to face, and wet clay was put between them. The clay was allowed to dry. They were then put into finely powdered charcoal and heated to 925°C for three hours. On examination it was found that carburization had only taken place on the surfaces in contact with the charcoal, the faces at the joint filled with clay had not hardened. Hardness tests were carried out to determine hardness and compare the results with the original. The original sample had a hardness value of 238VPN; the experimental sample a value of 231VPN. The experiment was repeated six times and in each experiment only the outer layer was carburized.

Conclusion

If the two pieces of iron are wired together face to face with clay in between them and carburized, then carburization will only take place on the outside face. This is one method that will produce the same microstructure that is seen on some types of Roman armour.

Notes

1 Excavated by Museum of London Archaeological Service at 30 Gresham Street. London in 2001.
2 Original sample from Durham Ref number M15 CAROO.

Glossary

Annealing: Heating steel to a high temperature (red hot) and holding at this temperature for a time, followed by slow cooling. This renders the steel in the softest possible condition and relieves stress. The blacksmith's method of annealing is to keep the steel in the forge for five to seven minutes, then to bury it in ash.
Bar: A length of iron forged to a cross section, (round, square, rectangular, etc) suitable to be forged into artefacts.
Blank: A section of metal roughly shaped to the form of the finished item.
Billet: A block of purified iron with only a small quantity of slag present.
Bloom: Iron which has been produced in a semi-solid state, as a product of the direct process of iron production, or reduction of the iron ore. A bloom is a mass of unrefined wrought iron with large quantities of entrapped slag and voids in the structure.
Bloom-smithing: A secondary operation that is carried out after direct production of bloom iron to consolidate the bloom produced by the expulsion of entrapped slag.
Blunt force trauma: The tissue damage caused by the transfer of kinetic energy is called blunt force trauma.
Brow band: A decorative strip of sheet metal, usually copper alloy but occasionally silver that runs along the front rim of the bowl of a helmet, usually with a simple embossed motif.
Brow guard: A metal peak riveted to either side of the helmet bowl in the region of the temples, which projects forward from the bowl. One function is to deflect downward blows away from the face of the wearer.
Carburizing: See case hardening.
Case hardening: A method of hardening the surface of a metal while keeping the interior soft. This is usually accomplished by heating the metal while it is in contact with a carbon rich material and holding it at this temperature for several hours (see steeling or cementation).
Cast iron: Iron which has been produced from its liquid state, and which contains between 1.8% to 4.5% carbon. The product is extremely brittle and is unsuitable for forging but suitable for casting.
Cementation (steeling): A process used for carburizing soft iron bars to make steel. The bars were heated for several days in contact with carbon.
Charge: The ore and fuel, of the correct weight ratio, which are loaded into the shaft furnace prior to smelting.
Cheek piece: (Buccullae) A hinged, shaped plate on either side of a helmet which offered protection to the cheek and jaw of the wearer. The shape of a cheek piece is largely dictated by the line of the jaw, the cheekbone, and the forehead, with cut-outs (see cusps) in the region of the eye and mouth. Some pieces had flanges on their rear and lower edges to deflect blows outwards.
Cinder: The drossy solid material that collects at the top of the molten slag. This has never achieved a free-flowing condition in the furnace.
Cusp: A cut-out in the front edge of a cheek piece positioned to accommodate the eye and the mouth of the wearer, whilst allowing the rest of the cheek piece to offer maximum protection to the wearer's face.

Cold chisel: Chisel for cutting metal that is in the cold condition.
Development: In sheet metal working pattern development is the production of a blank from which a product is created. The development is the blank.
Drawing down: The process where the cross-section of a bar is reduced by heating and hammering. During the process the length of the bar increases correspondingly.
Drifting: A process carried out after punching to bring a hole to an accurate size and shape. The drift is a piece of hard steel forged to a taper.
Falx: Single bladed weapeon with a sharpened inside edge.
Ferrite: Pure iron consists of 100% ferrite and ferrite is the principal constituent of low carbon steel.
Fire welding: See Welding.
Flaring: Hammering the end of a bar into a dovetail shape.
Flat: The term used to describe the rectangular cross-section formed on the end of the bar by hammering.
Flatter: Similar to a hammer but is held and struck with a sledge hammer to smooth out surface irregularities in the bar.
Flux: Substance mixed with or applied to metal surface to promote fusion.
Foil: A very thin sheet of metal that has been formed by hammering or rolling.
Forge welding: See Welding.
Form tools: Made in pairs that are the reverse shape of the finished product. A blank of hot metal is placed between them and struck with a heavy force thus forming the desired shape.
Fullering: Metal is placed between two shaped tools that are struck with a hammer; this decreases the cross section and increase the length.
Gangue: The unwanted component of the iron ore which can either be removed during preparation or during smelting. Gangue minerals such as silica, calcia and alumina which are slagged-off during smelting take a proportion of the iron with them as flux.
Hardening: Steel is heated to a suitable temperature depending on carbon content; 870°C for 0.2% carbon to 760°C for 1.0% carbon and is then rapidly cooled by quenching it in water or oil. The resulting hardness will depend on the original carbon content of the steel.
Hardy hole: Square hole in an anvil to receive tools such as bottom swages, or chisels.
Hammer scale: Iron oxide that forms on the surface of iron when heated during forging.
Hot set: Blacksmith's chisel used for cutting metal in the hot condition (red heat and above).
Lap: A defect caused by a portion of steel being folded over on itself and failing to weld on further working.
Lapped: Obtaining a precision fit by rotating male and female parts with an abrasive material between them.
Lobate: Lobed, usually used in the context of the lobate hinges of segmental armour.
Mandrel: Metal rod round which other metal items are forged to shape.
Neck guard: That part of the helmet at the rear of the bowl, usually protruding at an angle below the horizontal, and designed to deflect blows outwards and away from the shoulders.
Punching: A punch is driven through metal to create a hole the same shape as the punch (see drifting).
Pein (of a hammer): One face of a hammer head that is shaped to perform a special task, i.e. a ball for making hemispherical indentations in the surface of a piece of metal.
Piled wrought iron: Wrought iron is rolled into strips, and then cut into short lengths. The

lengths are built up into a pile, placed into a furnace called a balling furnace and heated until the strips fuse. At this point it is removed and welded under a power hammer. The quality of the iron is determined by how many times this process is repeated i.e. once piled, twice piled and so on.

Plastic condition: When a metal is in its most malleable condition.

Punctim: Punched decoration or identification marks.

Repousé: A method of decorating metalwork by the use of various shaped punches applied to the back face of sheet.

Scarfed: A method of joining ends of a piece of metal by bevelling or notching so that they overlap without increasing the thickness.

Silvering: The application of a thin foil of silver, often held in place by tin solder (so its traces can be confused with tinning).

Slag: The silicate complex formed by the combination of earthy material amalgamated with the ore, in conjunction with some of the iron oxide in the charge acting as a flux.

Steel: An alloy of pure iron and carbon. Steels containing more than 0.3% carbon can be flame hardened.

Steeling: A process by which wrought iron is converted into steel by packing the iron with carbon in a container and heating it for long periods. The carbon is absorbed into the wrought iron thus converting it to steel.

Stress raisers: A point in a material where stresses are concentrated and where it will fracture, i.e. at a sharp corner, a sharp change of section, or a slag inclusion

Striker: Blacksmith's assistant who stands opposite the blacksmith and wields a heavy sledge hammer.

Stringers: Present in wrought iron in the form of slag. Slag starts as large inclusions and as the bloom is reduced in cross-section and increases in length, the slag does the same and forms long string-like inclusions within the iron.

Swaging: Metal is worked to the desired shape by a series of blows from a hammer onto a pair of suitably shaped dies.

Tap slag: The slag which has been removed from the bloomery furnace in a molten state, during the smelting process. This is a prerequisite of the use of a slag-tapping furnace.

Tempering: Hardened steels are brittle. The brittleness is removed by heating the steel to between 210°C and 330°C then quenching in oil or water. This removes the brittleness at the expense of some of the hardness.

Tinning: The application of a thin wash of molten tin to a copper alloy or iron object for decorative or protective purposes.

Tuyère: The tube, normally of clay, passing through the wall of the furnace to take the air blast from the bellows.

Ultimate tensile stress: The highest load applied in breaking a tensile test piece divided by the original cross-sectional area of the test piece.

Upsetting: Metal is heated and forged in such a way that the length decreases and the cross-section increases.

Welding: The process in which two pieces of iron are heated to white heat and hammered together causing them to fuse.

Wrought iron: Iron produced by the direct (bloomery) process. The structure is iron with 0.04% carbon and 0.2% slag. It is ductile and malleable.

Latin Terms

Ansa: Horizontal handgrip for a shield.
Armamentarium: Area for weapons storage.
Armicustos: Soldier responsible for the administration and supply of weapons and equipment.
Artifex: Artisan.
Auxilia: Auxiliaries.
Auxiliaris: An auxiliary soldier.
Balteus: The military belt.
Bucculla: A helmet cheek piece.
Cassis: Helmet
Caliga: Military footwear.
Centuria: From the Latin for a 'hundred'; military unit of some thirty to two hundred foot soldiers.
Centurio: The centurion, or 'commander of hundred'.
Clipeus: Buckler.
Comminus: Close quarter fighting.
Conditorium: Depot.
Conductor: A supply contractor.
Congeries armorum: A quantity of military equipment.
Cornicen: A junior officer in the Roman army whose role was to signal salutes to officers and sound orders to the legions using the *cornu*.
Cornu: A military horn.
Cratis: A shield of wickerwork.
Crista: The helmet crest.
Crista transversa: A transverse helmet crest used as an identification for a centurion during the first century AD.
Cristatus: Crested.
Cura copiarum: Supply management.
Custos armorum: The soldier responsible for the registration and supply of weapons and equipment.
Digmata: The shield decoration.
Exuviae: Plundered weaponry and equipment.
Fabrica: A workshop.
Fabrica ballistaria: An artillery workshop.
Fabrica cohortis: A cohort's workshop.
Fabrica legionis: The legionary workshop.
Forma: A pattern or mould for casting.
Galea: Helmet.
Incus: An anvil.
Insignia scuti: The designs found on shields.

Lorica: The generic term for body armour (also used to refer to a parapet).
Lorica hamata: Ring mail body armour.
Lorica plumata: 'Feathered armour' could represent the small scale and mail combination armour.
Lorica segmentata: Modern terminology for segmented plate body armour, articulated on internal leather straps.
Lorica squamata: Scale body armour.
Loricatus: Armoured.
Manica: The arm protector.
Manubiae: Spoils and plunder.
Malleus: Hammer.
Minister bello: The logistical officer.
Ocrea: A greave.
Opera vacans: Soldier exempt from fatigue duty. This terminology was used in first century AD, by the second century AD this type of soldier was called an *immunis*.
Panoplia: Armour.
Parma: A small round shield.
Parma equestris: A cavalry shield.
Pectorale: Body armour.
Praeda: Plunder and spoils.
Praefectus castrorum: The military camp commandant.
Praefectus fabrum: The officer in charge of artisans.
Pteryges: From the Greek for 'wings', these were leather or linen strips for the protection of upper arms and thighs.
Quadrata: A rectangular shield.
Scutum: A shield.
Scutum publicum: A government issue shield.
Signifer: A standardbearer.
Spina: Reinforcing spine on shield.
Spolia: Spoils; plunder.
Sub aquila: Literally 'under the eagle', meaning on active service.
Subarmalis: An arming doublet.
Subsignanus miles: A soldier on active duty.
Summus curator: The senior administrator in charge of supply.
Symmacharis: An ally; auxiliary.
Tector: A cavalry trooper equipped with large shield.
Tegimentum: A protective garment worn over armour.
Tegimentum scuti: The protective shield cover, usually made of leather.
Thoracomachus: padded armour.
Tibiale: A legging or greave.
Umbo: The shield boss.
Umerale: Shoulder armour.
Vitis: The vine stick used to indicate the rank of centurion.

Bibliography

Aitchison, L. (1960) *A History of Metals Vol.* 1. Macdonald and Evans: London.

Alexander, W. and Street, A. (1979) *Metals in the Service of Man*. Penguin: Harmondsworth.

Allason-Jones, L. and Bishop, M. C. (1988) *Excavations at Roman Corbridge: the Hoard.* English Heritage Archaeological Report 7. English Heritage: London.

Allen, D. (1967) Iron currency bars in Britain. *Proceedings of the Prehistoric Society* 33, 307–35.

Allen, J. R. L. (1986) Interpretation of some Romano-British smithing slag from Awre in Gloucestershire. *Historical Metallurgy* 20(2), 97–104.

Allen, J. R. L. (1988) Chemical compositional patterns in Romano-British bloomery slags from the wetlands of the Severn Estuary. *Historical Metallurgy* 22(2), 81–6.

Angus, N. S., Brown, G. T. and Cleere, H. F. (1962) The iron nails from the Roman Legionary Fortress at Inchtuthil, Perthshire. *Journal of the Iron and Steel Institute,* 200(2), 956–67.

Bachman, H. G. (1982) *The Identification of Slags from Archaeological Sites*. University of London Institute of Archaeology Occasional Publications 6. London.

Bailey, F. W. J. (1967) *Fundamentals of Engineering Metallurgy*. Cassell: London.

Baker, P. A. (2004) *Medical Care for the Roman Army on the Rhine, Danube and British Frontiers in the First, Second and Early Third Centuries AD*. British Archaeological Report S1286. Archaeopress: Oxford.

Barber, A. J. and Walker, G. T. (1992) A bust of Mars or a hero from Cirencester. *Britannia* 23, 217–18.

Bealer, A. W. (1995) *The Art of Blacksmithing*. Castle Books: Edison.

Biek, L. (1963) *Archaeology and the Microscope; the scientific examination of archaeological evidence.* Butterworth: London.

Biringuccio, V. (1540) *The Pirotechnia of Vannoccio Biringuccio*, C. S. Smith (ed. 1959). Basic Books: New York.

Birley, A. R. (1979) *The People of Roman Britain*. University of California Press: Berkeley and Los Angeles.

Bishop, M. C. (1985) The Method, in M. C. Bishop (ed.), *The Production and Distribution of Roman Military Equipment*. British Archaeological Report S275. Archaeopress: Oxford, 1–42.

Bishop, M. C. (2002) *Lorica segmentata. Volume 1: A handbook of articulated Roman plate armour*. Armatura Press: Braemar.

Bishop, M. C. and Coulston, J. C. N. (1993) *Roman Military Equipment: from the Punic Wars to the fall of Rome*. Batsford: London.

Bishop, M. C. and Coulston, J. C. N. (2006) *Roman Military Equipment: from the Punic Wars to the fall of Rome*, 2nd edition. Oxbow: Oxford.

Blackburn, T. P. D., Edge, D. A., Williams, A. R. and Adams, C. B. T. (2000) Head protection in England before the First World War. *Neurosurgery* 47(6), 1261–86.

Blyth, P. H. (1993) Metallurgy of two fragmentary Archaic Greek helmets. *Historical Metallurgy* 27(1), 25–36.

Boon, G. C. (1974) *Silchester: the Roman town of Calleva*. David and Charles: London.

Bradley, K. (1994) *Slavery and Society at Rome*. Cambridge University Press: Cambridge.

Brailsford, J. W. (1951) Roman helmet from London. *British Museum Quarterly* 16(1), 17–19.

Brailsford, J. W. (1962) *Hod Hill: antiquities from Hod Hill in the Durden Collection*. The Trustees of the British Museum: London.

Bromehead, C. E. N. (1947) Practical geology in ancient Britain. *Proceedings of the Geological Association* 59, 345–67.

Bronson, B. (1986) The making and selling of Wootz, a crucible steel of India. *Archeomaterials* 1, 13–52.

Brewer, C. W. (1976) Metallographic examination of six ancient steel weapons. *Journal of the Historical Metallurgy Society*, 10(1), 1–10.

Bruet, B. J. F., Song, J., Boyce, M. C. and Ortiz, C. (2008) Materials design principles of ancient fish armour, *Nature Materials*. http://web.mit.edu/cortiz/www/Ben/nmat2231–rev.pdf.

Buchwald, V. F. (2005) *Iron and Steel in ancient times*. Special-Trykkeriet: Viborg.

Bull, S. (2007) *Triumphant Rider: The Lancaster Roman cavalry tombstone*. Carnegie Publishing: Lancaster.

Burgess, M. (1953) The mail-maker's techniques. *Antiquaries Journal* 33, 48–55, 193–202.

Burstall, A. F. (1970) *A History of Mechanical Engineering*. Faber and Faber: London.

Bushe-Fox, J. P. (1913) *Excavations on the Site of the Roman Town at Wroxeter Shropshire in 1912*. Society of Antiquaries: Oxford.

Cambell, J. B. (1984) *The Emperor and the Roman Army 31BC–235AD*. Clarendon Press: Oxford.

Campbell, B. (2000) *The Roman Army*. Routledge: London.

Campbell, J. and Fahy, F. (1984) A metallurgical study of the pile shoes from the Roman bridge at Minturnae. *Journal of the Historical Metallurgy Society* 18(1), 21–9.

Carroll, M. (2006) *Spirits of the Dead: Roman funerary commemoration in Western Europe*. Oxford University Press: Oxford.

Cave, J. K. (1977) A note on Roman metal turning. *History of Technology* 2, 77–94.

Charles, J. A. (1998) Development and use of layered ferrous microstructure. *Materials Science and Technology* 14(6), 496–503.

Child, I. B. (1983) Analysis of a coal sample taken from the Roman furnace at Icklesham on 25th September 1978, in Vahey, Z. (ed.) The Roman Road at Icklesham. *Hastings Area Archaeological Research Group* 4.3, 19–20.

Chilton, J. P. and Evans, U. R. (1955) The corrosion resistance of wrought iron. *Journal of the Iron and Steel Institute* (October), 113–22.

Clay, P. (1984) A cheek-piece from a cavalry helmet found in Leicester. *Britannia* 15, 235–8.

Cleere, H. F. (1963) A note on Roman bloomery tuyères. *Sussex Archaeological Collections* 101, 48–53.

Cleere, H. F. (1970) *The Romano-British Industrial Site at Bardown, Wadhurst*. Sussex Archaeological Society Occasional Paper 1: Chichester.

Cleere, H. F. (1971) Iron making in a Roman furnace. *Britannia* 2, 203–17.

Cleere, H. F. (1972) The classification of early iron smelting furnaces. *Antiquaries Journal* 52(1), 8–23.

Cleere, H. F. and Crossley, D. (1995) *The Iron Industry of the Weald* (2nd edition). Merton Priory Press: Cardiff.

Clemetson, J. (1993) Roman Scale Armour. *ARMA* 5(1), 8–10.

Clough, R. E. (1986) *Iron: aspects of the industry during the Iron Age and Romano-British periods*. Unpublished PhD thesis, University of London.

Coghlan, H. H. (1977) *Notes on Prehistoric and Early Iron in the Old world*. Occasional Papers on Technology 8(2). Pitt Rivers Museum: Oxford.

Collingwood, R. G. and Wright, R. P. (1991) *The Roman Inscriptions of Britain* 3. Alan Sutton: London.

Congdon, L. (1971) Steel in antiquity: A problem in terminology, in D. G. Mitten, J. G. Pedley, and J. A. Scott (eds), *Studies Presented to George M. A. Hanfmann*. Cambridge University Press: Cambridge, 17–27.

Connolly, P. (1988) *Greece and Rome at War*. MacDonald: London.

Cornel, T. and Matthews, J. (1992) *Atlas of the Roman World*. Facts on File: Oxford.

Cornell, T. J. (1995) Warfare and urbanisation in Roman Italy, in T. J. Cornell and K. Lomas (eds), *Urban Society in Roman Italy*. University of London Press: London, 121–34.

Coulston, J. C. N. (1988) *Military Equipment and the Identity of Roman Soldiers*. British Archaeological Report S394. Archaeopress: Oxford.

Coulston, J. C. N (1992) A preliminary note on scale armour from Carpow, Perthshire. *Arma* 4(2), 21–3.

Craddock, P. T. (1995) *Early Metal Mining and Production*. Edinburgh University Press: Edinburgh.

Craddock, P. T. and Lang, J. (2005) Charles Dawson's cast-iron statuette: the authentication of iron antiquities and possible coal-smelting of iron in Roman Britain. *Historical Metallurgy* 39(1), 32–44.

Crew, P. (1991) The experimental production of prehistoric bar iron. *Journal of the Historical Metallurgy Society* 25(1), 21–36.

Crew, P. (1993) Early iron-working workshop, Plas Tan Bwlch. *Historical Metallurgy Society News* 24(1), 1–2.

Crew, P. (1998) Laxton revisited: a first report on the excavations. *Journal of the Historical Metallurgy Society* 32(2), 49–53.

Cronyn, J. M. (2004) *The Elements of Archaeological Conservation*. Routledge: London.

Croom, A. (2000) The wear and tear of third century military equipment. *Journal of Roman Military Equipment Studies* 11, 129–34.

Cunnington, M. (1933) Mineral coal in Roman Britain. *Antiquity* 7, 89.

Curle, J. (1911) *A Roman Frontier Post and its People: the fort of Newstead in the parish of Melrose, Glasgow*. James Maclehouse: Glasgow.

Dakin, G. F. (1968) Romano-British ironworks at Bedford Purieus. *Journal of the Historical Metallurgy Society* 2(2), 67–8.

D'Amato, R. and Sumner, G. (2009) *Arms and Armour of the Imperial Roman Soldier*. Frontline Books: London.

Davies, O. (1935) *Roman Mines in Europe*. Oxford University Press: Oxford.

Dawson, T. (2002) Klivanion revisited: an evolutionary typology and catalogue of Middle Byzantine lamellar styles. *Journal of Roman Military Equipment Studies* 12/13, 89–95.

Dearne, M. J. and Branigan, K. (1995) The use of coal in Roman Britain. *Antiquaries Journal* 75, 71–106.

Debrebant, S. (2009) First person: Josef Loffl. *Financial Times weekend magazine* 31 October 2009, 7.

Doig, A. (2002) *Military Metallurgy*. Maney Publishing: London.

Driel-Murray, C. van (1988) A fragmentary shield cover from Caerleon, in J. C. N. Coulston (ed.) *Military Equipment and the Identity of Roman Soldiers*, 51–66.

Drescher, H. (1981) Untersuchung des Rinneflechtes aus Sorup, Grab K10. *Raddatz, Sorup1 Offa Bucher NF 46*. Karl Wacholtz Verlag: Neumunster.

Durman, A. (2002) Iron resources and production for the Roman frontier in Pannonia. *Historical Metallurgy* 36(1), 24–32.

Eadie, J. W. (1967) The development of Roman mailed cavalry. *Journal of Roman Studies* 57, 161–73.

Ehrenreich, R. M. (1985) *Trade Technology and the Iron Working Community in the Iron Age of Southern Britain*. British Archaeological Report 144. Archaeopress: Oxford.

Enckevort, van H. and Willems, W. J. H. (1995) Roman cavalry helmets in ritual hoards from the Kops Plateau at Nijmegen, the Netherlands. *Journal of Roman Military Equipment Studies* 5, 125–37.

Engelhard, C. (1866) *Denmark in the Early Iron Age illustrated by the recent discoveries in the Peat Mosses of Slesvig.* Williams and Norgate: London.

Fell, V. (1993) Examination of four Iron Age hammer heads from Bredon Hill (Hereford and Worcester), England. *Historical Metallurgy* 27(2), 60–70.

Ferris, I. (2009) *Hate and War: The Column of Marcus Aurelius.* The History Press: Gloucestershire.

Finley, M. I. (1965) Technical innovation and economic progress in the ancient world. *Economic History Review* 2 series 18, 29–45.

Forbes. R. J. (1956) Metallurgy, in ed C. Singer *et al.* (eds) *A History of Technology.* Oxford University Press: Oxford.

Forbes. R. J. (1958) *Metallurgy in Antiquity.* E. J. Brill: Leiden.

France-Lanord, A. (1980) *Ancient Metals.* ICCROM: Rome.

Frank, T. (1940) *Rome and Italy of the Empire. An Economic Survey of Ancient Rome* V. The Johns Hopkins Press: Baltimore.

Frankland, T. (1795) On welding cast steel. *Philosophical Transactions of the Royal Society of London* 85, 296–7.

Franzius, G. (1995) Die Römischen funde aus kalkreise 1987–95. *Journal of Roman Military Equipment Studies* 6, 69–88.

French, D. H. and Lightfoot, C. S. (1989) *The Eastern Frontier of the Roman Empire.* British Institute of Archaeology at Ankara Monograph 11/British Archaeological Report S553. Archeopress: Oxford.

Frere, S. S. and Wilkes, J. J. (1989) *Strageath. Excavations within the Roman Fort. 1973 to 1986.* British Monograph Series 9. Society for the Promotion of Roman Studies: London.

Fuegère, M. (1994) *Casques Antiques, les visages de la guerre de Mycènes à la fin de 'Empire Romaine,* Paris.

Fulford, M. G. and Allen, J. R. L. (1992) Iron making at the Chesters villa Woolaston Gloucestershire: survey and excavation 1987–1991. *Britannia* 23, 159–215.

Fulford, M., Sim, D. and Doig, A. (2004a) The production of Roman ferrous armour: a metallographic survey of material from Britain, Denmark and Germany, and its implications. *Journal of Roman Archaeology* 17, 197–220.

Fulford, M., Sim, D. and Doig, A. (2004b) In defence of Rome: a metallographic investigation of Roman ferrous armour from Northern Britain. *Journal of Archaeological Science* 32, 241–50.

Gale, W. K. V. (1971) *Iron and Steel Industries, a Dictionary of Terms.* David and Charles: Newton Abbot.

Garlick, M. (1980) The reconstruction and use of a lorica hamata, *Exercitus* 1(1), 8.

Gibson-Hill, J. (1980) Cylindrical shaft furnaces of the early Wealden iron industry: circa 100 BC to AD 300. *Journal of the Historical Metallurgy Society* 14(1), 21–7.

Gibson-Hill, J. and Worssam, B. C. (1976) Analyses of Wealden iron ores and their archaeological significance. *Bulletin of the Institute of Archaeology of London* 13, 247–63.

Gilliver, K. (2007) Display in Roman warfare: The appearance of armies and individuals on the battlefield. *War in History* 14(1), 1–21.

Gordon, R. (1996) *American Iron 1607–1900.* Johns Hopkins University Press: Baltimore.

Gordon, R. (1997) Process deduced from ironmaking wastes and artefacts. *Journal of Archaeological Science* 24, 9–18.

Goldsworthy, A. (2003) *The Complete Roman army.* Thames and Hudson: London.

Gralfs, B. (1988) *Metallverarbeitende produktionsstatten in Pompeji.* British Archaeological Report S433. Archaeopress: Oxford.

Greenough, A. P. (1987) An examination of Roman iron working residues from Loughor, West Glamorgan, Wales. *Journal of Historical Metallurgy* 21(1), 25–7.

Hannah, I. (1932) Roman blast furnaces in Lincolnshire. *Antiquaries Journal* 12, 262–8.

Hanson-Davis, V. (1989) *The Western Way of War.* Alfred A. Knopf: New York.

Hartley Leather, E. (1950) *Combat without Weapons.* Gale and Polden Limited: Aldershot.

Healy, J. F. (1978) *Mining and Metallurgy in the Greek and Roman World.* Thames and Hudson: London.

Higgins, R. A. (1976) *Engineering Metallurgy.* Hodder and Stoughton: London.

Hodge, A. T. (1990) A Roman factory. *Scientific American* 263(1), 58–62.

Hodges, H. (1989) *Artefacts: an introduction to early materials and technology.* Duckworth: London.

Hošek, J., Cleere, H. and Mihok, L. eds (2011) *The Archaeometallurgy of Iron. Recent developments in archaeological and scientific research.* Prague.

Huntingford, G. W. B. (1980) *The Periplus of the Erythraean Sea.* The Hakluyt Society: London.

Hyland, A. (1990) *Equus: the horse in the Roman world.* Batsford: London.

Jackson, D. A. and Tylecote, R. F. (1988) Two new Romano-British ironworking sites in Northamptonshire – a new type of furnace? *Britannia* 19, 275–98.

Jackson, R. (2000) *Doctors and Diseases.* British Museum Press: London.

James, S. (1988) *The fabricae: state arms factories of the Later Roman Empire.* British Archaeological Report S394. Archaeopress: Oxford.

Jones, P. N. (1984) A short history of the attack of armour. *The Metallurgist and Materials Technologist* May 1984, 247–50.

Jurisic, M. (2000) *Ancient Shipwrecks of the Adriatic: maritime transport during the first and second centuries AD.* British Archaeological Report S828. Archaeopress: Oxford.

Junkelmann, M. (1999) Roman helmet in the Axel Guttmann-Collection, Berlin. *Journal of Roman Military Equipment Studies* 10, 81–5.

Kaminski, J. (1996) *The Environmental Implications of Romano-British Iron Production in the Weald.* Unpublished PhD thesis, University of Reading.

Kaminski, J. and Sim, D. N. (2007) The production of the Chichester helmet. *Sussex Archaeological Collections* 145, 217–21.

Kapp, L., Kapp, H. and Yoshindo, Y. (1987) *The Craft of the Japanese Sword.* Kodansha International: Tokyo.

Keller, W. (1975) *The Etruscans.* Book Club Associates: London.

Kendal, R. (1993) *A Discussion of Some of the Logistical Problems Associated with the Building of Hadrian's Wall: with particular reference to transport.* Unpublished MA dissertation, University of Reading.

Keppie, L. (1984) *Making of the Roman Army from Republic to Empire.* Batsford: London.

Köhne, E., Ewigleben, C. and Jackson, R. (2000) *Gladiators and Caesars: The Power of Spectacle in Ancient Rome.* University of California Press: Berkeley.

Landels, J. G. (1978) *Engineering in the Ancient World.* Chatto and Windus: London.

Lane Fox, R. (2006) *The Classical World.* Penguin Books: London.

Lang, J. (1988) Study of the metallography of some Roman swords. *Britannia* 14, 199–216.

Lendon, J. E. (2005) *Soldiers and Ghosts: a history of battle in classical antiquity.* Yale University Press: Yale.

Lemmon, C. H. (1952) Fieldwork during the season 1952, *Transactions of the Battle and District History Society,* 27–9.

Lepper, F. and Frere, S. (1988) *Trajan's Column: a new edition of Cichorius plates.* Allan Sutton: London.

Lewis, M. J. T. (1997) *Millstone and hammer: the origins of water power.* The University of Hull: Hull.

Lynnerup, N., Astrup, J. G. and Sejrsen, B. (2005) Thickness of the human cranial diploe in relation to age, sex and general body build. *Head and Face Medicine* 1:13, 1–7.

MacMullen, R. (1960) Inscriptions on armour and the supply of arms in the Roman Empire. *American Journal of Archaeology* 64, 23–40.

McCarthy, M., Bishop, M. and Richardson, T. (2001) Roman armour and metalworking at Carlisle, Cumbria, England. *Antiquity* 75, 507–8.

McCartney, E. S. (1912) The genesis of Rome's military equipment. *Classical Weekly* 6(10), 74–9.

Maddin, R. Hauptmann, A. and Baatz, D. (1991) A metallographic examination of some iron tools from Saalburgmuseum. *Sonderdruck aus dem Saalburg-jahrbuch* 46. Verlag Philipp von Zabern: Mainz am Rhein, 5–23.

Manning, W. H. (1972) Ironwork hoards in Iron-Age and Roman Britain. *Britannia* 3, 224–50.

Manning, W. H. (1976) *Catalogue of Romano British ironwork in the Museum of Antiquities, Newcastle-upon-Tyne*. Department of Archaeology, University of Newcastle-upon-Tyne: Newcastle-upon-Tyne.

Manning, W. H. (1985a) *Catalogue of the Romano-British Iron Tools, Fittings and Weapons in the British Museum*. British Museum Publications: London.

Manning, W. H. (1985b) The iron objects, in L. F. Pitts and J. K. St. Joseph (eds), *Inchtuthil: the Roman Legionary Fortress*. Britannia Monograph Series 6, 289–99.

Marsden, E. W. (1971) *Greek and Roman Artillery: technical treatises*. Clarendon Press: Oxford.

Maryon, H. (1949) Metal working in the ancient world. *American Journal of Archaeology* 53(2), 93–125.

Mays, S. (1998) *The Archaeology of Human Bones*. Routledge: London.

Meiggs, R. (1982) *Trees and Timber in the Ancient Mediterranean World.* Clarendon Press: Oxford.

Meijers, R. and Weller, F. (2007) *Achter het zilveren masker: Nieuw onderzoek naar de productietechnieken van Romeinse ruiterhelmen.* Museum Het Valkof: Nijmegen.

MLA (2004) *Portable Antiquities Scheme: Annual Report 2003/4.* MLA: London, 47–8.

Money, J. H. (1974) Iron Age and Romano-British iron working site at Minepit Wood, Rotherfield, Sussex. *Bulletin of the Historical Metallurgy Group* 8(1), 1–20.

Mouritsen, H. (1988) Elections, magistrates and the municipal elite: studies in Pompeian epigraphy. *Analecta Romana Instituti Danici* Supplement 5. Rome.

Nash Williams, V. E. (1932) The Roman Legionary Fortress at Caerleon in Monmouthshire. Report on the Excavations carried out in the Prysg Field, 1927–9. Part II: The Finds. *Archaeologia Cambrensis* 87, 48–104.

Niblett, R. (2002) A lorica fragment from Verulamium. *Journal of Roman Military Equipment Studies* 12/13, 67–73.

Northover, J. P. 1995: Late Bronze Age drawplates in the Isleham hoard, in B. Sshmid-Sikimi and P. della Casa (eds.), *Trans Europam: Beiträge zur Bronze- und Eisenzeit zwischen Atlantik und Altai – Festschrift für Margarita Primas*. Bonn: Dr Rudolf Habelt, 15–22.

Oddy, W. A. (1991) Gilding: an outline of the technological history of the plating of gold on to silver or copper in the Old World. *Endeavour* 15(1), 29–33.

Olson, S. D. (1991) Firewood and charcoal in classical Athens. *Hesperia* 60, 411–20.

Pantosa, E., Kockelmann, W., Chapon, L. C., Lutterottic, L., Benneta, S. L., Tobina, M. J, Mosselmans, J. F. W., Pradell, T., Salvado, N., Butí, S., Garner. R. and Prag, A. J. N. W. (2005) Neutron and X-ray characterisation of the metallurgical properties of a 7th century BC Corinthian-type bronze helmet. *Nuclear Instruments and Methods in Physics Research Section B: beam interactions with materials and atoms* 239(1–2), 16–26.

Parker, A. J. (1992) *Ancient Shipwrecks of the Mediterranean and the Roman provinces*. British Archaeological Report S580. Archaeopress: Oxford.

Payne, S. (2010) The shadow in the old smithy. *British Archaeology* 111, 11–15.

Penrose, J. (ed) (2005) *Rome and her Enemies*. Ospray: Oxford.

Piggott, S. (1965) *Ancient Europe: from the beginnings of agriculture to classical antiquity*. Edinburgh University Press: Edinburgh.

Pleiner, R. (1969) Experimental smelting of steel in early medieval bloomeries, Pamatky. *Archeologicke* 60, 459–487.

Pleiner, R. (2000) *Iron in archaeology: the European bloomery smelters.* Archeologicky Ustav Avcr: Prague.

Raddaz, K. (1968) Religionsgeschichtliche Probleme des Thorsberger Moorfundes, in H. Jankuhn (ed.), *Vorgeschichliche Heiligtumer und Opferplatze in Mittel-und Nordeuropa.* Symposium: Rheinhausen, 190.

Radman-Livaja, I. (2004) *Militaria Sisciensia: finds of Roman military equipment in Sisak in the holdings of the Archaeological Museum in Zagreb.* Archaeological Museum in Zagreb: Zagreb.

Rankov, B. (1999) The Roman ban on the export of weapons to the Barbaricum: a misunderstanding. *Journal of Roman Military Equipment Studies* 10, 115–20.

Rees, S. (1979) *Agricultural Implements in Prehistoric and Roman Britain.* British Archaeological Report 69. Archaeopress: Oxford.

Rehder, J. E. (1986) Primitive furnaces and the development of metallurgy. *Historical Metallurgy* 20(2), 87–92.

Richmond, I. A. (1982) *Trajan's Army on Trajan's Column.* British School at Rome: London.

Richter, G. M. A. (1944) Five bronzes recently acquired by the Metropolitan Museum. *American Journal of Archaeology* 48(1), 1–9.

Robertson, A., Scott, M. and Keppie, L. (1975) *Bar Hill: A Roman fort and its finds.* British Archaeological Report 16. Archaeopress: Oxford.

Robinson, H. R. (1975) *The Armour of Imperial Rome.* Arms and Armour Press: London.

Rostoker, W. (1986) Ancient techniques for making holes in sheet metal. *American Journal of Archaeology* 90(1), 93–4.

Rostoker, W. (1990) *Pre-industrial Iron: its technology and ethnology.* Archaeomaterials Monograph 1. Philadelphia, 93–288.

Rostoker, W. and Dvorak, J. (1991) Some experiments with co-smelting to copper alloys. *Archaeomaterials* 5(1), 5–20.

Rostoker, W., Bronson, B. and Dvorak, J. R. (1989) Smelting to steel by the Japanese Tatara process. *Archaeomaterials* 3(1) 11–25.

Royal Athena Galleries (2007) *Art of the Ancient World: Greek, Etruscan, Roman, Egyptian and Near Eastern antiquities* Vol. 18. Royal Athena Galleries: New York.

Rudling, D. (1986) The excavation of a tilery on Great Cansiron Farm. *Britannia* 17, 220–2.

Salter, C. and Ehrenrich, R. (1984) Iron Age metallurgy in central and southern Britain, in B. Cunliffe and D. Miles (eds), *Aspects of the Iron Age in Central Southern Britain.* University of Oxford Committee for Archaeology: Oxford, 146–61.

Sander, E. (1962) Der praefectus fabrum und die Legionsfabriken. *Bonner Jahrbücher* 162, 139–161.

Scarth, H. M. (1864) *Notices of Roman Bath.* Simpkin, Marshall & Co: London.

Schioler, T. (1980) Bronze Roman piston pumps. *History of Technology,* 17–38.

Schoff, W. H. (1915) The eastern trade of the Roman Empire. *Journal of the American Oriental Society* 35, 224–39.

Schrüfer-Kolb, I. (1999) Roman iron production in the East Midlands, England, in S. M. M. Young, A. M. Pollard, P. Budd and R. A. Ixer (eds), *Metals in Antiquity.* British Archaeological Report S792. Archaeopress: Oxford, 227–33.

Schrüfer-Kolb, I. (2004) Roman Iron Production in Britain. British Archaeological Report 380. Archaeopress: Oxford.

Schubert, H. R. (1957) *History of the British Iron and Steel Industry from c. 450 B.C. to A.D. 1775.* Routledge and Kegan Paul: London.

Scott, D. A. (1991) *Metallography and Microstructure of Ancient and Historic Metals.* Getty Conservation Institute: Los Angeles.

Senn, M. and Fasnacht, W. (1991) Experimental iron smelting and smithing documented by the department of Prehistory, University of Zurich, Switzerland. *Materialy Archeologiczne* 26, 27–31.

Shirley, A. M. (2000) *The Construction of the Roman Legionary Fortress at Inchtuthil.* British Archaeological Report 298. Archaeopress: Oxford.

Sim, D. N. (1992a) Some misunderstandings concerning the use of blacksmith's tongs. *Historical Metallurgy* 26, 63–5.

Sim, D. N. (1992b) The manufacture of disposable weapons for the Roman army. *Journal of Roman Military Equipment Studies* 3, 105–19.

Sim, D. N. (1994) *Beyond the Bloom: bloom refining and artefact production in Roman Britain.* PhD thesis, University of Reading.

Sim, D. N. (1995a) Weapons and mass production. *Journal of Roman Military Equipment Studies* 6, 1–3.

Sim, D. N. (1995b) *Beyond the bloom: bloom refining and artefact production in Roman Britain.* PhD thesis, University of Reading.

Sim, D. N. (1997a) Roman chain-mail: experiments to reproduce the techniques of manufacture. *Britannia* 28, 359–71.

Sim, D. N. (1997b) Experiments to produce Roman *styli* by forging and machining on a pole lathe. *Antiquity* 71, 1011–15.

Sim, D. N. (1998a) The reproduction of a Roman hammer. *Tools and Trades History Society* 60, 17–23.

Sim, D. N. (1998b) *Beyond the bloom: bloom refining and iron artefact production in the Roman World.* British Archaeological Report S725. Archaeopress: Oxford.

Sim, D. N. (1998c) The use of domestic hearths as a means of annealing carbon steel. *Historical Metallurgy Society News Letter* 39, 5–6.

Sim, D. N. (1998d) Report on two sections of lorica segmentata found at Vindolanda. *Arma* 10, 9.

Sim, D. N. (2000) The making and testing of a falx also known as the Dacian battle scythe. *Journal of Roman Military Equipment Studies* 11, 63–4, 77–82.

Sim, D. N. (2002) Reinforcing a Roman helmet during the Dacian Wars. *Journal of Roman Military Equipment Studies* 12/13, 105–7.

Sim, D. N. and Ridge, I. (2002) *Iron for the Eagles.* Tempus: Stroud.

Simkins, M. (1990) *Warriors of Rome.* Blandford: London.

Singer, C., Holmyard, J. and Hall, A. R. (eds) (1954) *A History of Technology.* Clarendon Press: Oxford.

Smith, R. L. and Sandland, G. E. (1922) An accurate method of determining the hardness of metals, with particular reference to those of a high degree of hardness. *Proceedings of the Institution of Mechanical Engineers* 1, 623–41.

Souchopova, V. and Stransky, K (1989) Experimental iron smelting in the Blansko Region, Czechoslovakia. *Archeomaterials* 3(2), 149–61.

Southern, P. (2006) *The Roman Army: a social and institutional history.* Oxford University Press: Oxford.

Sprague de Camp, L. (1963) *Ancient Engineers.* Tandem: London.

Stephenson, I. P. (1999) *Roman Infantry Equipment of the Late Empire.* Tempus: Stroud.

Straker, E. (1931) *Wealden Iron.* Bell and Sons: London.

Ström, C. (1992) Injuries due to violent crimes. *Medical Science Law* 32, 123–32.

Swift, G. (1986) The local Roman iron working background, in D. R. Rudling (ed.), The Excavation of a Roman tilery on Great Cansiron Farm, Hartfield, East Sussex. *Britannia* 17, 193–194.

Thomsen, E. G. and Thomsen, H. H. (1974) Early wire drawing through dies. *Transactions of the ASME Journal of Engineering for Industry* Series B 96(1), 1216–21.

Thomsen, E. G and Thomsen, H. H. (1976) Drawing solid wires through soft dies in antiquity *Transactions of the ASME Journal of Engineering for Industry*, Paper No. 75-WA/Prod-6, 1–5.

Thomsen, R., Naumann, F. K. and Pliner, R. (1971) *Metallografisch Untersuchungen an wikingerzeitlichen Eisen barren aus Haithabu*, in K. Schietzel (ed.), Berichte über die Ausgrabunger in Haithabue, Bericht 5. Karl Wachholz Verlag: Neümunster, 9–29.
Thorland, E. (1971) Evidence of the use of carburized steel and quench hardening in Late Bronze Age Cyprus. *Opuscula Atheniensia* 10, 15–22.
Treloar, A. (1971) The Roman shield: Polybius vi. 23. 2. *Classical Review* 21(1), 3–5.
Tylecote, R. F. (1962) Roman shaft furnaces in Norfolk. *Journal of the Iron and Steel Institute* 201(1), 19–22.
Tylecote, R. F. (1975) *Metallurgy in Archaeology*. Edward Arnold: London.
Tylecote, R. F. (1976) *A History of Metallurgy*. Metals Society: London.
Tylecote, R. F. (1986) *The Prehistory of Metallurgy in the British Isles*. Alard: Dorking.
Tylecote, R. F. (1987) *The Early History of Metallurgy in Europe*. Longman: London.
Tylecote, R. F., Austin, J. N., and Wraith, A. E. (1971) The mechanism of the bloomery process in shaft furnaces. *Journal of the Iron and Steel Institute* 209, 342–63.
Varoufakis, G. J. (1975) Materials testing in Classical Greece: Technical specifications of the 4th century BC. *Journal of the Historical Metallurgy Society* 9(2), 57–63.
Vetters, H. (1996) Ferrum Noricum. Anzeiger der Österreichischen Akademie der Wissenschaften in Wien. *Philosophische-Historisches Klasse* 103, 167–85.
Wacher, J. S. (1971) Roman iron beams. *Britannia* 2, 200–2.
Wagner, D. B. (1990) Ancient carburisation of iron and steel: A comment. *Archaeaomaterials* 4(1), 111–7.
Ward, J. (1911) *Roman Era in Britain*. Methuen: London.
Watson, G. R. (1969) *The Roman Soldier*. Thames and Hudson: London.
Webster, G. (1955) A note on the use of coal in Roman Britain. *Antiquaries Journal* 35(3), 199–217.
Webster, G. (1998) *The Roman Imperial Army*. University of Oklahoma Press: Norman.
Wheeler, R. E. M. and Wheeler, T. V. (1932) *Report on the excavation of the prehistoric, Roman and post-Roman site in Lydney Park, Gloucestershire*. Reports of the Research Committee of the Society of the Antiquaries of London, 9. Oxford University Press: Oxford.
White, J. H. (1968) *The Extraction of Metals*. Macmillan: London.
White, K. D. (1984) *Greek and Roman Technology*. Thames and Hudson: London.
Williams, A. R. (1977) Roman arms and armour: a technical note. *Journal of Archaeological Science* 1(4), 77–87.
Wilson, A. (2002) Machines, power and the ancient economy. *Journal of Roman Studies* 92, 1–32.
Wright, J. H. (1972) Metallurgical examination of a Roman iron beam from Catterick Bridge, Yorkshire. *Journal of the Historical Metallurgy Society*, 6(1), 24–8.
Young, G. K. (2001) *Rome's Eastern Trade: international commerce and imperial policy, 31 BC–AD 305*. Routledge: London.

The Publisher's authorised representative in the EU for product safety
is Authorised Rep Compliance Ltd, Ground Floor, 71 Lower Bagot St,
Dublin, Ireland, D02 P593

Printed and bound by CPI Group (UK) Ltd, Croydon, CR0 4YY
11/02/2026
02052078-0005